SURVIVING LITERARY SUICIDE

June 1999

For Joe and Jean,

In gratitude and friendship.

Warmly,

Jeff

Surviving Literary Suicide

JEFFREY BERMAN

University of Massachusetts Press
AMHERST

Library of Congress Cataloging-in-Publication Data
Berman, Jeffrey, 1945–
Surviving literary suicide / Jeffrey Berman.
    p.   cm.
ISBN 1–55849–195-3 (cloth : alk. paper). —ISBN 1–55849–211 (pbk. : alk. paper)
1. American literature—History and criticism.
2. American literature—Study and teaching.
3. Suicide in literature.
I. Title.
PS169.S85B47   1999
810.9'353—dc21   98–32202
                                        CIP

British Library Cataloguing in Publication data are available.

Excerpts from "To a Tragic Poetess" in *88 Poems* by Ernest Hemingway, copyright ©
1979 by The Ernest Hemingway Foundation and Nicholas Gerogiannis, are reprinted
by permission of Harcourt Brace & Company; "Résumé" by Dorothy Parker, copyright
1926, 1928, renewed 1954, © 1956 by Dorothy Parker, from *The Portable Dorothy Parker*,
by Dorothy Parker, introduction by Brendan Gill, is used by permission of Viking Penguin, a division of Penguin Putnam, Inc.

To the memory of Leonard Port, 1936–1968

I think we ought to read only the kind of books that wound and stab us. If the book we're reading doesn't wake us up with a blow on the head, what are we reading it for? So that it will make us happy, as you write? Good Lord, we would be happy precisely if we had no books, and the kind of books that make us happy are the kind we could write ourselves if we had to. But we need the books that affect us like a disaster, that grieve us deeply, like the death of someone we love more than ourselves, like being banished into forests far from everyone, like a suicide. A book must be the axe for the frozen sea inside us.

FRANZ KAFKA

Contents

Acknowledgments

I am grateful to the many friends, colleagues, and students whose enthusiasm and support for this project never wavered. I want to single out two of my colleagues at the University at Albany who made valuable suggestions for improving the substance and style of the book: Professor Randall Craig of the English department and Professor Emeritus Jerome Eckstein of Judaic studies. True friends, they did not hesitate to point out problems with my argument and suggest solutions. On some pages, their commentary exceeded my own. They alone know the extent of my indebtedness to them. I am also grateful to Professor Joseph Adamson of McMaster University, Professor Emerita Sophie Freud of Simmons College, and Professor Daniel Ross of Columbus College for reading the entire manuscript and sharing their impressions with me. In addition, Professor Carl Eby, author of the recently published *Hemingway's Fetishism: Psychoanalysis and the Mirror of Manhood,* and James Nashold, M.D., author of a forthcoming biography on William Styron, were helpful in their comments on those two writers. Thanks also to Professor Marjorie Pryse for her responses to the Kate Chopin chapter. I am grateful to William Styron for allowing me to reprint his letter to Julie.

I am deeply indebted to the graduate students who took my 1994 course on literary suicide and who allowed me to use their diaries and reader-response paragraphs. This book could not have been written without their insightful and moving commentaries. Those students who have given me permission to acknowledge their names include Hal Crimmel, Rebecca Fiske, Irene Geel, Kristin Lindemann, Alina Luna, Jennifer McGrath, Lisa Mastrangelo, Tom Nespeco, Nancy Rullo, Perla Sasson,

Jonathan Schiff, Naoko Selland, Jennifer Snell, and Tim Walter. Jonathan Schiff and Tim Walter read the entire manuscript and alerted me to some classroom issues that I had forgotten. Special thanks go to Alyssa Colton, Alina Luna, and Jonathan Schiff for allowing me to use a substantial amount of their signed writings here and elsewhere. I thank Julie not only for her extraordinary "Letter to William Styron" but for her lasting friendship.

A University at Albany Faculty Research Grant-in-Aid offered timely financial assistance. I appreciate the wise counsel of Jeffrey Cohen, the human subjects research officer.

I am once again grateful to the staff of the University of Massachusetts Press, especially Clark Dougan, senior editor. At a time when academic publishing has become increasingly cautious about undertaking controversial projects, Clark was willing to take a risk publishing this book and its predecessor, *Diaries to an English Professor.* I will always be indebted to him. Thanks also to Anne Gibbons for her expert copyediting.

Part of chapter 3, "Virginia Woolf and the 'Embrace in Death,'" appeared in my 1990 book *Narcissism and the Novel,* published by New York University Press. Part of chapter 5, "Sylvia Plath and the Charge of Art," appeared in my 1985 book *The Talking Cure: Literary Representations of Psychoanalysis,* published by New York University Press. I am grateful for permission to reprint these sections. A portion of chapter 7, "William Styron and the Landscape of Depression," first appeared in *The Critical Response to William Styron* (1995), edited by Daniel Ross and published by Greenwood Press, an imprint of Greenwood Publishing Group, Inc., Westport, Connecticut. The information on how to help a suicidal friend appears in "'ASAP'—An Adolescent Suicide Awareness Programme" by Diane M. Ryerson, in *Suicide in Adolescence* (1987), edited by Rene F. W. Dykstra and Keith Hawton and published by Martinus Nijhoff. Reprinted with permission of Comprehensive Behavioral Healthcare, Inc.

My greatest indebtedness is to my wife, Barbara, and my daughters, Arielle and Jillian. They provided me with a support system that was especially welcome for a project such as this. They have not only insured my own survival but have also brought me the greatest joy.

SURVIVING LITERARY SUICIDE

Introduction
SOUL MATES AND SILENT SUFFERING

Literature is filled with countless numbers of suicidal characters, many of whom are studied every day in high schools and colleges without any discussion of how their deaths affect readers. Does a fictional character's suicide awaken the same emotions within us as a real character's suicide? What are the conditions in which a reader's identification with a suicidal character may lead to heightened vulnerability? In an age when the suicide rate has jumped dramatically, does a story's glorification of suicide pose special dangers to readers? If so, can we identify those who may be at risk and take appropriate measures to avert a tragedy? Can literature play a role in suicide prevention?

These questions assume greater urgency when reading novels and poems by authors who later take their own lives. The high incidence of suicide among twentieth-century writers is well known and includes John Berryman, Tadeusz Borowski, Paul Celan, Hart Crane, Romain Gary, Ernest Hemingway, William Inge, Randall Jarrell, Jerzy Kosinski, Primo Levi, Vachel Lindsay, Ross Lockridge Jr., Jack London, Vladimir Mayakovsky, Yukio Mishima, Cesare Pavese, Sylvia Plath, Anne Sexton, John Kennedy Toole, and Virginia Woolf. Less well known is the extent to which many of these writers romanticized suicide in their work. Given what clinicians call the contagion effect—suicide's ability to "infect" other people, rendering them susceptible to self-death—should literature teachers take special precautions when discussing self-destructive authors?

If these questions seem alarming, consider Virginia Woolf. She never extolled suicide in her voluminous diaries, letters, critical writings, or even in the suicide notes written in the final days of her life, but she does portray Septimus Warren Smith's leap into oblivion in *Mrs. Dalloway* as an act of heroic defiance against an oppressive psychiatric establishment. Clarissa Dalloway not only approves of the suicide, which she regards as preferable to institutionalization, but also regards it as a cause for celebration. Woolf includes a line in the American edition of *Mrs. Dalloway* about Clarissa's reaction to Septimus's suicide that is omitted from the English edition: "He made her feel the beauty; made her feel the fun." Although the editor of the new edition of *Mrs. Dalloway* deletes this line on the grounds that it is "gratuitous" to think that Clarissa could feel this way about a serious subject (*Mrs. Dalloway*, "Textual Notes" 213), the novel consistently justifies Septimus's suicide—with the explicit approval of many literary critics.

Suicide preoccupied Ernest Hemingway from the beginning of his writing career in 1920. His earliest stories contain suicidal fears and desires that antedated his father's suicide in 1928 and shaped his reaction to it. Unable to forgive his father for killing himself, Hemingway condemned him as a coward and created a larger-than-life persona to ward off his own fears of disintegration. He could empathize with some of his suicidal characters, such as the old man in "A Clean, Well-Lighted Place," but not with others, such as Robert Jordan's father in *For Whom the Bell Tolls*, who is modeled on his own father. Many of Hemingway's characters, including Robert Jordan, are disguised suicides: they reject suicide as an act of cowardice but then proceed to create situations that lead to their own destruction. Hemingway portrays Robert Jordan's death wish as heroic, but he felt no compassion for Dorothy Parker, whose suicide attempts he mercilessly satirized in his 1926 poem "To a Tragic Poetess." The poem reflects and reinforces several dangerous myths about suicide, including the belief that those who talk about taking their own lives do not actually go through with it. "To a Tragic Poetess" also suggests that a woman's suicide attempt should be taken less seriously than a man's.

Sylvia Plath's suicide at the age of thirty occurred when she was writing the best poems of her life. She regards herself as an escape artist in "Daddy" and "Lady Lazarus" and views suicide there and in her autobiographical novel, *The Bell Jar*, as part of a pattern of death and rebirth. It is easy to see why so many readers have celebrated these brilliant poems, with their incantatory rhythms, resurrection imagery, and feminist themes. Yet if death precedes rebirth in "Daddy" and "Lady Lazarus," there is no such affirmation in Plath's last poem, "Edge," written two or three days before her self-asphyxiation. To judge from the poem, which eerily foreshadows her own suicide, Plath may have also considered killing her two infant children, for she depicts them in "Edge" as each coiled, like a white snake, at an empty pitcher of milk. Though Plath took pains to protect the sleeping children from the gas that snuffed out her life, "Edge" raises the most vexing questions about the boundary between healthy and unhealthy art. To view "Edge" as a celebration of mystical transcendence, as many critics do, is to ignore the shattering interpersonal implications of suicide, the devastation experienced by relatives and friends.

Anne Sexton refuses to glorify mental illness or suicide in her early poems, regarding herself instead as a survivor. She believed that the writing of poetry saved her life and could save the lives of others. In her late poems, however, we see a darkening of Sexton's vision and an increasing attraction to death. Her poem "Sylvia's Death," written a few days after Plath died, glamorizes suicide as an irresistible longing. The news of Plath's death has created a "terrible taste for it, like salt" (*Complete Poems* 127), and the poem embraces suicide as a solution to the problems of life. Sexton's pro-suicide poems implicate the reader in the poet's suicidal crisis, and by portraying death as more attractive than life, they may prove disturbing to those at risk.

Can a suicidal poem or story literally endanger a reader's health? It is not likely that a psychologically stable reader will be imperiled by a literary text, but if a reader is depressed, might a text that glorifies suicide further weaken his or her precarious health? This is, admittedly, a difficult question to answer, and I acknowledge here that there are no definitive answers to this or to the other related questions I pose throughout the present study. The best way to address this question is to look at individual writers and readers, and when we do so, we find some evidence to suggest that the glorification of suicide may endanger certain people.

A recent example of this may be seen in Elizabeth Wurtzel's autobiographical *Prozac Nation* (1994), subtitled *Young and Depressed in America*. Wurtzel does not romanticize mental illness, but she does become, in her own words, "downright rhapsodic" when describing her elaborate suicide fantasy to her psychiatrist. After giving precise details about the most effective way to slash her wrists without botching the job, she lingers over the appropriate background music. She rejects the more obvious soundtracks that would accompany her immersion in a sepulchral hot bath—Janis Joplin and Billie Holliday would be too clichéd. Nor would she play her usual melancholy favorites like the Velvet Underground or Joni Mitchell. She considers briefly Judas Priest's *Stained Glass,* which formed the background music to a failed suicide attempt by a young man who later "sued the band, claiming the lyrics made him do it" (281). She would not play her all-purpose favorites like Bob Dylan or Bruce Springsteen, though *Blood on the Tracks* or *Darkness on the Edge of Town* would be poetically suitable, as would be John Lennon's song "Strawberry Fields," with the ominous words "Let me take you down." Wurtzel's psychiatrist is horrified by her patient's deadly serious fantasy and insists she must be hospitalized immediately, upon which Wurtzel panics, thinks of the lines from Sexton's poem "Wanting to Die"—"But suicides have a special language. / Like carpenters they want to know *which tools.* / They never ask *why build"*—and then rushes to a bathroom, where she locks the door and swallows a full bottle of powerful antipsychotic medication.

Despite literature's long interest in suicide, few attempts have been made to discover how suicidal characters and themes affect readers. For this reason, my own teaching experiences may prove interesting to readers. In 1992 and 1994 I taught a graduate seminar on literary suicide at the University at Albany. The reading lists were identical in both years. We spent the first two weeks of the semester discussing clinical and theoretical aspects of suicide. We read selections by Emile Durkheim, Sigmund Freud, Karl Menninger, and Edwin Shneidman, some of the leading theorists in the field. We read a novel by a writer who did not commit suicide, *The Awakening,* by Kate Chopin, and then spent two weeks apiece on Woolf, Hemingway, Plath, and Sexton. Both classes ended with *Darkness Visible,* William Styron's memoir of his own suicidal depression and recovery.

The only difference between the two courses was that the 1992 students were reluctant to share their feelings about suicide with their classmates and teacher—largely because I neglected to provide them with an appropriate means to do so. I emphasized the importance of reader-response issues, but they felt uncomfortable speaking about their feelings either during class discussions or in their formal essays. There was little personal engagement with the material: suicide was simply one more academic subject they were learning to theorize. We live and teach in a highly theoretical age in which, all too often, the personal element of learning is ignored, resulting in education that is increasingly abstract and impersonal. Suicide remained a theoretical and textual issue, removed from the real world.

For example, despite my repeated encouragement to talk about their reactions to Septimus Warren Smith's decision to plunge to his death in Woolf's *Mrs. Dalloway* rather than enter a rest home ordered by his psychiatrist, the students remained silent, as if a question about the reader's feelings or fantasies were inappropriate in a graduate seminar. They were also reluctant to explore the extent to which they felt complicit in the speakers' suicide attempts in "Daddy" and "Lady Lazarus," both of which blur the distinction between victim and victimizer.

There are many explanations for silence, but I suspect that my students' silence was due to the taboo surrounding suicide. For most people suicide is a morbid topic, and they experience so many conflicting emotions that they have difficulty speaking about it. I have found that both undergraduate and graduate students feel uneasy discussing suicide, as do their teachers. Many students have told me that their teachers studiously avoid any discussion of suicide when reading *The Awakening*, which ends with Edna Pontellier walking into the sea.

Julie: A Letter to William Styron

One student in the 1992 course, however, did speak personally about suicide—Julie, the only undergraduate. She had asked me if she could do her class presentation on a personal response to *Darkness Visible*, and I agreed. A graduating senior who had been in two of my earlier courses, Julie was an outstanding student: bright, conscientious, and witty. She was also perfectionistic and depressed. I was apprehensive when she asked me if she could take the literary suicide course, for I knew she was experiencing a personal crisis and that she had been self-destructive in the past. I agreed to let her into the course when she told me that both she and her physician thought it might be helpful to her therapy.

For most of the semester Julie said little, feeling intimidated, as she later told me, by the graduate students. In her presentation, written in the form of a letter to William Styron, Julie revealed to her classmates that in the preceding weeks she had struggled with suicidal thoughts and had been living in the University Health Center. She recounted a long history of depression and expressed frustration that none of the other students had really spoken about the terrible suffering that drives people to kill themselves. Only Styron, she felt, had captured this pain, and that was why she was giving her presentation on him. Julie has allowed me to reproduce her essay.

10 December 1992

Dear Mr. Styron:

I am writing to you for at least a couple of reasons. I have to present your book Darkness Visible *to a graduate class on literary suicide. For your information, we're also reviewing* Sophie's Choice. *For your further information, you are the only living author on the syllabus and as such, I consider myself the most fortunate student in the class: to be able to present on life, even at its darkest, as opposed to death.*

Anyway, I've known about this requirement for some time, and now that the day is fast approaching, I can honestly say that I really have not procrastinated. Instead, in the midst of my own murk, I have also felt myself both at a loss for what to say: how to add to yet another of your masterpieces and then settling on feeling nothing but inept. To avoid beating myself down into the ground any further, however, I have decided to join you instead. I decided that I, too, would put myself on the line, personally, as you did by having Darkness Visible *published for the world to read. In so doing, I would spare myself from having to add to what you already have said so eloquently and thoroughly.*

Thus, while my presentation is geared toward a tiny population of graduate students compared to the world of your presentation, I am hopeful that I might help you drive home the seriousness of the depression you describe as well as to loosen the stigma associated with those afflicted. Of course, there is really no way for me to be certain that I will have accomplished my task, but like you, I figure it cannot hurt to try and do my part for maybe that one classmate who is afflicted but cannot vocalize or even recognize it.

Finally, this may end up being a cathartic experience for me, writing to you, and as such, I can only say that it is about time I participated in some healthy self-indulgence as opposed to that destructive kind to which I have become so comfortably accustomed.

The second reason I am writing to you is because it is about time that my pen hit the paper, for I have been writing letters to you in my mind since the summer. Yes, after reading and rereading and picking myself up off the floor after Sophie's Choice, *I felt as though in some strange way I was connected to you as much as I was to Sophie, Nathan, Stingo, and even Morris Fink. In class now, we discuss how autobiographical information is often buried in an author's novels or poems: for example, Anne Sexton's confessional suicide poems, Virginia Woolf's Septimus Warren Smith, and now your Sophie.*

Sophie's Choice *has to be one of the greatest masterpieces of our time, Mr. Styron. What you need to know from me or what I need to let you know is that not only did I become enthralled with and want to embrace Sophie, but also, to some extent, I felt the same way about you. See, I just knew from my own depressive illness that there was simply no way you could have been so crisp in your description of Sophie's descent unless you had been there yourself. You quoted Sophie as saying to Stingo, "Anyway, I felt this emptiness. It was like finding something precious in a dream where it is all so real—something or someone, I mean, unbelievably precious—only to wake up and realize the precious person is gone. Forever! I have done that so many times in my life, waking up with that loss! And when this music stopped, it was like that, and suddenly I knew: I had this premonition that I would never hear such music again."*

Later on you describe Sophie's situation in the camp, when "[s]he rose to her feet and continued the climb upward, feeling feverish and unstrung. Too many things crushing down upon her all at once. Too many thoughts to sort out, too many swift shocks and apprehensions. If she didn't take hold of herself, make every effort to keep her composure, she knew she might simply collapse today like a puppet that has performed its jerky dance on strings, then, abandoned by its master, falls into a lifeless heap."

Mr. Styron, you were there. You were Sophie for flickered moments in the novel. As I said, there's no way to describe those passages without having your own heart thrown in there. Speaking of your heart, I have to say I envision it to be as large as the ocean. So, Sophie's Choice *and* Darkness Visible *meet at a crossroad in that the former might be your real memoir of madness and the latter its justification.*

It's like the difference between someone who has never had an abortion trying to describe the details as opposed to someone who truly has experi-

enced one. Need we wonder whose description will be the more crisp and accurate?

So, I needed to write to tell you, at the risk of sounding like some loony, that in some ways you have a soul mate out there: one whom you will undoubtedly (and maybe thankfully, on your part) never meet but who wanders about thinking about you every now and then and knowing she is not alone because, after all, Mr. Styron has also been there and is still alive to talk about it. You have a soul mate in that, without knowing you, I already know that I would help you and listen to you with whatever capacity I had. That may be a fantasy of grandeur, but the point is that when you've traveled the path we have and do end up choosing life, you almost automatically acquire a host of silent comrades who serve to buoy you up when that murky cloud threatens to descend again. Kind of like your prologue, where you quote Job about that "thing which" we "greatly feared" which comes upon us. Some lyrics by Bob Dylan come to mind; he says something like, "Strange how those who suffer together make better ties than those who appear most content." So I speak of a silent suffering, nevertheless, together.

So now I will turn to Darkness Visible, *which, globally, seems to be your attempt to purge the stigma associated with depression and those who are afflicted with it. You speak in the beginning about how, unless one has suffered from it personally, there is no way to really comprehend its depths; it is like that peripheral description of the abortion I mentioned earlier and so much more than the blues. But I still wonder along with you if we will ever get to that point you mentioned in which we attach no more reproof to the victims of depression and suicide than we do to cancer victims. Certainly, when I think of the task of having to convert even one person to this way of thinking, then I know we have a long way to go.*

Even in my class, where once a week we talk about the tragedy of famous suicides for three hours, I notice these almost urgent attempts to explain the suicide away: to justify it in some way, to look at the contributing factors as the actual causes. Never have I felt we truly recognize the tragedy in its fullest sense. For example, one student described Anne Sexton as overdosing every night because of the amount of medication she required in order to get, at least what you and I know as, a semblance of obliviated, unwracked sleep. The horrors you mentioned about depressive insomnia are too difficult, I guess, to comprehend unless one has been awake for a solid month and finally is willing to kill for sleep.

Another student questioned what really could have prevented Anne Sexton's suicide, as though her repeated attempts and habitual overdosing created her destiny or was the equivalent of her fate. Personally, that statement frightened me when I looked at my own history, and even though I am not famous, I wondered if friends and family would reach the same conclusion about my seemingly inevitable suicide. Would they say I was bound for it? Then I quickly race back to Darkness Visible, *where you say, "Through the healing process of time—and through medical intervention or hospitalization—most people survive depression, which may be its only blessing." But still, Anne Sexton had time and the best intervention. So what do we conclude? Again, we return to* Darkness Visible, *where you say, "To discover why some people plunge into the downward spiral of depression, one must search beyond the manifest crisis, and then still fail to come up with anything beyond wise conjecture." Obviously, there's some biochemical imbalance, which you address most thoroughly in* Darkness Visible, *but maybe too an imbalance of time and intervention: not the right combination. As I wrote in my journal the other day, "if only I had just a little more time." Right, if only . . . .*

But back to this question of a biochemical/metabolic imbalance as it appears in Darkness Visible. *Certainly, those suffering from it feel some reprieve from the guilt of not being able to "straighten up," as my mother so comfortingly put it at one time. Your observations are on target about the science of medicating the mentally ill and the necessity of doing so. Yet, this science seems to suffer its own depression, touting only and mainly its success story for the treatment of manic-depression with Lithium. Hooray for manic-depressives. But what about those of us who are atypical?*

Like you, I suffered the horrors of waiting at least three weeks for my body to register a medication, enduring the unendurable throughout only to find out that it was the wrong medication and so had to wait another two weeks to be weaned off and then start that gruesome process all over again. It's like telling the guinea pig not to have low self-esteem. All of this when a minute seems like a day, and yet, we're asked to wait for weeks. Unreal. However, we plod on with some hope, albeit diminished but hope just the same. However, for me, that hope became diminished, and I failed to make the decision you made, to leave your internal madhouse for an institutional one. No, instead, professionals made that decision for me, and there I went, involuntarily, twice. I have smartened up at least a bit, caught up to you after having had all my freedom usurped and fear instilled in me. I was finally able to make that decision under more rational conditions at least two times more. More on that later.

You also discuss the inappropriateness of the word "depression" to define our reality. You're right in saying that we'll have to be "saddled" with it until a better word comes along, but I must say that they should add your thoughts to the DSM-IIIR, when you said, "it is hopelessness even more than pain that crushes the soul. And so the decision-making of daily life involves not, as in normal affairs, shifting from one annoying situation to another less annoying—from discomfort to relative comfort—or from boredom to activity—but from moving from pain to pain. One does not, even briefly, abandon one's bed of nails, but lies upon it wherever one goes."

All of what you say is right. I know when you sat mute at that small dinner party of yours that it was because you simply had no choice. What do we say at those times when the mask is beyond reach? "Excuse me, I cannot concentrate on anything but trying to remain still to prevent these nails from gouging any deeper than they already have." Thus, our inertia. It's not that we don't want to move; it's that we cannot.

You wondered how it started for you or where it started. It is good that your strength allowed you such a clear retrospective view, where you saw your use of alcohol and abrupt cessation as a possible point of origin, at least for the depression to manifest itself full-blown. Furthermore, your knowledge of incomplete mourning, revealed both in Sophie's Choice *and here in* Darkness Visible, *shows the havoc it can create. So your vice, friend, and killer was alcohol. Mine was eating disorders. Yes, they created in me at times that same "magical conduit to fantasy and euphoria, and to the enhancement of the imagination," that alcohol did for you. Yes, my own retrospective view allows me to see that I was dying all the time, as were you, not so much directly from our vices but rather from the depression that we were blanketing via those vices. To reduce my twelve-year eating disorder into a sentence, I recognize it now as a symptom of something far greater, which became most obvious when my body, after years of torture and abuse, like yours, rose up and said, "No more, no more."*

But what were we left with, you without your alcohol, and me without my eating disorder? Well, you made it clear that you were left spiraling downward due to mourning the loss of your friend in alcohol, which was a mask in itself. The real problem, the depression, became like a seething monster ready and almost eager finally to take center stage, now that you had made some room for it. Similarly, when I finally realized my body would no longer succumb to the self-inflicted pain, I also realized that there was no way I was equipped to face my real monster in the eye. What eye? It has a fly's eye with a million facets. So I attempted suicide and have many times—impulses, gestures, and true attempts. I lost count by now, like Anne Sexton doing it almost reflexively, habitually, recreationally, and always ambivalently—and always hoping that I had taken enough to put me out only long enough for my monster to disappear when I finally awoke. But like you, every time I awoke, I realized I was only "in the first stage—premonitory, like a flicker of sheet lightning barely perceived—of depression's black tempest." The war was always yet to be waged. First, we have to deal with internal conflict amongst our own home troops before we can hope they can get their shit together and fight the real battle. Such a war.

I guess this is where the professionals and medications come in. Combined, they are hardly the cure; they are merely the ammunition with which we will still have to confront that monster, ultimately, by ourselves.

As I review Darkness Visible *herein, I so hope you don't think I'm diminishing it. I'm still finding myself feeling pretty inept compared to every remarkable word you wrote. I just go through it and say, "yes, yes, yes, you've hit it on the head" every time—when you mention that "immense and aching solitude" that feels like physical pain.*

I write to you from the non-clinical setting of my university's infirmary, my short-term holding tank to save me from myself. My academic and work schedule as well as my ability to give some semblance of having my shit together prevent me from yet another formal hospitalization. But I return to my cozy little one-bedroom apartment for a fresh change of clothes and then maybe a weekend pass just the way you returned to your beloved farmhouse in Connecticut after having been on Martha's Vineyard. And like you, instead of being met with the awe of some simple beauty, we were met with that Dickinsonian "certain slant of light": death everywhere.

So I race into the apartment and try to ignore the loudness of the silence, but then when, on a weekend pass, I am forced to dally, I sit in fear of being swallowed by that silence, which turns out to be even louder than my sobbing. As you said, "that gray drizzle of horror induced by depression takes on the quality of physical pain." So how do I concentrate? You spoke about the lack of concentration that persists. How am I to figure out what to buy for dinner? Will I like my choice if I ever make a decision? Should I do my laundry now or later? What type of music am I in the mood for? Am I in the mood for music? Needing my address book to dial the most frequently dialed numbers? And what's more, how can I possibly study when my mouth still feels dry from my last overdose?

Speaking of which, I get sent home with a small bundle of Valium, which you also addressed with regard to your Halcion prescription—the overmedicating of or the wrong kind for the depressed patient so that sometimes the cure only exacerbates the problem. So now, does this little bundle replace my eating disorder? A new blanket to cover and avoid that monster? That biochemical monster. Yes, I reiterate biochemistry again because even as I sit here with no intention of going on this Valium binge, I also know that if I started, like Sexton, I would not be able to stop. You spoke of having a double, a "wraithlike observer" who watches you commit these crazy dramatic acts—and this is exactly what it is like. One part of me says, "Don't even take one," while the other part says, fifteen to twenty pills later, "This really might not be quite enough," because as you said, by that point I have begun to think only "ceaselessly of oblivion."

You know what the most redeeming quality of Darkness Visible *is? It is when your humor returns. You begin almost staunch, urgent, with an incessant need to convince the world of the multifacetedness of depression. Yet, when you finally turn and focus on yourself and your ordeal, eventually your humor returns. It's our sign of health, indeed.*

I will tell you that a fellow patient and I stole our charts and did some speed reading. On the last recorded day on my chart, the doctor wrote, "Still suicidal but has ability to laugh; humor has returned." And your humorous descriptions of how in the midst of the depression we can find ourselves attaching to the most "ludicrous" little things and giving them utmost importance. For you, no wonder, it was your writing instrument. For me, I became obsessed with my socks, sometimes changing them three or four times before I left my apartment in the morning. Had to have the right socks. These oddities in themselves are not so funny as when we finally recognize them, but hey, at least I wasn't choosing from a pile of same-colored socks for then it would turn from funny to frightening. I've chilled out considerably regarding socks since then.

Later on your humor continues to shine through as you described the "institutional sitcom" of group therapy—those depressed women in curlers having to spill their guts out and produce satisfactory tears for that young, smug shrink. And then you made me hysterical when you described art

therapy as "nothing more than organized infantilism." I had an art therapist who actually allowed a fellow patient to hold up his crayoned drawing, which consisted of a black dot in the middle of a large piece of cheap
newsprint paper. The therapist then proceeded to ask how it made us feel.
How to respond without causing that patient to require another few weeks
of hospitalization? And then to look around the room and find that people
actually responded to that stupid dot. What was it, his family portrait? I
forget. And yes, I laughed when you said of your teacher, "not even a teacher
of very young retarded children could have been compelled to bestow, without deliberate instruction, such orchestrated chuckles and coos." Mine was
quite the same, acting as if my scribbles were Picasso's.

The only difference I faced was that my art teacher was also anal reten-
tive and became overly anxious about us getting the crayons back into the
proper boxes before we even had a chance to get them out. We're smiling
now, though. It's over, but it was at this time when your humor returned
that you recognized your emergence into light: shaky but emerging. I hope
so deeply in my heart of hearts that I will be able to write about emerging
into the light someday, even if it's only in my journal.

And then there's your closing, where you confirm what I said earlier
about incomplete mourning and grief. You recognized first your ability to
create "landscapes of depression" in the women of your novels and then
how your accuracy stemmed from the loss of your own mother at the age of
thirteen. You speak of the "insufferable burden of which rage and guilt and
not only dammed-up sorrow are a part, and becomes the potential seeds of
self-destruction." You made me remember how my grieving when I was five
years old over the death of my beloved grandfather was abruptly brought to
an end by a smack in the face out of the darkness. I was told I had cried
enough. I stopped crying at five. Where are those tears? Hidden in an eating disorder or a bottle of Valium? I suppose quite possibly.

I have some tears now because I'm just about to close this letter to you.
But first let me not close without reiterating how fortunate I consider myself to have been able to present Mr. Styron's Darkness Visible to my class:
William Styron, the one who made it through, the one who did not succumb. While I still identify more with Anne Sexton, it is you toward whom
I gravitate because you are breathing. And while it probably sounds mushy
to say I love you, I will say it anyway because you are my silent comrade;
and you made it through and weren't ashamed to tell the world.

I'm so thankful that, on the night the heat went out in your house, when *you sat all bundled in a blanket, you were forced to look around. You were able to gather yourself together enough so that you did not abandon the memories created by the children and animals who ran through these rooms, memories of the holidays of yesteryear and the possibility of more cheer. Nor did you consent to abandon those who helped create those memories.*

I've read your Darkness Visible. *I have only one suggestion. You should most definitely consider a sequel so we know how you're doing. I'm sure your honesty would reveal that the struggle persists, but it would also reveal that you as a human being have persisted as well and maybe give even more hope to those of us who have trouble seeing why it's worth that persistence in the first place. As I said, I don't know you but you must know that you have enlightened and sustained me a great deal in such a short time. Thank you, Mr. Styron, for not giving up.*

Fondly yours,
Julie

P.S. This was my presentation.

Julie's presentation occurred during the last class of the semester, and few of us were dry-eyed when she was finished. There was a long silence followed by comments praising her courage, insight, and humor. It was the most memorable class I have experienced as a student or teacher. *Darkness Visible* was not for Julie merely another recovery narrative, to be analyzed and categorized; rather, she read the story as if her life depended on it. Her letter to Styron affirms literature's power to move readers deeply, heightening their connection to life. Like Styron, Julie deromanticizes and destigmatizes suicide while offering the realistic hope that those suffering from severe depression will overcome it. Students began for the first time in the semester to talk about the course's impact upon them and to relate literature to personal experience.

I told Julie afterward that if she gave me permission I would send a copy of her paper to Styron. She was surprised by the suggestion that a famous writer might be interested in her letter but agreed without hesitation. She wrote a cover letter indicating that the honesty and openness of *Darkness Visible* had encouraged her to speak with the same candor to her classmates. Julie wanted Styron to realize that he had acquired a "silent comrade" in her and that a response from him would be the high

point in her college life. Julie later told me that Styron's warm, supportive letter to her, written while she was still in the hospital, was vital to her
recovery:

14 February 1993

Dear Julie,

*I was very moved by your generous letter besides being enormously im-
pressed by the wisdom and insight you've brought to bear on the nature of
the illness we've both suffered from. I understand that at the moment you're
in a hospital and I can only say that I'm with you in spirit and proud to be
your "silent comrade." Your letter was splendid in its articulate awareness
of both the anatomy and the wellsprings of depression; such perception
will certainly help you weather the ordeal. I'm glad you saw the humor in
my little book since some of the critics didn't; you are obviously blessed by
humor yourself and it's plainly a large component in your ability to survive
and eventually destroy the demons.*

*Thank you for your expression of love, which is what I continue to need
and which I send back to you.*

Ever yours,
William Styron

Julie's presentation emboldened me to teach Literary Suicide again in
1994, this time with a personal writing component. I was now able to
explore the ways in which the reader becomes, in Julie's words, the writer's
"silent comrade," a bond that can be helpful or harmful to the reader,
depending upon whether the writer survives or succumbs to a suicidal
depression. The class proved to be a unique learning experience, and
readers may be interested in my efforts to ensure each student's "survival." Chapter 1 begins with a discussion of the prevalence of suicide in
our culture, the myth and reality of suicide, and the ways to respond to a
person who experiences a suicidal crisis. I then focus on some of the
personal and pedagogical issues that arose in the 1994 course. Many students wrote about how suicide touched their lives, and their diaries, which
they gave me permission to quote, reveal the characteristic emotions elicited by suicide: grief, confusion, guilt, and anger. Curiously, although
students do not generally romanticize suicide in life, they often do so in

literature, a phenomenon that raises questions about the contagion or "Werther" effect. Chapter 2 is devoted to *The Awakening,* and subsequent chapters concentrate on individual authors: Woolf, Hemingway, Plath, Sexton, and Styron. I have chosen these writers because they are taught in many high schools and nearly all colleges, and because their writings pose challenging pedagogical and reader-response issues.

In each chapter I discuss the writer's shifting attitude toward suicide, readers' responses, and the impact of writing about suicide on the artist's life. Writers' suicides cannot be predicted, but in retrospect one can almost always see an extended history of self-destructive behavior, an imaginative preoccupation with the subject, or both. As Norman Holland observes, "the writer who destroys himself leaves in his works a long record of ego strategies and choices, a picture of his style in action large and clear enough for us to infer for him an identity theme" (290). While some critics have argued that Woolf, Hemingway, Plath, and Sexton were victimized by the creative process, they themselves believed, with justification, that writing held in check their suicidal feelings and prolonged their lives.

I have tried to tell two parallel stories here: the story of literary works on suicide and the story of students' responses to these texts. There are several other overlapping stories: the story of authors' wrestling with suicide in their own lives; the story of the role that writing may play in allowing authors to act out or work through their suicidal impulses; the story of the multiple causes of suicide, the treatments of suicidal depression, and the consequences of suicide; the story of students grappling with a subject that evokes powerful anxieties, fantasies, and defenses. Each of these stories is extraordinarily complex and interrelated. I hope that *Surviving Literary Suicide* will enable teachers and students to begin discussing a subject that has remained for too long enshrouded in fear and silence.

CHAPTER 1

English 745
LITERARY SUICIDE 1994

The eighteen men and women enrolled in the 1994 Literary Suicide course were likely representative of most graduate students in literary studies attending a relatively large northeastern public university. They were a thoughtful and diverse group, attracted to the course because of the subject and reading list. Some were masters' students, interested in secondary education; others were doctoral students, hoping to complete their degrees and receive a college teaching appointment. They ranged in age from the early twenties to the fifties, with several years of teaching experience in high school or college. Fourteen were women, a ratio slightly higher than the department's graduate student population as a whole. As with most contemporary graduate students in literary studies, some were interested mainly in literature, others in theory, and still others in creative writing or composition theory.

Students in all my classes write several formal essays throughout the semester, but in addition, I introduced a diary component to the 1994 course, hoping it would encourage students to explore their feelings about suicide and make connections between their own lives and those of the fictional characters studied in class. I also asked them to write brief reader-response paragraphs in class. These were the only two changes I made between the 1992 and 1994 courses, but they proved decisive.

I have used introspective diaries in other courses, with intriguing results. Students in my psychoanalytic literary criticism courses have been writing introspective diaries for me since 1976. The diaries are the "laboratory" part of the course, encouraging students to pursue the Delphic Oracle's injunction, Know thyself. In *Diaries to an English Professor* I explored the major subjects students write about, including divorce, eating disorders, sexual conflicts, and suicide. About one-third of the students in each course write about suicide: most write about a relative's or friend's attempted or completed suicide, but in every class a few write about their own past or present suicidal crisis. Before teaching Literary Suicide, I wondered whether the course would attract a disproportionately high percentage of students who were suicidal. I asked the students, in an anonymous questionnaire on *The Awakening*, whether they had thought seriously about committing suicide. I distributed the same questionnaire to 11 professors in my department who regularly teach *The Awakening* and to 102 students in four undergraduate classes who were reading the novel. The responses were remarkably similar. Twenty-nine percent of the undergraduates, 29 percent of the Literary Suicide students, and 36 percent of the faculty indicated that they had thought seriously about committing suicide; 64 percent of the undergraduates, 59 percent of the Literary Suicide students, and 45 percent of the faculty indicated that they had not thought seriously about committing suicide; and 6 percent of the undergraduates, 12 percent of the Literary Suicide students, and 18 percent of the faculty indicated that they were not sure.

The Prevalence of Suicidal Thinking

These responses are consistent with national figures. According to the 1991 national school-based Youth Risk Behavior Survey, sponsored by the U.S. Centers for Disease Control (CDC), 27 percent of all high school students thought seriously about committing suicide in 1990; 8 percent of all students actually attempted suicide; and 2 percent of all students sustained injuries in the course of a suicide attempt serious enough to warrant medical attention (633–35). The CDC also noted that the suicide rates for adolescents fifteen to nineteen years of age have quadrupled in the last forty years, from 2.7 per 100,000 in 1950 to 11.3 per 100,000 in 1988. The suicide rate for fifteen- to nineteen-year-olds is now at the highest level ever (Holinger 4).

Diaries to an English Professor was published at the end of 1994, too late for me to use in my Literary Suicide course, but I gave the students a photocopy of the chapter "Suicide Survivors" so they could understand how the subject touches so many lives in both expected and unexpected ways. The term "suicide survivor" refers to those who have lost a relative or friend: there are several million suicide survivors in the United States. The graduate students were thus reading diaries of undergraduates at the same university, and they were also reading about my own experience as a suicide survivor.

The Legacy of Suicide

Words like "devastated" or "traumatized" do not begin to describe how I felt when my best friend committed suicide thirty years ago. Len had often talked about suicide, each time rejecting my encouragement to speak to a therapist, but I was not prepared for his telephone call on Labor Day 1968, telling me that he had taken an overdose of sleeping pills. Unable to convince him to hang up and call an ambulance, and knowing only that he was calling from his parents' house in New York City, a five-hour drive from Ithaca, New York, where I was living, I felt helpless and panicky; and when, contrary to his stated wish that I remain on the phone, I hung up to call the police, I felt I was betraying him. He carried out his threat to slash his wrists if I attempted to intervene: his body was discovered the next day in his automobile. For years I was haunted by his death, unable to talk about it with anyone. The driving force behind my teaching and writing has been the need to work through the paralyzing guilt, anguish, and confusion that are the legacy—or illegacy—of suicide.

Coming to terms with a loved one's suicide is a lifelong experience for most people, and just when they believe they understand their convoluted feelings, events prove otherwise. These conflicts may express themselves unexpectedly, as I can demonstrate with the following example. Two dear friends who read the present book in manuscript pointed out a revealing typographical error I made in the chapter on Virginia Woolf. In a 1903 diary, Woolf quotes a suicide note attached to the body of a woman who drowned herself. In Woolf's words, "It was blurred but the writing was still legible. Her last message to the world—whatever its import, was short—so short that I can remember it. 'No father, no mother, no work' she had written 'May God forgive me for what I have done tonight'" (*A Passionate Apprentice* 212). I had typed the words "May God forbid me," an error that both readers were quick to detect. One wrote: "A perfect example of the unconscious working! Freud would have loved this example"; the other wrote: "If this is a typo, you're in trouble!" I had indeed committed a Freudian slip. I had used every argument to talk Len out of killing himself, and while neither of us believed in God, I tried to convince him that suicide was, existentially, a forbidden act. Thirty years after his death, I still mourn his loss and have difficulty forgiving him.

A Suicide Diary

Before asking my 1994 students to write a weekly diary, I sought permission from the University Human Subjects Research Review Board, the committee that reviews all requests involving human research. The committee recommended that students not sign the diaries with their real names and that the diaries be voluntary. After receiving approval from the review board, I distributed to each student a copy of the guidelines for the diary:

> Perhaps no subject provokes more intense debate on the meaning of life and death than suicide. In order to explore reader-response issues arising from what I call suicidal literature (that is, literature in which a character attempts or commits suicide), I would like you to keep a weekly diary. Each week you will be requested to turn in to me a diary entry (one or two pages, typed, double spaced); you will receive the entry back, with my comments, the following week. Before I hand the diaries back to you, I will read about five of them aloud to the class. I will always read the diaries anonymously, and there will be no class discussion of the diaries afterward. Each person in the class will thus draw his or her own conclusions about the diaries read aloud: the diarists' identities will never be revealed. If you give me permission to read your diary to the class, please indicate so at the bottom of the diary with the word *yes*.
>
> In order to maintain absolute confidentiality, do not put your real name on the diary entry. Instead, make up an imaginary name—or number—and place that name or number on a separate cover sheet attached to each entry.
>
> I will not grade your diaries, nor will I know the identities of the diarists. If you do not wish to discuss your personal responses to literature, you can use your diaries to explore ideas for your formal essays or discuss how critics have responded to literary suicides. You can also use your diaries to comment on our class discussions or on other diary entries that I have read aloud in previous weeks. You alone will determine the degree to which your diaries will be self-disclosing.
>
> At the end of the semester, after I have told you your final grade in the

course, I will ask you for permission to photocopy your diaries for possible use in a book on suicidal literature. I am interested in exploring questions such as the conditions under which a reader identifies or counteridentifies with a suicidal character, the emotions and fantasies awakened within readers by fictional suicides, and the conditions under which the reading of suicidal literature may be therapeutic or countertherapeutic. If you do give me permission to use one or more diaries for my book, I will ask you to fill out a permission slip at the end of the semester. If I do use your diary, I will not refer to you by your name and I will make whatever factual changes you suggest to prevent others from identifying you.[1]

The students took diary-writing seriously and turned in an entry every week or two. Most gave me permission to read their diaries to the class. They wrote about reactions to friends' and relatives' suicides (as well as Kurt Cobain's, which occurred during the semester), their own struggles against suicide, and—to use a term coined by one of them—their suicideophobia. Some wrote about the contradictory tendency to romanticize suicide in literature while deploring it in life. They were astonished by the degree of self-disclosure. The diaries turned out to be, for many, the most important part of the course, allowing them to explore feelings about which they had never previously written.

Suicide Information Test

I felt it was important for my students to have the latest clinical knowledge, and so on the first day of class I gave them a copy of the "suicide information test" appearing in Scott Poland's book *Suicide Intervention in the Schools*. The students were able to answer correctly most of the twenty-eight true-false questions, which applied mainly to adolescent suicide. They knew, for example, that the following statements are *true*: the incidence of teenage suicide has increased almost 300 percent since the 1950s; there are more than one hundred attempts for every completed suicide; suicide is the second leading cause of death among adolescents; most suicides occur at home between the hours of 3 P.M. and midnight; as many as eight to ten of every one hundred adolescents have

1. I have adhered to these guidelines; in addition, I sent students a copy of the sections of the present book in which their diaries appeared so they could see how I have used their writings. I have not edited the diaries except to make necessary disguises to preserve students' anonymity.

attempted suicide; females make more suicide attempts than males and use less lethal means; males and females are becoming more alike in method and completion of suicide.

The students also knew that the following statements are *false*: teenagers who make plans to commit suicide keep their thoughts to themselves; suicide occurs without warning; suicidal teenagers are fully intent on dying; a person who is suicidal will always be suicidal; there is no causal relationship between drugs/alcohol and suicide; there are one or two causes or motives that explain most suicides; teenagers who threaten suicide and make suicidal gestures are attempting to manipulate others and should be ignored; there is a certain type of person who commits suicide; suicide is always the act of a mentally ill or psychotic person; talking openly about suicide may cause a suicidal person to commit suicide; improvement following a suicidal crisis means that it will not recur; everyone who commits suicide is depressed; young children never commit suicide; suicidal adolescents will be angry at those who attempt to stop them from committing suicide;[2] the religious belief that suicide is wrong will prevent someone from committing suicide; teenagers who are suicidal will tell adults instead of their friends about their suicidal thoughts or actions; suicide is only a problem among teenagers.

Four questions proved troublesome. Most students did not know that removing the means of suicide (such as handguns and poisons) would prevent many suicides. Few realized that deaths by firearms account for most suicides. Contrary to what they believed, there is no particular time of year in which most suicides occur. They were also surprised to discover that suicidal tendencies are not inherited. There is no evidence of a "suicide gene," although there is growing evidence that illnesses such as manic depression, which has a genetic component, may lead to suicide when left untreated.

One of the questions on the "suicide information test" calls for moral rather than factual judgments: "each person has a right to commit suicide, and it is wrong to intervene." Most of my students judged this statement to be false, as do I.

---

2. What makes this statement false is the implication that adolescents do not wish to be prevented from committing suicide. They may be angry at their rescuers—but relieved at the same time.

I should state here my own feelings toward suicide, as I did on the first day of the semester. I believe that one has the right to commit suicide; I also believe, even more strongly, that others have the right to intervene whenever possible to save a life. I realize these are conflicting rights and that in some situations there is no simple resolution to whose rights take precedence. If I can intervene to save a life, I will do so, and I would urge others to do the same. I can imagine extreme situations in which suicide may be warranted, such as during war, when one may be tortured into betraying one's comrades, but in the great majority of cases, suicide is a permanent solution to a temporary problem, particularly among young people. Most attempted and completed suicides are impulsive—including those of many fictional characters we examine in this book—and while someone who is recovering from a suicidal crisis may experience a setback, there is a good chance that the crisis will never recur.

Attitudes toward suicide vary widely throughout history and culture, and my own point of view has been influenced by Edwin Shneidman. He writes in his 1996 book *The Suicidal Mind* that in his fifty-year career as a researcher and clinician, he has concluded that suicide is caused, in almost every case, "by pain, a certain kind of pain—*psychological* pain," which he calls *psychache* (4). He notes that though there are perhaps exceptions—events such as hara-kiri, suicidal terrorists, and religious martyrs—nearly all people who attempt or commit suicide are trying to escape from psychological pain. "Suicide is never born out of exaltation or joy; it is a child of the negative emotions" (7). Suicide is a "lonely act, a desperate and, almost always, unnecessary one" (160).

Suicide Prevention

After giving the students a copy of the suicide information test, I discussed the signs of suicide. They include giving away treasured possessions, changes in sleeping patterns, withdrawal from friends, alcohol and drug abuse, risk taking, and verbal expression of suicidal intent or depression, such as "I won't be around here much longer" or "You won't have to bother yourself with me soon." I gave each student a copy of the following do's and don'ts appearing in Diane Ryerson's essay, " 'ASAP'—An Adolescent Suicide Awareness Programme":

DO

If you think a friend is very depressed or suicidal, try to follow these suggestions:

1. Take your friend seriously—consider the warning signs of suicide.
2. Talk to him about his feelings. Be a good listener and let your friend know that you really care and want to understand how he feels.
3. Be open and ask your friend if she is thinking of hurting herself. If so, how, where, and when does she plan to do so? The more thought your friend has given to the method, time, and location, the greater the degree of risk.
4. Stay with your friend until you can get help.
5. Urge your friend to get professional help.
6. Get help for your friend if he can't or won't. Speak to someone immediately—a school counselor, a clergyman, a family member, a mental health professional.
7. Let your friend know that depression can be helped and trained people are available who can help her overcome depression and resolve problems.
8. If your friend is in a suicidal crisis, call the emergency number.
9. If your friend is momentarily attempting to harm himself, call the police.
10. Try to remain calm.

DON'T

1. Don't ignore the warning signs.
2. Don't promise not to tell—a life may be at stake.
3. Don't try to make your friend feel guilty or tell them that everything is really fine or they're overreacting.
4. Don't leave the person until you get help if the crisis is imminent.

(Ryerson 180–81)

It may seem odd to discuss suicide prevention in a literature course, but there are good reasons to do so. Though most of the recent public attention on suicide has focused on physician-assisted death, youth suicide remains a grave national problem. Each year more than a quarter of a million U.S. high school students make a suicide attempt serious enough to require hospitalization. How can educators reduce youth suicide? The CDC concluded its Youth Risk Survey by recommending several strategies, including educating youths about the warning signs of suicide and the availability of suicide prevention services. This recommendation is consistent with the U.S. Department of Health and Human Services'

1989 *Report of the Secretary's Task Force on Youth Suicide:* "[E]fforts to reduce suicide by improving the general coping skills of high risk youth — e.g., helping youth to recognize and talk about their feelings, ask for help when needed, identify how and where to get help for oneself and others—should be beneficial in preventing a wide range of problem behaviors" (38).

And yet despite the pervasiveness of suicidal thinking and the need for public education, suicide remains a taboo subject inside and outside the classroom. One can understand why students feel uncomfortable talking about suicide, but it is less easy to understand why teachers are reluctant to discuss the subject, even when they teach suicidal literature. Teachers' silence may reflect the widespread myth that talking or writing about suicide will heighten a student's vulnerability. The silence may also betray the anxiety that suicide awakens even in clinicians, who must guard against projecting their own fears onto patients. Teachers are not trained to be therapists, but they inadvertently confirm the stigma attached to suicide by avoiding appropriate discussions.

The inability to talk about suicide heightens the loneliness and despair of those who are at risk. Unable to express their fears, they may conclude that their situation is hopeless and that they are better off dead. Their deaths are devastating to suicide survivors. Clinicians report that survivors are often overwhelmed by grief, anger, confusion, and guilt. Survivors also have an increased risk of committing suicide. No death is more difficult to mourn than suicide: survivors generally feel that a loved one's death has killed part of themselves. Teen suicide is probably the most tragic of all deaths.

Literature teachers can play a vital role in suicide prevention, for they are among the first to realize from a diary or personal essay that a student may be depressed. Given the vast number of stories, plays, and poems containing characters who perish by their own hand, literature teachers can educate students about the pervasiveness of suicide and its complex psychological and social dynamics. Without being falsely optimistic, teachers can inform their students of the progress that has been made in understanding the risk factors for suicide. With the help of psychotherapy, support groups, appropriate intervention, and effective antidepressants, most suicides can be averted.

The Werther Effect

In addition to educating students about suicide prevention, literature teachers can deromanticize suicide. Teachers should be aware of the possibility that real or fictional suicide can lead to other suicides through imitation or identification. The most famous literary example is *The Sufferings of Young Werther* (1774), Goethe's confessional novel about a passionate youth who kills himself because of unrequited love. Goethe based some of the details of Werther's suicide on a friend who took his own life, but the novelist was also writing about his own tormented feelings. He was actively suicidal when writing the story and "even kept a dagger at his bedside and made repeated attempts to plunge it into his breast" (Steinhauer 20). Goethe may not have romanticized suicide to the extent that Werther does, but he identifies so closely with his hero that he blurs the separation between author and character. Werther views himself as a Christ-like martyr and, before shooting himself, tells his beloved Lotte, who was modeled closely on Goethe's Charlotte, that she will be better off without him. Werther also offers a long philosophical justification of suicide, claiming that it leads to eternal freedom.

Goethe was later embarrassed by the novel and distressed that it provoked numerous readers to imitate the event. "Sentimental young men sported Werther's costume: blue coat and yellow trousers and vest; some lovelorn creatures followed his example and committed suicide with copies of the novel in their pockets" (Steinhauer *The Sufferings of Young Werther* 24). Goethe healed himself through the telling of the story and lived a long and productive life, but this consolation came too late for those readers whose identification with his suicidal hero proved fatal.

Emile Durkheim argued in his monumental 1897 book *Le Suicide* that the suicide rate is not influenced by imitation or suggestibility. His assertion remained unchallenged until David Phillips demonstrated, in his 1974 essay "The Influence of Suggestion on Suicide," that the suicide rate increases after the publication of suicide reports in newspapers. The longer a story remains on the front pages of a newspaper, the larger the rise in the suicide rate. Phillips, who coined the expression the "Werther" effect, after Goethe's hero, has estimated that celebrity suicides raise the suicide rate by an average of 1 percent for about a month. "The largest increases in British and American suicides occurred after the deaths of Marilyn Monroe, the actress, and Stephen Ward, the British osteopath involved in the Profumo affairs. In the United States, suicides increased by 12% in the month after Marilyn Monroe's death and by 10% in England and Wales" (Phillips 306). Though few poets or novelists have the celebrity status of actresses or rock singers, we have already seen the impact of Sexton's poem "Wanting to Die" on Elizabeth Wurtzel's suicide attempt, and we will come across other examples of the Werther effect, including that of Assia Weevil, the woman with whom Ted Hughes lived after leaving Sylvia Plath and who, in imitation of her female rival, asphyxiated herself (and her young child) in 1969.

Reactions to "Suicide Survivors"

The week after I distributed copies of "Suicide Survivors" along with Freud's essay "Mourning and Melancholia" and selections from Edwin Shneidman's book *Definition of Suicide,* I received a diary from the following student who was troubled by the discussion of my friend's suicide:

After having read this packet I am left haunted, disturbed, even a bit frightened. I well know how to consider theory and how to attempt to apply theory to case studies or works of literature: these sorts of tasks seem healthy and satisfying, seem challenge enough. But this packet is far more than "Mourning and Melancholia" and Definition of Suicide. *Good lord, attempting a response to either of these pieces, even a diary response, is task enough. What do I do with your* Diaries to an English Professor? *I can't get beyond it; I can't look away; I can't pretend that I haven't read something I feel I should not have read. Ah, so many negatives in that last string of independent causes—what would Freud do with such a blatant display of ambivalence? All I can do is try to tell you what my initial, emotional response is to your chapter.*

First, somehow, the form of this piece reminds me of the coffin, of the womb, of the enveloping parental body. You begin and end with yourself embracing the empty space of the lost other: with "Like many people who study suicide, I do so out of a need to understand a personal tragedy . . ." and "Good luck with the book." In this way I am left sensing an author (you) who is incomplete, having been hollowed out perhaps by loss: the loss which springs from suicide and the loss which springs from writing. Forgive me for being so presumptuous, but I am compelled to say what I am thinking. Further then, the body of your chapter contains the stories (touching, powerful, enlivening) of others' loss. Each story preserves a memory of a dead one so that your experience of Len's suicide opens a place for Joan's mother, Wayne's friend, Ralph's lover, and the rest. I often love how writing captures what is lost, and I often hate how writing slaughters as it captures. How can I explain?

It is your telling of Len's story which disturbs me the most. Perhaps I need to get used to hearing such things. Right now, I feel you are exposing him, exploiting him, forcing him to reconnect, refusing to allow him to "go some-place else to die." Fort-da. But this is not fair; I presume too much. My impulse is to wonder at the violence of such control. Also, the core image here, the image of Len (bloody, dead) within his old Plymouth, hurts me.

I was not aware of creating a verbal coffin in "Suicide Survivors," but I agree that I was "embracing the empty space of the lost other." I memorialized my friend and acknowledged for the first time in print my love for him and the anguish I experienced over his loss. I tried to bring him back to life while simultaneously exorcising his haunting specter. His death left me incomplete, hollowed out by loss. All suicide survivors probably feel this way, as do survivors of other tragedies.

Is the loss arising from suicide comparable, as the diarist suggests, to that which springs from writing? It was wrenching to write about Len's suicide, but afterward I was glad I had made the effort. I was not conscious, then or now, of a loss that springs from writing, apart from my inability to capture more than a hint of Len's complex personality. I tried to tell a story of the devastating aftermath of suicide, and despite the imprecision of my language, I created a verbal portrait of Len that had not existed previously. As the diarist suggests in her allusion to Freud's repetition-compulsion principle, writing is a "fort-da" ritual in which we cast off a person only to make him or her symbolically reappear. Whether we write memorially or counterphobically (that is, to overcome feelings of dread), writing allows us to come to terms with injury and loss.

Students' Experiences with Suicide

Sixteen students indicated that they knew a person who had attempted or committed suicide, and nine wrote about this experience in their diaries. Some of these diaries were written at the beginning of the semester, others during the middle or the end. What follows are the diaries of eight students, each describing his or her reactions to an attempted or completed suicide. The diaries reveal many of the characteristic responses to suicide.

(1)

I'm not sure why I was drawn to this class. I had you before, and I enjoy your teaching, so that was one reason. But I didn't feel like the topic of suicide really touched me on a personal level, simply for the fact that I have never been close to anyone who has killed themselves, and I have never seriously considered suicide myself, despite a long-standing battle with my own pretty severe depression. When I went home after class and read the "Suicide Survivors" chapter of Diaries to an English Professor, *and started thinking about my own life and my relationships, I realized that suicide has really touched me, and that I have been denying this for a long time.*

Since I was a small child I always had a certain connection for what my mom calls "strays," unwanted animals and people. I often made friends with the foreign exchange student or the girl that nobody liked because she was too fat or slightly obnoxious. I'm not sure why I felt this connection with people in distress, but it continued into my adolescent and later adult life. I had a very close friend in tenth grade who was a wonderful artist, but she always seemed as if she were in a constant tortured state. She used to come to class with her face painted or in outlandish outfits. There was something very odd and very likable about her. I made it a point to try to understand her. As our friendship evolved, she shared a lot with me, including her suicidal thoughts.

It's hard for me to remember all of this, because I have blocked most of the experience out. I didn't know what to do with this unwanted knowledge she had given to me. I was her only friend; she wouldn't talk to anyone else, no matter how much I pleaded. I was so angry with her for putting this burden on me. I started actually to dislike her, although I felt responsible for her at the same time.

Finally, I met with a youth counselor in my town whom I was good friends with at the time. I just sat in his office and cried, explaining to him the situation in which I found myself. It was great just to share this information with someone else; it was as if a great burden had been lifted. He suggested that I anonymously refer my friend to one of the school counse-

lors—she was a cool lady, not like a typical guidance counselor. I did so, not entirely sure if I was betraying a trust, or if I was, whether it was justified.

A few days later my friend called me at home and asked me if I had made the referral. (I suppose it didn't take her too many guesses; the anonymous referral was pretty stupid now that I think of it.) Caught by surprise, I told the truth. We talked after that, but things were never the same. I was angry at her. That sounds so selfish and stupid—but I hated being put in this position.

Last year I saw her mother at a job-related event. She ran up to me and said, "Oh, aren't you Lauren's friend?" I didn't know what to say, so I said yes. She said it like I was the only one, and I may have been. I feel guilty about allowing this to ruin our friendship, especially at a time when she needed someone so badly. I hear that she is doing well. I wish her well. I didn't realize that I was going to spend this long on one person, but it is something that I have never really talked about, much less written about. There are other reasons why I think this class will touch me, but I will save them for future entries.

(2)

When I was a kid I was scared by the idea of suicide as if it were a ghost. That was mainly because of Mishima's suicide, which happened when I was in the third grade. Before he killed himself, I knew him by his name, which was frequently spoken on TV or appeared in magazines. I believed that he was a strange, even slightly crazy person, based on information from the media and my father. A few months before Mishima's death, my father ran across him at the airport in the white uniform of the Shield Society. After coming home, my father reported to my mother how maniacally Mishima kept talking to his friends in a loud voice. My father said that Mishima was insane.

Next morning after Mishima's seppuku, all the newspapers had articles about this sensational event in the front pages. The newspaper which we subscribed to at that time did not have the picture of his body, but another newspaper showed Mishima's beheaded body. When I saw the picture, which our neighbor kindly brought to us, I felt like my back was stroked by a cold hand. The picture was taken against the light from a distance, probably from the door of the room where he committed suicide with his partner. His head, separated from the body, was rolling on the bloody floor, and the body was lying with its back to the camera. The setting sun was shining into the room. That night I could not go to the bathroom by myself. I could not believe that a human being could ask someone to decapitate him. I felt that a huge ghost controlled by madness was seeking for the spirits to get their heads. I had never been so scared before.

In those days scary comics were popular among kids. I also liked them very much, and when I read them, I could not go to the bathroom by myself at night. There was a scary comic in which the ghost's name was Tamami. Whenever I remembered this name—when I was playing hopscotch with a pebble, or when I was in class, or when I was taking piano lessons—I felt like my heart was grabbed by a cold hand. But maybe I enjoyed this scary sensation. I liked testing my ability to control this scariness by remembering the name Tamami. However, the name Mishima was so scary that I could not enjoy remembering it; I tried hard to forget the name. The image which I had in those days was a bloody figure of Mishima's white body.

Later, in about the sixth grade, I saw a wax sculpture of Mishima's naked body with a sword in a wax museum in Tokyo Tower. I assume that at that time, I could remember the scary feelings I had three years before. But because of that childhood experience, I could not get rid of my early prejudice that Mishima was only a crazy person. I maintained this belief until I read Mishima's novel The Sound of Waves (Shiosai) *in junior high school.*

I forget the details, but it was a love story between a young man and a young woman in a small village on the sea. I was surprised knowing how pure and beautiful the story was. In both high school and college I read all of Mishima's stories, and there was a brief period when I tried to imitate his style. But after writing a few lines, I realized that I did not have either Mishima's extremely accurate brain or his extremely sensitive mind. Now, I usually have three post-its defining genius in my mind, and I often put one of them on Mishima as well as on Picasso.

Another memory of suicide is connected to Mishima. When I was in high school, one of my friends committed suicide. Sakura was the first student who I vowed would be my closest friend, but I gradually became annoyed by her strong jealousy. As I became used to the new school and made new friends, she did not like it, and she tried to monopolize me. I forget why, but one day I yelled at her and said that we were no longer the closest friends. She became panicky and apologized to me many times. She was unpopular with other students because she was always working hard for good grades. Her nickname was "Gariben," which means "only working without playing."

Later I knew that Sakura worked hard because she was pressured by her mother. In a composition class, she wrote how she adored comic books and how she read them secretly without making her mother aware of it. "I know which step on the staircase creaks when my mother puts her foot on it. When I hear the sound, I immediately hide the comic book I was reading under the desk." She wrote that kind of thing. She was very good at drawing cartoons, but only a few people, including me, knew about her talent.

During junior high school we did not talk to each other at all. As with most other private schools, we were supposed to wear school uniforms. Since Sakura's mother was a tailor, her uniform was handmade. I recognized her only because her skirt was a different color from that of the other students. In both elementary school and in junior high school, she was a hard worker and hardly ever played with the other students. After that we went to different high schools, so I totally forgot about her until I was informed of her suicide.

When a friend telephoned me that Sakura jumped from a building, the first feeling I had was guilt. I wondered whether she would not have died if I still were her closest friend. However, that feeling turned into the slight excitement of knowing about a friend's suicide. I also felt guilty about this excitement. Shortly after that, I read Mishima's essay titled "Anti-Moral Education Seminar" in which he wrote that human beings have the nature to be excited by other people's tragedy. I agreed with him and tried to believe that my indifference to Sakura's death was the proof of my intelligence. When I remember the feeling I had at that time, I cannot help thinking that I am a cold person.

When my father passed away five years ago, Sakura's father visited my mother after the funeral. I heard from her that he apologized that he did not know about my father's death and said that he could not help grieving because Sakura and I were very good friends in elementary school. At that time, I felt strong shame. I have a lot of shameful feelings for other reasons, but this was the worst I've ever had.

(3)

When I got to know Jimmy, he was twelve, and I was twenty-four. The difference in our age was odd. I didn't realize it until later—I didn't realize much about Jimmy until later—that he was drawn to me because his family was falling apart. His parents were about to undergo a bitter divorce. Part of what I saw in Jimmy was that I always wanted a brother or a son.

Jimmy had that rare combination of black hair and blue eyes. But he had far more than that. He was bright, good-looking, athletic, musical, and had a keen sense of humor. People were pulled toward him like a magnet. In retrospect, I leaned too hard on Jimmy and confided too much in him for someone his age. In any case, as his parents divorced, he was drawn into a drug-using crowd and away from me. I bitterly bid him, "Have a nice, druggy life."

I didn't see him much after that. He continued to develop his musical talent and became a remarkable lead guitar player. But this is about Jimmy's death, not his life.

The last time I saw Jimmy, I was with a date in a bar. My date and I were sitting at a little table when I spotted Jimmy returning to the bar from the men's room. I went over and spoke with him briefly. I went back to my date, and we decided to ask him to join us at our table. When I went back to the bar to get him, he was gone.

About four years after that a friend of mine called to tell me that Jimmy had died in a car crash. It was totally out of the blue. Jimmy was just twenty-four, my age when I got to know him. I have never been so shocked and upset by a death. I got on my hands and knees and pounded the floor with my fists as I cried profusely.

Apparently Jimmy had been at a bar, drinking. Alone, he got into his little green Carmen Ghia with a white convertible top and sped into a telephone pole so fast that he broke the pole in two and cut off the electricity in about half the town. He must have died instantly. I don't know if he had a seat belt on—I doubt it—and the car, which was a shambles, was quickly whisked out of town before I could see it. But later I paced off the spot where it happened, and I figure Jimmy must have been going at least eighty miles per hour.

I stayed with a friend the night it happened, and we went to the funeral together. It was a traditional service with a closed coffin at the front of the church, which was packed. I lost it when I saw Jimmy's electric guitar lean-

ing against the coffin. The minister said Jimmy had recently visited Cape Cod and that he wanted to keep making sand castles. At the end of the service they carried the coffin down an aisle, and I thought it was over.

But then they placed the coffin on a cart and wheeled it across the street to the town cemetery. Much of the crowd followed it, including my friend and me. We stood around the grave as they lowered the coffin in. Then, starting with the family members, each person who knew Jimmy took a shovel full of dirt and dumped it onto the coffin. To me it felt like the hand each one of us had in Jimmy's death. It may have been a suicide, but with those shovels of dirt on Jimmy's coffin, it was a burden borne by all.

(4)

I had planned to devote a whole diary to each of the people I knew who had committed suicide. Especially difficult would have been the diary about George, because I felt, however incoherently, that I may have been the cause of his jumping out of a fifteenth-story window. He had been severely depressed for a long time, months actually, during which time I had no contact with him. He was in New York City. He called to ask me to take a small but important role in a play he was directing that summer. I was unavailable. However, knowing through the grapevine how depressed he was, I talked to him for as long as possible, expressed my eternal gratitude for his having thought of me, told him how I looked forward to seeing him again, etc. etc.

I am aware that he did not jump because of my refusal. There was all of his large group of Equity actors to choose from. There was not and had never been the possibility of a romantic involvement. But of course I did feel guilty. Was I just the straw that broke the camel's back? Should I have said I would do it just to help him out of his depression? Should I have known that he was suicidal? When I had been told of his severe depression no one mentioned the S word. Damn! How can we eliminate the fear of this word?

When I once worked as a volunteer on a help line, we all had to be trained to be able to say the word suicide to our depressed clients. This was a countywide line that dealt with many problems aside from suicidal clients, but the big phone calls, the scary ones, were from suicidal people. I did learn to say "Have you been thinking about suicide?" I probably surprised the client as often as I surprised myself by saying the word. As a society we have to learn that words don't kill people.

(5)

Since *'s suicide, I haven't returned to * College, not once. I cannot bring myself even to walk the paths, to open the big gray and glass doors of * Hall, to walk up the three flights of stairs, to turn right, to walk one two three four five offices down the hall, to stand at her office door, to knock gently, to hear her say, "Ah, you're late! Let's get out of here. I'm starved. Indian Place OK?" to hug her, to walk out into the open air with so much to say. . . . I just cannot bring myself to, even in my imagination.

Why can I see the long, slender, white fingers pointing, gesturing, waving, tracing all the words of hours and hours of secret conversations? Why was her mouth so tiny, so plump, so alive? Did you know that she taught me how to paint acorns and pine cones with gold? Did you know she showed me her first villanelle, that she blushed when I read it aloud? Did you know that she loved the same books you do: Hardy, Lawrence, Conrad. Once, we spent an entire lunch talking about Jude and the crows. Did you know she was the only woman I know who entered into psychoanalysis? Did you know that her suicide has left a hole in my life that will never be filled? Did you know that I will never forgive her? Did you know that I love her in spite of my anger?

(6)

The diaries that were read last week triggered a memory of a story I had heard years ago. I had been working with someone who had spent time in a juvenile detention facility. One night, for whatever reason, we spoke about the subject of suicide. He told me a story about a young man in the facility who had been showing signs of self-destructiveness for a while. One day he approached one of the counselors with a razor blade pressed to his throat and threatened to kill himself. After failing to calm him down the counselor decided to call the young man's parents. (I can't recall whether he demanded this or the counselor did it on his own initiative.)

After getting through to the parents and explaining the situation, the counselor prepared to hand the phone over to the young man. They both then heard one of the parents shouting something to the effect that they wanted nothing to do with their rotten bastard of a son and couldn't care less what happened to him.

Reacting instantly, the young man pulled the razor across his throat. According to the storyteller, his last words were, "No, I didn't mean . . ."

before the blood began pouring from his jugular. He died almost instantly.

I hadn't questioned the truthfulness of the story at the time, though I now wonder if it may have been more of an urban myth than an actual event witnessed by the teller. Regardless of this, what struck me most about the story was how powerfully and poignantly it expresses the ambivalence of a suicidal individual, even in the final instant of his decision.

(7)

After having read about Septimus Warren Smith and the trauma of war that was responsible for his suicide in Mrs. Dalloway, I somehow drew a parallel with Marty's suicide.

Marty grew up in my neighborhood. He was always friendly and playful since early childhood. He attended college for two years and then was sucked up in the infamous Vietnam War. There, he saw death, won promotion, and, above all, as a hero was awarded the Medal of Honor. Unfortunately, however, he acquired a habit—drugs. Was it to drown out the numbness, the sight of death and fear all around him?

When he returned home, Marty encountered no sense of anyone being proud, no glory attached to his feats. He was given a stipend by the government and moved away from his parents' home.

I lost touch with him until one day I heard that he had been arrested for dealing drugs. He was given a prison sentence, and I heard no more of him until the day he committed suicide.

On the morning of his discharge from prison, a guard went to his cell to get him but found instead his body hanging from the ceiling. I later learned that the prison guards had for some time noticed that Marty seemed despondent and very depressed. His parents blamed the prison system for not having him seen by a prison psychiatrist.

My feelings at the time were of horror and sadness. I also felt anger. Anger not only toward the system but toward his parents as well. I hope that I am wrong, but I cannot [help but] wonder if they gave him the support and love he needed when he was most vulnerable. Did he experience a sense of abandonment and aloneness, perhaps a feeling of shame of having to face his friends? Did his parents visit him often? Couldn't they see a distinct change in him—a withdrawal perhaps? Of course the prison system was very much to blame. They admitted that Marty seemed depressed just before his discharge. Why, then, didn't they try to help him?

(8)

When I wrote my first diary on my friend's suicide and heard it read aloud, I was shocked at my own reaction. It struck me to hear my own words, and through them to hear my own pain. I had written about his life before, but this was my first attempt to express in writing his death. And there was my pain, confronting me. I had never realized how difficult it was for me to lose him.

Your questionnaire asked if we viewed people who commit suicide as victimizers of others. Yes, oh yes. My friend's attempt was successful. He left behind so many of us.

My unconditional response to your question is prompted by another experience, this one fortunately an unsuccessful attempt. Judith had been my best friend in college. She was a French major, bright, witty, fun to be around with, understanding, etc. But for some reason that I never quite came to understand, Judith had regrets not just about her current life, but about the fact that she had ever been born. She was beginning to face questions about her future and the "real world" after graduation. Inwardly, she slowly became more depressed. She began to be afraid of sleeping at night, afraid of the dark. Many nights she slept on my floor. Eventually she began spending every evening in my room, venting her depression, searching for its causes, and looking for possible answers from me. Suddenly I realized that she had become suicidal. The signs were clearer and clearer, and I became more and more afraid for her. Comments like: "If I'm not here in the morning, there is a list of things I want my friends to have on my desk"; "I've really enjoyed our friendship. I hope that the rest of your life is happy." I heard them over and over again.

What could I do?

What could I say?

She was my closest friend. Soon three to five hours every night were devoted to listening to her. I soon grew more and more worn out, no longer able to entirely stand the emotional drain on myself. Now, I would find excuses for some time to myself in the evenings, call my mother or my boyfriend, looking for support and venting my own emotional stress. After two months of this I was a wreck, and my family convinced me to call the Health Center (as anonymously as one can when there is only one person who really knows what is going on). They came within fifteen minutes, removed

Judith from the dorm, and kept her for twenty-four hours for emergency care and observation.

I was exhausted, mentally and physically. I alternately slept and cried the twenty-four hours that she was across campus and in someone else's care.

She never forgave me for it. She still hasn't, and I assume she never will. She came to my room immediately when she was released. She screamed at me, expressing hatred I did not know she was even capable of. I had broken her trust, how could I have taken a solution to a problem that wasn't mine to solve? How could I do such a thing, she yelled, when she had finally decided that she felt better about living?

I stopped dead in my tracks. I might as well have been slapped in the face.

For three months this woman had shared her anguish, pain, depression, regrets, and fears. Never once had she said, "I think I'm feeling better today." I was so hurt, so angry, so relieved to see her standing in front of me still alive. I did not and still do not understand why she trusted me enough that she might share her death with me. (She had often told me that she wanted me to find her body if she ever killed herself, because she thought I could "handle it.") But she had not trusted me enough to share her life.

We patched things up as best we could. She was required to go to therapy twice a week, something she resented and did not get much out of. She didn't put much into it as far as I could see. Life became calmer all around. She graduated, and we kept in touch. She went to graduate school in another state. Suddenly I received a call: she wanted to spend a week with me. I had not seen her in a year. Would she have adopted a different outlook on life, or would we fall back into our old pattern of me as confidant, social worker/mother figure? I was scared about how things would go, but I did not voice my apprehensions to the people I lived with.

She arrived, and things seemed to be going well. A few days into her visit, my friend Ken offered to cook for us. Having eaten his cooking before, I immediately took him up on his offer. After the meal and several glasses of wine, however, things began to sour. Judith had had far too much to drink. As we sat down to watch TV, she began to hurl coded insults at me. She told Ken never to trust me with his life. (She didn't mention the possibility of him sharing his death, but I decided not to bring it up.) She told me what a traitor I had been. On it went for about fifteen minutes. I sat mute. She left the room, saying she was going for a walk. I burst into tears. Ken *was fortunately a good listener, as the tale was long. Judith left, and I have not seen or contacted her since.*

On occasion I have had suicidal thoughts myself. None of them were ever very serious. But I am constantly haunted by my memories of that awful year. I did the only thing that I felt I could do, and it apparently wasn't good enough. I don't know which was worse, being uninvolved in my friend's suicide and therefore feeling guilty about not being given a chance to help, or being involved in someone's suicidal feelings and helping the only way I knew how, and still being told that I was destroying things.

I am glad she is still alive. I hope that she has learned that I considered her worthy of living and that if no one else cared enough to stop her from hurting herself, I had tried. According to her, I tried the wrong way, but I did my best.

Yes, unconditionally yes, a person's suicide or even suicide attempt victimizes other people. My only possible exception to this is one of the saddest thoughts I think I ever had: that someone might be so truly alone and isolated in the world that their death went unnoticed by the people around them. Suicide has affected most of us, more than some of the people who have tried it ever can know.

Reading Suicide Diaries

I have quoted the preceding diaries because they demonstrate so many of the turbulent emotions of suicide survivors. Nearly all the diarists express sadness, guilt, anger, and confusion. Two students use the same word to describe the aftermath of an attempted or completed suicide: diarist 1 writes, "I was so angry with her for putting this burden on me," and diarist 3 observes, Jimmy's death was a "burden borne by all." A common response among suicide survivors is the feeling that if they had been a better friend, more alert to the signs of suicide, they might have been able to avert a tragedy. Paradoxically, the more one helps a friend who later attempts or completes suicide, the more one tends to be self-blaming. "I did the only thing that I felt I could do," writes diarist 8, "and it apparently wasn't good enough." Self-reproach makes the mourning process problematic. Suicide is among the most painful tragedies to mourn because, unlike other deaths, suicide creates guilt that, when inadequately understood and worked through, may remain frozen in time.

In addition, the diarists felt implicated in suicide, drawn in against their will. Suicide usually implies a dyadic relationship involving a person ambivalently intent upon death and a would-be rescuer, and whether the victim leaves a note or calls another person, as occurs in about one-quarter of all suicides, the act has interpersonal implications. Suicide thrusts a relative or friend into a Catch-22 situation: either do nothing and possibly let a person die, or intervene and incur his or her anger. For this reason, suicide survivors often feel a sense of complicity despite the fact that they are not responsible for the actions of others.

Sarah: "Romanticizing the Suicidal Ending"

Significantly, none of the diarists idealizes suicide or describes it as a heroic, defiant, or transcendent act. Of the scores of diaries I have received from undergraduate and graduate students, none has glorified suicide. This would not be surprising were it not for the fact that those who refuse to romanticize suicide in life often do so in literature.

Sarah is a striking example of this contradiction, and I want to look at three of her diaries. She was the ninth student who wrote about her reactions to a person who had attempted or completed suicide. Her opening diary described her reactions to her sister's suicide attempt two years earlier, an event Sarah still could not come to terms with.

I'm in this class for two reasons. The first, straightforward reason is that the reading list appealed to me, purely in its literary content. The second reason is longer, more convoluted, more personal. I am curious about the nature of suicide, the mental workings of a person who wills death.

I think my first encounter with anyone's suicide came in high school. A boy in my history class shot himself when we were in tenth grade. I remember all the hysteria, the sudden availability of adults "to talk to," the empty chair in our classroom the rest of the spring. I didn't know the boy very well, but it was horrible just the same. I joined a peer group called "Human Relations" that was formed to encourage students to talk about their feelings and concerns. Nothing I learned from this experience (and from the intervening years' observations of humanity) prepared me for what happened two years ago.

A week before Thanksgiving, my mother phoned me with the news that my sister was in a hospital in New York City, where she went to school. She had been out drinking with her roommates and left the bar early to come back to the dorm. When her roommate returned to their room hours later, she found my sister unconscious in a pool of blood. She had hacked her wrists open with a pair of scissors (thankfully, a pair that was not too sharp). She was admitted to the hospital for alcohol poisoning and attempted suicide. The doctors kept her on a locked psychiatric ward for five days' observation, until she convinced them that she did not really want to die.

The important detail missing here is that my father had died the preceding year. My sister had worshiped the man, and she continued worshiping him after he died. I theorize that this suicide attempt, rather than being an effort to join him, was done more out of anger than grief. At the "scene," my sister's roommate found a picture of my father which looked like it had holes punched in it with a pencil—definitely not an expression of love. I think my sister was finally becoming angry at him for leaving her. Alcohol enhanced her emotions, and she became self-destructive. (I'm almost ready to make the leap that she was really trying to do some harm to him—out of angry abandonment—in attempting to kill herself.)

Where am I in all of this? Even though I seem to have weathered my father's death, I have not been able to shake the anger I feel toward my sister. I believe I have intellectualized her suicide attempt quite well, but the emotional aspect of it escapes me. I have a very hard time empathizing with her pain. I DO NOT UNDERSTAND life being so unbearable that you want to die. I don't even believe she really wanted to die: the alcohol factor looms too large for me here. I just don't get it. And I haven't forgiven her for throwing my family into another circle of hell this year. I'm sure that colors my relationship with her; it's not one of sunshine and benevolence. I'm here in this class out of curiosity about suicide, and to learn enough about this subject to change my resentment to understanding.

Sarah's next diary was written in response to *The Awakening*, a novel that elicited a far different attitude to suicide.

I had read The Awakening *before, and all I could remember was the idea of a woman languishing. I didn't remember too many of the details; even the love of Robert didn't register too strongly. In my memory it was a novel of slow quietness, not a lot of action, not a lot of dialogue: just this woman slowly fading away.*

Rereading the book, here are my thoughts. I identify with Edna in some important ways. I know the feeling of yearning for something, of loving someone so consumingly. I know of being awakened to something and wanting to change my life because of it. I love how Edna thumbs her nose at Léonce by sleeping in the hammock and by refusing to honor her Tuesday open house ritual. Léonce is not a demon, but I admire Chopin's understated portrayal of the couple's battle of wills.

When I read the novel for the first time, I was surprised by Edna's method of suicide. I think I knew she would have to die (because nineteenth-century women with heightened sensibilities never fare too well), but I pictured it as a more gradual withdrawal from life (i.e., just sleeping into death with laudanum). With a second reading, I appreciate Chopin's method much more. It seems more appropriate that Edna die at Grand Isle, the site of her awakening, and even more appropriate that she die in the sea, which has been a source of sensuousness and seduction for her. The ending is coherent. I believe she would do this.

I know that here I am probably romanticizing the suicidal ending. How can I do such a thing?! Well, first of all, this is fiction. Oh, hell, that's not a very good excuse, now, is it? Do I have a fantasy about this Edna experience? It is awesome to be so committed to yourself and your passions that you refuse life if they are thwarted. (I must warn you, I have a penchant for passionate people—I really admire this quality.) But, really, though, the woman is dead. It's troubling and ironic that the only salvation of Edna's self is the obliteration of the self. That really is nothing to admire. I suppose I can rationalize Chopin's killing her off by noting that there really weren't many alternatives for nineteenth-century Southern women. So maybe I can empathize with Edna only in her historical context. I wouldn't choose the same response for myself today, but then I couldn't quite duplicate her plight (thankfully).

Now that I think about it, one thing that probably helps me to like this book so much is that Kate Chopin didn't waltz off into the idea herself. I'm comforted by the fact that Edna's fate is that of a character and not a real woman; I like knowing that Chopin, who understood so well Edna's struggle, was not a suicide herself. (I have a lot of trouble with people killing themselves.) It makes me sad to realize this, because I like the idea of taking fiction seriously. I think I'm being utterly logical in separating real human lives from fictional ones in my sympathies with suicidal behavior, but the mere fact of my own logic has never been a comfort to me.

Sarah's responses demonstrate that one can romanticize literary sui-cide only if one remains safely distanced from the terrible suffering asso-ciated with it. Such a response implies the radical separation of literature from life, a separation that reduces literature to the realm of fantasy or escape. The fact that Chopin did not commit suicide in real life, as her heroine does at the end of *The Awakening,* makes it easier to accept the idea of heroic death. As Chopin's biographer observes, "My students like to know that Kate Chopin did not walk into the sea and that long after her death, she has been resurrected for us" (Toth 65). But when authors do commit suicide, it becomes more difficult to accept their romanti-cized portrayals of suicide in their fiction, as Sarah remarked in her next diary, written in response to Mishima's short story "Patriotism," a highly eroticized account of ritualized self-disembowelment. In a chilling ex-ample of art prefiguring life, Mishima later committed suicide in a par-ticularly gruesome way. The story jolted Sarah, prompting the following diary entry.

So much for the romance of suicide! Just when the nature of literary sui-cides (or suicide contemplators) was becoming perhaps too beautiful and seductive for me, you throw Mishima's "Patriotism" at me. What a horrible little piece.

Yet there is still something ennobling about Shinji's motives and actions, don't you think? Despite the details Mishima offers, though, I don't think it's particularly clear how the author wants me to take the couple's deaths. I find the title ironic, and the mix of sex and death in the story is intriguing. But if I were Japanese and imbued with the historical sense of such acts, my reaction would be different. I sympathize with Shinji initially because he is incapable of leading the charge against his friends. But the cause of his suicide gets lost in the story; I have to keep reminding myself of it. When the suicide gets all mixed up with sex and shame and appearances, somehow it becomes less easy for me to sympathize with Shinji.

This response may arise out of my weird desire to perceive suicide as romantic. Let me think about this for a minute. Suicide (in life and litera-ture) can be so perceived because of its links with pain, love, yearning, disappointment, tragedy, separation, desire, and unfulfillment. To witness someone's pain and suicidal resolution of that pain on PAPER is a mental experience. I appreciate the separation of my own life from that aching person's hellish experience. When someone IN LIFE has all that pain, it's not romantic—witness my sister's suicide attempt and my anything-but-sentimental reaction to it. I try a lot harder to feel what the aching person went through, but the separation isn't there. I'm too close to it.

I am living the repercussions of this lack of separation. But I am also regretting my romanticizing of literary suicides because they mean I'm not taking literature seriously enough. It's important for my sanity to realize the difference between life and literature. But I value (or want to value) literature too much to relegate it to the category of "just a story."

I agree with Sarah that we do not take literature seriously when we approach it as purely fantasy or escapist; I also agree with her that we should not glorify a subject in literature that produces so much suffering in life. Several of the characteristic fantasies surrounding suicide have a powerful appeal, including the desire for rebirth, the wish for reunion with a lost loved one, and the quest for heroism and transcendence. These fantasies are seductive because they conceal the violence inherent in suicide and its destructive impact on society.

Apart from actually experiencing suicidal depression, probably the best way to understand its mind-chilling horror is through literature. Creative writers generally succeed in exploring suicide without romanticizing it, and their writings affirm, for the most part, the richness of life and the value of survival. But when poets and novelists do glorify suicide, I believe it is the critic's and teacher's responsibility to comment on this. My refusal to romanticize literary suicide does not imply the belief that this literature should be ignored or banned—I am not proposing a new censorship based on "suicidal correctness." On the contrary: I seek a fuller discussion of suicidal literature and its impact on readers and society.

Roger Shattuck does not confront directly the subject of suicide in his 1996 book, *Forbidden Knowledge*, but many of the questions he raises on pornography and violence are relevant to our study. Shattuck notes that the two most influential approaches to crime and evil in art derive from Plato's theory of infection and Aristotle's theory of catharsis. He then cites two conflicting and controversial U.S. government reports: the 1970 *Report of the Commission on Obscenity and Pornography*, which suggests that there is no empirical evidence that pornography contributes to criminal behavior, and the 1986 *Final Report*, which asserts that sexually violent pornography may encourage criminal behavior among a small group of people. Shattuck agrees with the two reports' different though not opposed conclusions and argues that freedom of speech must be preserved except in the case of child pornography. Yet he also worries about the consequences of forbidden knowledge. "The world teems with salutary influences and with poisonous influences. The critic's minimum responsibility is to recognize writings for what they are and to puncture false claims" (289).

Shattuck invokes the medical analogy of infection and immunity to suggest that literature can either weaken or strengthen a reader's general health. "As a child can be given vaccinations at predetermined ages to activate its immune system against polio, for example, so certain spectacles and stories introduce a child to aspects of violence and evil to which it can develop a resistance. Or it may become infected" (297). Since more than one-quarter of all high school students are depressed enough in any given year to consider suicide seriously, it is likely that many of them will be exposed to poems and stories that speak to their own conflicts. Exposure to this literature may help students to develop a "resistance" to suicide—or a heightened susceptibility to it.

Like violence and pornography, suicide represents forbidden knowledge and must be approached with caution. Whereas homicide or rape is rarely described as heroic, transcendent, or empowering, suicide is often viewed this way. Of all the novels that romanticize suicide, none is taught more often on college campuses than *The Awakening*, to which we now turn.

CHAPTER 2

Romanticizing Suicide in Kate Chopin's *Awakening*

I remember the first time I read The Awakening *in the context of a class. I was an undergraduate, taking a course on women's literature. It was the first time I had been exposed to such a phenomenon; mostly my education consisted of courses on dead white men (some suicidal, some not). So I was excited. I had read the book as a high schooler, thanks to the woman I baby-sat for, who decided that I should be enlightened to such works. But I never had the opportunity to discuss it with anyone, since at that time no one had ever really heard of it.*

There I was, anticipating the class, which was taught by a woman, and feeling sure that the discussion would be inspirational. I had been extremely struck by Edna's suicide. It had seemed somehow natural to Edna, somehow in step with her character. To look at her in context with the rights that a woman had at that time, the scandal that occurred when she moved into the Pigeon House, and how her husband had to save face by ordering construction on the house, among other factors, was really striking. So I was prepared to discuss it.

So I sat there, astounded, as Ms. Wilson, of Ye Olde School of Instructors, discussed the plot, characters, the symbolism of the water, and the bird with the broken wing. Not once did she mention Edna's suicide as being tragic, moving. Not once did she ask how it affected us. She did not put the story into an historical context to explain what Edna's rights would and wouldn't have been as a woman in society (Southern society, no less) at the time. Nothing. I was crushed.

I wanted to ask her if this story actually meant anything to her. I know the impact it had on me—Edna's discussions of having feelings that were completely foreign, of learning what it was finally to be in control of her own inside thoughts. Except that she was not allowed to act on her sexual impulses: her fate to that effect had been sealed by her marriage to Léonce. And I thought about myself, at a woman's college, finally gaining a sense of myself and my own independence, my own capabilities and freedoms. Yet Ms. Wilson never said a word about anything that I thought really mattered.

"She's from the old school," one of my friends explained. "That's just the way she was trained, probably." Trained not to explore? Trained not to recognize that there were more important things to Edna than the fact that the water could be seen to recognize an unconscious state? How sad I was when I left that class, how truly saddened that this woman could not incorporate more than what was simply on the surface of The Awakening.

It was not until I shared my feelings with a few classmates, expressing my utter dismay about what I saw to have been a totally failed class discussion, that I began to realize that everyone else felt the same way. We were almost as equally struck by Ms. Wilson's response to it as we were by Edna's suicide itself. And where to go from there? For coffee, for a heated discussion about whether Edna truly had any other options, whether she intended to kill herself when she went back to the island, or whether it just seemed like a good idea at the time. Was Edna scared out there in the water? What would we have done in a similar situation? Were there modern situations that presented the same kind of constrictions? Overwhelmingly, no one seemed to condemn Edna for killing herself. It seemed to be her choice, and she took full advantage of the option. The questions were endless, the answers from all different perspectives. But I was thrilled. Someone else was upset by Edna's suicide, saddened by it, touched by it, and was ready to admit it. I felt that I understood suicide and Edna, as well as myself and the constrictions of the educational institution around me, much better.

LIZZIE

It seems hardly possible to talk about Edna Pontellier's suicide in Kate Chopin's celebrated novel *The Awakening* without discussing the many questions Lizzie raises in her diary, yet this is precisely the situation that exists in many classrooms today. Despite the extensive body of literary criticism on *The Awakening,* most of it written after the story's rediscovery in the 1960s, few critics have investigated the reasons for Edna's suicide and its impact on readers. For example, of the more than forty study questions on *The Awakening* appearing in the popular anthology *Nine Short Novels by American Women*, edited by McMahan and Funk, not one is concerned with Edna's suicide, an omission that highlights our cultural anxiety over self-inflicted death.

"It Is Not a Healthy Book"

Reviewers were not afraid to comment upon Edna's suicide when *The Awakening* first appeared in 1899. They were so appalled by Edna's abandonment of her husband and children that they condemned her suicide without trying to understand it. In ending the story with Edna's swim into the unknown, Chopin openly defied her society's ban against self-inflicted death, a prohibition that did not apply equally to both sexes. Whereas male suicide roused shock and indignation, female suicide, far less common, provoked horror and outrage. The vast majority of the suicides in the 1890s—like those in the 1990s—were committed by men, and as tragic as a father's suicide was, it was not as cataclysmic to the family as a mother's suicide. Unlike men, women were expected to devote themselves to their children and were held to a higher moral standard. Women were deemed to have greater fortitude and patience than men and thus were required to endure life's inevitable suffering.

This double standard can be seen in an unsigned article called "Women and Suicide" appearing on the woman's page of the influential New Orleans newspaper the *Daily Picayune* on 8 October 1899, six months after the publication of Chopin's story. Without mentioning *The Awakening*, the reviewer, presumably Dorothea Dix, one of the first advice columnists in the United States, begins by disagreeing with a distinguished lawyer who had recently argued that under certain conditions people have the right to commit suicide. To judge from her examples, Dix has no sympathy for male suicide. Rather, she reserves her compassion for women, who, stoically bearing their hardships, rarely commit suicide. "Women seldom take their own lives, and so we have the curious and contradictory spectacle of the sex that is universally accounted the braver and stronger, flinging themselves out of the world to avoid its troubles, while the weaklings patiently bear theirs on to the bitter end" (qtd. in Culley 150). Dix condemns suicide as a "coward's deed" and concludes by suggesting that women are the stronger sex: "The babe salutes life with a wail, and the dying man takes leave of it with a groan. Between there is no time that has not its own troubles, and cares, and sorrows, and it is our part to bear them with courage, and it should be part of our pride in our sex that so many women sustain this brave attitude towards life under circumstances that might well tempt them to play the coward's part" (qtd. in Culley 151).

If women, then, were expected to be less self-centered than men, more inclined to subordinate their desires to the preservation of their families, we can understand why nearly all the early reviewers of *The Awakening* were horrified by Edna's rejection of home and hearth. Readers expressed the wish that Kate Chopin had never written *The Awakening:* illicit passion and family dissolution were profoundly unsettling to the Victorian sensibility. "At the very outset of the story one feels that the heroine should pray for deliverance from temptation," wrote the reviewer for the *St. Louis Daily Globe-Democrat* in May 1899, adding, "when, having removed every vestige of clothes she 'stands naked in the sun' and then walks out into the water until she can walk no farther, and then swims on into eternity, one thinks that her very suicide is in itself a prayer for deliverance from the evils that beset her, all of her own creating" (qtd. in Culley 163). Declaring that *The Awakening* is "not a healthy book," the critic makes no attempt to sympathize with a woman in Edna's situation.

Edna's suicide affronted other readers. "[W]e are well satisfied when Mrs. Pontellier deliberately swims out to her death in the waters of the gulf," concluded a critic in *Public Opinion* (qtd. in Culley 168), voicing an opinion shared by the reviewer in *Literature:* "The awakening itself is tragic, as might have been anticipated, and the waters of the gulf close appropriately over one who has drifted from all right moorings, and has not the grace to repent" (qtd. in Culley 168). Even Willa Cather, who reviewed Chopin's novel for the *Pittsburgh Leader*, felt that *The Awakening*, with its affinity to Flaubert's *Madame Bovary*, was not a subject for respectable readers. "Edna Pontellier, fanciful and romantic to the last, chose the sea on a summer night and went down with the sound of her first lover's spurs in her ears, and the scent of pinks about her. And next time I hope that Miss Chopin will devote that flexible iridescent style of hers to a better cause" (qtd. in Culley 172).

The early reviewers assumed that suicide is a violation of both human and divine law; those who chose to end their own lives thus deserved everlasting condemnation. Viewing Edna as selfish, spoiled, and sensual, critics could not understand why she might be driven to desperate remedies. They saw her suicide as the inevitable conclusion to an immoral life rather than as an indictment of a patriarchal society. As Elaine Showalter observes in "Tradition and the Female Talent," "Readers of the 1890s were well accustomed to drowning as the fictional punishment for female transgression against morality, and most contemporary critics of *The Awakening* thus automatically interpreted Edna's suicide as the wages of sin" (qtd. in Walker 186). One reviewer actually refused to concede that Edna's suicide was motivated by desperation; his denial of adequate agency and motivation deprived her of any sympathy or pity: "It is not a pleasant picture of soul-dissection, take it anyway you like; and so, though she finally kills herself, or rather lets herself drown to death, one feels that it is not in the desperation born of an over-burdened heart, torn by complicating duties but rather because she realizes that something is due to her children, that she cannot get away from, and she is too weak to face the issue" (qtd. in Culley 162).

Negative Countertransference

Edna's suicide awakened in early readers of the novel the negative feelings that suicidal patients often elicit in therapists. Two related psychoanalytic terms, *transference* and *countertransference*, are relevant here. Transference refers to patients projecting their emotional responses on their analysts, while countertransference refers to analysts projecting their emotional responses on their patients. Transference and countertransference are generally unconscious and reveal the extent to which past relationships influence present ones. As psychoanalysts John Maltsberger and Dan Buie have argued, suicidal patients evoke feelings of malice and aversion in the therapist, feelings that, if not analyzed, may form a major obstacle in treatment. "When the countertransference is fully conscious it can stimulate introspection in the analyst, can usually be controlled, and can direct his attention to details of his patient's behavior, the meaning of which might otherwise remain obscure. Otherwise, when unconscious, countertransference may generate well rationalized but destructive acting out by the therapist" ("Countertransference Hate" 270).

Readers, too, may find themselves unable to empathize with a character whose suicide is morally or psychologically offensive. Late nineteenth-century reviewers saw Edna's suicide as a threat to society rather than as a symptom of a personal or interpersonal crisis. The malicious and aversive tone of their writings is striking. I believe they were right to recognize the shattering relational implications of Edna's suicide but wrong not to empathize with her struggle for a more fulfilling life. The early readers of *The Awakening* were relieved that Edna had terminated her existence because it seemed to rid society of a virulent contagion. Edna literally turns her back on society in moving toward the sea, and critics responded by wishing she had never come into existence.

Rejecting Edna

The early reviewers acted like the characters in *The Awakening,* all of whom fail to understand Chopin's heroine. Edna is different from the other women in the novel, in part because she is not one of the "mother-women." "They were women who idolized their children, worshiped their husbands, and esteemed it a holy privilege to efface themselves as individuals and grow wings as ministering angels" (*The Awakening,* ed. Walker 26). Unlike her friend Madame Adele Ratignolle, who is radiant in her maternal instincts and who gives birth every other year, Edna is not overly attached to her children: "She was fond of her children in an uneven, impulsive way. She would sometimes gather them passionately to her heart; she would sometimes forget them. . . . Feeling secure regarding their happiness and welfare, she did not miss them except with an occasional intense longing. Their absence was a sort of relief, though she did not admit this, even to herself" (37). Many contemporary readers are able to identify with Edna's feelings toward her children, but readers a century ago were shocked.

Edna's extramarital passion also disturbed Chopin's early readers. Léonce Pontellier is a stolid and respectable husband who remains devoted to his wife's well-being, but he looks upon her primarily "as one looks at a valuable piece of personal property" (21). A shrewd businessman, he becomes agitated whenever he believes Edna's actions devalue his considerable investment in her. He is a courteous husband as long as his wife remains acquiescent. Unable to fathom the changes in her, Pontellier consults with his long-time family physician, Dr. Mandelet, who hears Pontellier's complaint that Edna's "got some sort of notion in her head concerning the eternal rights of women" (85) and asks: "has she been associating of late with a circle of pseudo-intellectual women—super-spiritual superior beings?" (86). Upon being told that Edna has not been associating with any of these people, Dr. Mandelet reflects for a moment and then offers Léonce the following advice:

> Woman, my dear friend, is a very peculiar and delicate organism—a sensitive and highly organized woman, such as I know Mrs. Pontellier to be, is especially peculiar. It would require an inspired psychologist to deal successfully with them. And when ordinary folks like you and me attempt to cope with their idiosyncracies the result is bungling. Most women are moody and whimsical. This is some passing whim of your wife, due to some cause or causes which you and I needn't try to fathom. But it will pass happily over, especially if you let her alone. Send her around to see me. (86)

In echoing the prevailing turn-of-the-century medical dismissal of women's complaints, Dr. Mandelet dismisses the significance of Edna's unhappiness. No inspired psychologist, he seems to equate all women with moodiness and instability. Mandelet's attitude, symptomatic of a cultural attitude held by the majority of the physicians of his age, reveals itself in the belief that women are in essence mysterious and irrational creatures. Although he counsels Pontellier to remain hopeful about his wife's condition—"The mood will pass, I assure you. It may take a month, two, three months—possibly longer, but it will pass; have patience" (87)—Mandelet is, as we shall see, the first of a long line of physicians and psychologists in literature who fail to offer convincing therapeutic relief to their suicidal patients.

Nor does Edna's father support her. A colonel in the Confederate army and passionate about horse racing and liquor, he argues with Edna over her refusal to attend her sister's wedding, a decision that reflects her feelings about her own marriage. The Colonel criticizes Pontellier's unwillingness to order Edna to attend the wedding and declares: "You are too lenient, too lenient by far, Léonce. . . . Authority, coercion are what is needed. Put your foot down good and hard; the only way to manage a wife" (91). To which the narrator observes wryly: "The Colonel was perhaps unaware that he had coerced his own wife into her grave" (92).

Edna's two lovers, Robert Lebrun and Alcée Arobin, also fail her. Robert professes his hopeless passion for Madame Ratignolle early in the story, but he switches allegiances and becomes enamored of Edna. When she returns his affection, Robert becomes nervous and flees to Mexico. His absence fuels Edna's obsession, and once aroused, she turns elsewhere, consummating her passion with the story's Don Juan figure, Alcée Arobin. Robert's unexpected return awakens in Edna the hope of a joyful reunion, but his final departure and cryptic note—"I love you. Goodby—because I love you" (134)—deepen her despair. Shedding her clothes as she walks into the Gulf of Mexico, Edna repeats Robert's words to herself and then embarks upon her final journey.

Contemporary Views of Edna's Suicide

How do contemporary readers respond to Edna's suicide? To answer this question, I distributed an anonymous questionnaire to the 18 students in my Literary Suicide class. Eleven colleagues who regularly teach the novel agreed to fill out the questionnaire, as did 102 students in four undergraduate courses that I taught. I asked students and faculty to indicate whether they agreed or disagreed with the following statements, all of which condemn Edna's suicide. The first three are from early reviews previously quoted, while the fourth is by George M. Spangler. The results of the questionnaire are rounded off to the closet percentage. (Not all respondents answered every question.)

"[*The Awakening*] is not a healthy book"; it is a novel that is "too strong poison for moral babes, and [that] should be labeled poison."

	AGREE	DISAGREE	NOT SURE
Literary suicide	0	94%	6%
Faculty	0	100%	0
Undergraduates	1%	92%	7%

"One thinks that her very suicide is in itself a prayer for deliverance from the evils that beset her, all of her own creating."

	AGREE	DISAGREE	NOT SURE
Literary suicide	18%	35%	47%
Faculty	9%	91%	0
Undergraduates	26%	46%	28%

"The awakening itself is tragic, as might have been anticipated, and the waters of the gulf close appropriately over one who has drifted from all right moorings, and has not the grace to repent."

	AGREE	DISAGREE	NOT SURE
Literary suicide	6%	88%	6%
Faculty	0	91%	9%
Undergraduates	22%	54%	24%

"If then, the conclusion Mrs. Chopin chose for *The Awakening* allows for pathos and poetic justice to please the sentimental and moralistic—a dubious accomplishment indeed—it also leads to a painful reduction in Edna's character. For in the final pages Edna is different and diminished: she is no longer purposeful, merely willful; no longer liberated, merely perverse; no longer justified, merely spiteful." (qtd. in Culley 210–11)

	AGREE	DISAGREE	NOT SURE
Literary suicide	11%	56%	33%
Faculty	18%	73%	9%
Undergraduates	30%	40%	29%

These responses appear consistent with the judgments of contemporary literary scholars, who overwhelmingly reject the early reviewers' censure of Edna's suicide. As Suzanne Wolkenfeld observed more than twenty years ago, critical attitudes toward Edna's suicide have undergone a radical shift. Feminist critics praise Edna for her pursuit of freedom and view her suicide as an act of individualism. They do not, however, seem troubled by the relational implications of the suicide.

Why Does Edna Commit Suicide?

It is a tribute to the psychological realism of *The Awakening* that its presentation of Edna's suicide is consistent with the latest clinical research. Eight of the ten common characteristics that Edwin Shneidman has applied to most suicides clearly relate to Edna's suicide:

The common stimulus in suicide is unendurable psychological pain.
The common stressor in suicide is frustrated psychological needs.
The common purpose of suicide is to seek a solution.
The common goal of suicide is cessation of consciousness.
The common emotion in suicide is hopelessness/helplessness.
The common internal attitude toward suicide is ambivalence.
The common cognitive state in suicide is constriction.
The common action in suicide is egression.

(Shneidman, *Definition of Suicide* 124–49)

There is some evidence to suggest that Shneidman's ninth characteristic also applies to Edna's death: "the common interpersonal act in suicide is communication of intention." We do not know enough about Edna's early life to confirm the tenth characteristic: "the common consistency in suicide is with lifelong coping patterns."

Suicide is among the most complex acts and has multiple causes. As judged by the respondents to my questionnaire, the motives for Edna's suicide include, in order of decreasing importance, the need to (1) escape from an intolerable situation, (2) end her suffering, (3) regain control of her life, (4) achieve unity or self-transcendence, (5) take revenge on others, and (6) atone for her actions. Of these motives, critics have focused mainly on Edna's need for escape and her effort to achieve unity or transcendence. Cynthia Wolff's classic 1973 psychoanalytic essay explores Edna's fantasy of unity with the infinite. Fantasies of (re)union with a deceased love object, or with nature itself, are not uncommon in suicide, as Dan Buie and John Maltsberger have suggested: "Some patients anticipate the grave as a womb of eternal holding by mother earth. Some believe they can rejoin a dead self object by dying themselves. In some psychotic cases such ideas occur as delusions. Many suicidal patients not obviously deluded are very attached to such fantasies, which at moments of crisis may operate with delusional force" (62–63).

Contemporary readers emphasize the positive motives of Edna's suicide. They see her as an innocent or helpless victim striving for freedom, independence, unity, and self-fulfillment. Not one Literary Suicide student or professor (and only two undergraduates) believed that Chopin condemned Edna's suicide. Only about 20 percent of the Literary Suicide students and undergraduates (and none of the professors) viewed Edna as clinically insane at the end of the novel. There was disagreement over whether Edna had other viable options at the end of the story: 61 percent of the Literary Suicide students, 44 percent of the professors, and 77 percent of the undergraduates believed that other choices were available to her.

Significantly, few respondents believed there were darker motives behind Edna's suicide, such as revenge. Only about 10 percent of the Literary Suicide students and undergraduates and 18 percent of the faculty judged revenge as a strong motive in Edna's suicide, a much lower percentage than the first four motives. There was no clear agreement whether

Edna's last words, "Good-bye—because I love you," should be interpreted ironically.

Is Edna's Suicide an Act of Liberation?

Chopin originally intended to call her story "A Solitary Soul," and the change in title suggests that Edna's suicide is the inevitable conclusion to her awakening. The sea, the agent of Edna's death, is associated with rebirth imagery throughout the story, as the impassioned language intimates: "She felt like some new-born creature, opening its eyes in a familiar world that it had never known" (136). I asked my students and colleagues to indicate whether they agreed or disagreed with the following statements by Paula Treichler and John May, both of whom interpret Edna's suicide as an act of liberation.

In determining "never to belong to another than herself," and "to give up the unessential," she transcends the mythologies offered to her, and to us, and this is treated as a triumph, not a failure. (qtd. in Walker 328)

	AGREE	DISAGREE	NOT SURE
Literary suicide	76%	18%	6%
Faculty	60%	30%	10%
Undergraduates	39%	31%	29%

The ultimate realization that she has awakened to is that the only way she can save herself is to give up her life. She cannot accept the restrictions that nature and man have conspired to impose upon her, the perpetual frustration of desire that living entails. And so, paradoxically, she surrenders her life in order to save herself. (qtd. in Culley 216)

	AGREE	DISAGREE	NOT SURE
Literary suicide	67%	22%	11%
Faculty	73%	18%	9%
Undergraduates	68%	22%	10%

These two passages reflect the dominant contemporary attitude toward Edna's suicide. Most critics regard Edna's suicide as an act of release, rebirth, or transcendence, and though they may be troubled by the ending, they gloss over the darker implications of her death. Three critics whose essays appear in the Modern Language Association's 1988 volume *Approaches to Teaching Chopin's* The Awakening illustrate this tendency. Patricia Hopkins Lattin asserts that "Edna's 'self' is reborn, through a rebirth that is harder even than dying, since in the end she chooses death as a solution to the problems threatening her newly reborn self" (42). Though she refers to Chopin as a "scrupulously objective narrator [who] provides no solution to the ambiguity facing the reader" (44), Lattin nevertheless sees Edna's suicide as a welcome escape from despair. Barbara Solomon concludes her essay by suggesting that Edna's interaction with the other characters in *The Awakening* "helps to convince readers that Edna's problems are insoluble given the environment, the era, and the strength of her newly discovered, uncompromising identity" (119). The strongest affirmation of Edna's suicide comes from Joyce Dyer, who sees Chopin's heroine as fulfilling her heroic destiny: "Awakening is a serious matter. For what Edna's 'inward contemplation' at last has let her know is this: the only way to remain a romantic and hold onto our dreams and illusions is to die. Edna's dreams and ideals are so important to her that she refuses to give them up—in spite of the high price she has to pay. She rejects the very idea of compromise and walks into the gulf" (131).

I suggested earlier that *The Awakening* provoked in nineteenth-century readers the feelings of malice and aversion that are typical negative countertransference responses to suicidal patients. *The Awakening* provokes in many twentieth-century readers a different form of negative countertransference: feelings of relief and satisfaction that Edna made the right decision in ending her life. These feelings allow readers to affirm Edna's fantasies of rebirth and thus to distance themselves from her hopelessness and pain.

Romanticizing Edna's Suicide

Critics who argue that Edna's final action is an escape, rebirth, or transcendence overlook one of the most problematic aspects of *The Awakening:* its romanticization of suicide. The story idealizes suicide in at least three ways: first, by portraying Edna's drowning in strongly positive terms; second, by endorsing the dichotomous nature of Edna's suicidal thinking (*either* she commits suicide and remains true to her emancipated self *or* she rejects suicide and compromises her newly awakened desire for freedom and independence); and finally, by failing to describe the aftermath of Edna's suicide.

When asked whether Chopin romanticizes Edna's suicide, a large majority of the Literary Suicide students (76 percent), professors (64 percent), and undergraduates (58 percent) replied "yes." What makes this response puzzling is that when asked another question, "How is Edna's suicide portrayed?" a similarly high percentage of the Literary Suicide students (72 percent), professors (73 percent), and undergraduates (81 percent) believed that the suicide was treated ambiguously, as both a triumph and a defeat. If most respondents believed that Edna's suicide is portrayed ambiguously, why did they also believe that Chopin romanticized the suicide?

Drowning as Seduction

The reason, I suspect, is that while Chopin generally maintains narrative distance from Edna, viewing her heroine as dispassionately as possible, she describes the suicide itself as an impassioned, sensual act, devoid of violence and terror. The opening description of the sea foreshadows its mysterious attraction to Edna:

> The voice of the sea is seductive; never ceasing, whispering, clamoring, murmuring, inviting the soul to wander for a spell in abysses of solitude; to lose itself in mazes of inward contemplation.
> The voice of the sea speaks to the soul. The touch of the sea is sensuous, enfolding the body in its soft, close embrace. (32)

Edna's "sensuous susceptibility to beauty" (32) draws her to the gulf's irresistible waters. The alluring image of the sea is never seriously contradicted or qualified by any of the other characters in the story or by Chopin herself. Edna feels in the beginning a "certain ungovernable dread" while swimming, but this is mainly because she is an inexperienced swimmer. As she develops more confidence in her swimming ability, she feels "intoxicated with her newly conquered power." Swimming in the gulf is a mystical and transcendent experience for her, offsetting the loneliness and melancholy of her life. "She turned her face seaward to gather in an impression of space and solitude, which the vast expanse of water, meeting and melting with the moonlit sky, conveyed to her excited fancy. As she swam she seemed to be reaching out for the unlimited in which to lose herself." Overestimating her stamina and swimming further out in the gulf than prudence suggests, she finds herself in a dangerous situation; yet neither a "quick vision of death" nor a "flash of terror" fails to subdue her attraction to the sea (46–47).

The Circean power of the gulf never releases its hold on Edna. Using language identical to the earlier description, Chopin emphasizes the sea's capacity to soothe the troubled soul. "The water of the Gulf stretched out before her, gleaming with the million lights of the sun. The voice of the sea is seductive, never ceasing, whispering, clamoring, murmuring, inviting the soul to wander in abysses of solitude." Feeling reborn, Edna casts off her clothes and walks out into the sea, feeling its waters enfold her body in a "soft, close embrace" (136). Walking on and on, she recalls the terror she felt on the night when she had swum far out, but the memory quickly passes. *The Awakening* ends with Edna's mastering her fear and contemplating without regret or sadness the life she has now given up: "She looked into the distance, and the old terror flamed up for an instant, then sank again. Edna heard her father's voice and her sister Margaret's. She heard the barking of an old dog that was chained to the sycamore tree. The spurs of the cavalry officer clanged as he walked across the porch. There was the hum of bees, and the musky odor of pinks filled the air" (137).

Chopin depicts Edna as fully in control of her destiny, exquisitely attuned to the sights and sounds of life but willing to sacrifice everything for a final, transcendent unity with the sea. We are presented with an idealized vision of suicide, shorn of its violence and terror. What is concealed here is as telling as what is revealed. There is no awareness of the terrifying suffocation that accompanies drowning or of the body's involuntary resistance to prolonged submersion. Edna's suicide is eroticized but not in the way Mishima sexualizes suicide in "Patriotism." There we see dismemberment; here we see Edna merging with the circumambient universe. Because we never actually behold Edna's drowned body, we do not have to deal with the reality of death. Nor is there anything to indicate that if the sea can look seductive and inviting one moment, it can look angry and cruel the next moment. Edna's moods are mercurial, shifting from despair to joy and then back to despair in a matter of seconds; consequently, we would expect the sea, which is personified throughout the story, to reflect these changes. And yet the waters of the gulf remain quiescent and inviting.

Dichotomous Thinking

If Edna's problems are insoluble, then we may find ourselves seduced into the dichotomous thinking that is symptomatic of a suicidal crisis. "The primary thought disorder in suicide," Edwin Shneidman has observed, "is that of a pathological narrowing of the mind's focus, called constriction, which takes the form of seeing only *two* choices: either something painfully unsatisfactory *or* cessation" (*Suicide as Psychache* 21). Although she has far fewer options than her twentieth-century counterparts, we do not have to endorse Edna's suicide as the only acceptable choice, as Paula Treichler would have us do. "Learning to swim—awakening—made Edna's death inevitable" (327). Rarely if ever do we respond to a real-life suicide with such deterministic thinking. Nor would we react to the news of a suicide by saying, "He was remaining true to his newly awakened self" or "She was seeking transcendence"—particularly if that person is twenty-nine years old and in otherwise perfect health, as Edna Pontellier is.

Edna's suicide is not premeditated but impulsive. There are hints from the opening pages that she will leave home, as when the parrot repeats, *"Allez vous-en! Allez vous-en! Sapristi!"* (19), but most readers cannot predict until the final paragraphs that she will take her life. She cheerfully tells Victor Lebrun, moments before announcing her intention to leave for a swim, that she is hungry and is looking forward to dinner. It is never precisely clear when she decides to commit suicide: she does not have a clearly formulated plan, nor does she consciously think about ending her life. Indeed, she promises to be back from her swim in time for dinner. Her final action is consistent and in character, but the suicide is not an inevitable result of her awakening.

It may be argued that since she is a fictional rather than a real character, Edna owes her existence as much to the conventions of literature as to the probabilities of life. Susan Rosowski has suggested that the "prerequisites of the novel of awakening" include the "assumption that a woman does not have choice" (33). Yet even if this is true, most critics, including Rosowski, have assumed that Edna freely chooses to end her life.

The Aftermath of Suicide

The novel romanticizes suicide in another way, by omitting the aftermath of suicide. *The Awakening* concludes with a suicide in progress; we see neither the completed act nor its aftermath. One leading critic, Sandra Gilbert, has argued that since we do not actually observe Edna drown, it may not be a suicide at all. "Even in the last sentences of Chopin's novel, then, Edna Pontellier is still swimming. *And how, after all, do we know that she ever dies?*" (105). Yet Gilbert acknowledges that this reading is "of course hyperbolic" (105).

Few critics have dwelled on the relational implications of Edna's suicide, particularly its effect on her children. Her two young boys, "sturdy little fellows of four and five" (20), are not like the mother-tots of Grand Isle. "If one of the little Pontellier boys took a tumble whilst at play, he was not apt to rush crying to his mother's arms for comfort; he would more likely pick himself up, wipe the water out of his eyes and the sand out of his mouth, and go on playing" (26). Their sturdiness and independence seem to be a result of their mother's benign neglect of them. Despite Léonce Pontellier's criticisms of his wife's care of her children, the boys never appear to be disadvantaged.

Early in the story, for instance, Pontellier tells Edna that Raoul has a high fever and requires attention; Edna replies that she is certain that he does not have a fever, prompting her husband to scold her severely. Edna springs out of bed, enters her son's bedroom, and soon returns, refusing to answer her husband's questions. She then begins to cry, experiencing an "indescribable oppression" (25). The scene is interesting for at least two reasons: first, we sense that Edna's growing depression arises over her husband's treatment of her; second, there is nothing in the scene to indicate that Raoul is indeed ill or in need of attention. Edna's silence does not confirm her husband's allegation of motherly neglect. Edna may be an ambivalent mother, but her sons seem to be none the worse for it.

"I Would Give My Life for My Children"

The night before her suicide, Edna recalls Madame Ratignolle's last words to her: "Think of the children, Edna. Oh think of the children! Remember them!" (132). The urgent warning, intended to alert Edna to the consequences of marital infidelity, takes on added significance in light of the impending suicide. It is almost as if Madame Ratignolle unconsciously senses that Edna may intend to harm her children. But Edna cannot think about them: the subject is too painful. Edna recalls the next day a conversation in which she had told Madame Ratignolle that "I would give my life for my children; but I wouldn't give myself" (67). Edna regards the children at the end as persecutory objects from whom she must escape. "The children appeared before her like antagonists who had overcome her; who had overpowered and sought to drag her into the soul's slavery for the rest of her days. But she knew a way to elude them" (136).

Two clinical observations are relevant here: paranoid thinking and depression "are opposite sides of the same coin" (Allen 180); and "[s]uicide can be understood as an effort to rid oneself of intolerable hostile impulses originating from within, through attributing them to an inner enemy" (Maltsberger and Buie, "The Devices of Suicide" 407). Viewed from this perspective, Edna's suicide seems to be motivated, in part, by the wish symbolically to kill her own children. Critics who regard Edna's suicide as an act of liberation have tended to ignore or soften its impact on her children. It is difficult to accept Priscilla Leder's claim that Edna "contrives a suicide that will appear to be an accidental drowning, leaving her children motherless but respectable. Moreover, when she dies for her children, she does so out of conscious consideration for their futures" (244). Edna's attempt to escape from the responsibilities of motherhood has ironic consequences, for while she has never been one of the "mother-women" who efface themselves for their family, her last journey into the maternal sea is a far more radical self-effacement than the one she has rejected earlier.

How will Edna's suicide affect her children? When I asked my students and colleagues to speculate on this question, most chose the answer, "There's no way of knowing." If Edna's suicide is viewed mainly as a personal tragedy, then the life (and death) of only one character is affected. But if the suicide is viewed as an interpersonal tragedy, as suicide is in real life, then the lives of many characters are affected. A comparison of *The Awakening* with *Madame Bovary* is instructive here. Flaubert describes in one moving sentence Justin's reaction to Emma's suicide. "On the grave among the firs knelt a young boy, weeping and sobbing in the darkness, his heart overflowing with an immense grief that was tender as the moon and unfathomable as night" (386). So, too, does Goethe intimate in the last paragraph of *Werther* the aftermath of his hero's suicide: "Lotte's life was feared to be in danger" (Steinhauer 271). Had *The Awakening* described the children's reaction to their mother's death, readers would be less inclined to idealize the ending.

A Dangerous Book?

If *The Awakening* romanticizes suicide, is it a dangerous book? Might certain readers identify with Edna's suicide and find themselves at risk? Chopin's responses to this question are worth noting. She satirically distanced herself from her fictional projection in an often-quoted remark: "Having a group of people at my disposal, I thought it might be entertaining (to myself) to throw them together and see what would happen. I never dreamed of Mrs. Pontellier making such a mess of things and working out her own damnation as she did. If I had had the slightest intimation of such a thing I would have excluded her from the company. But when I found out what she was up to, the play was half over and it was then too late" (qtd. in Toth 344).

A more serious response appeared in an interview in the *St. Louis Post-Dispatch* while she was completing *The Awakening*. The newspaper had printed an editorial on 23 January 1898 called "The Killing Pace" publicizing the suicides of four young women of high society. "Does the conjunction of suicidal attempts indicate a tendency in that direction among the women of society? Has high society struck the pace that kills?" (qtd. in Toth 311). Two weeks later the newspaper returned to the subject and interviewed four prominent women including Chopin. She defended women's right to participate in society and attacked the double standard:

> Business men commit suicide every day, yet we do not say that suicide is epidemic in the business world. Why should we say the feeling is rife among society women, because half a dozen unfortunates, widely separated, take their own lives?
>
> The tendency to self-destruction is no more pronounced among society women than it ever was, according to my observation.
>
> The desire seems to come in waves, without warning, and soon passes away. The mere reading of a peculiar case of suicide may cause a highly nervous woman to take her own life in a similar manner, through morbid sympathy.

But do not men do the same thing every day? Why all this talk about women? (qtd. in Toth 312)

When she wrote these words a century ago, Chopin was more concerned with protesting women's social and political inequality than with the impact of her novel on "half a dozen unfortunates," but now, a century later, the suicide rate for men and women alike is many times higher. If she felt that the reading of a novel like *The Awakening* might cause a "highly nervous woman to take her life in a similar way, through morbid sympathy," then might not many more readers at the close of the twentieth century find themselves in a similar situation?

To answer this question, I asked my Literary Suicide students, colleagues, and undergraduates whether reading or talking about *The Awakening* triggered any serious conflicts or disturbances in them. The results were surprising: 20 percent of the Literary Suicide students, 36 percent of the faculty, and 25 percent of the undergraduates indicated "yes." I distributed the results of the questionnaire to the Literary Suicide students the following week and asked them to write brief paragraphs describing how *The Awakening* might prove disturbing to some readers. Several conclusions emerged. None of the eighteen students felt that reading or talking about Chopin's story produced suicidal feelings or increased vulnerability within them. None referred to *The Awakening* as a "dangerous" book or implied that it should not be taught or read. Nor did any one believe that the story was morbid or depressing. Several commented, however, on the need to read oppositionally in order to distance themselves from Edna's movement toward self-destruction.

I think the author makes it clear that she agrees with Edna's behavior, and I get sucked into it. Chopin says it's okay, so it shouldn't bother me. Now, I'm not that unsophisticated a reader, really. But I do think I'd feel more outright disturbance over Edna's act if Chopin had painted it more horrifically. There's such a peaceful aura about the suicide; I've been lulled by it.

I wasn't disturbed, though I did experience conflicts. I could understand and almost "permit" (for lack of a better word) Edna's struggle as a literary device. It was difficult because I struggle with moral and religious implications of suicide. One reason I can better accept Edna's suicide is that I try to read it in the mind frame in which it was written. I try to consider the

social responsibilities and limitations of a woman in the nineteenth cen-
tury. I therefore purveyed her attitude as an act of self-preservation: her
means to freedom. I may, however, interpret it differently had she been a
twentieth-century woman in similar conflicts.

I personally cannot foresee having an emotionally charged response in any
respect to The Awakening. *It seemed, as some of us said in class, to be such*
an aesthetic, symbolic suicide that, for me, it virtually denigrated the wrench-
ing guttural realism that I imagine to be implicit in any suicidal experi-
ence. That someone last week could have related her emotional response to
the suicide as "elated" is proof that this was an aesthetically designed ploy
of Chopin's. I guess it pretty much offends me, so if that's an emotional
response, I guess I did have one. (I don't mean to be totally callous about
this. I could see someone being disturbed by troubles in their life that reso-
nate in Edna's experience, but the suicide itself, no way.)
It reminded me, actually, of an episode of that cheesy syndicated show
called Baywatch. *One of the lifeguards almost drowns, and while having a*
near death experience ("seeing a bright light," etc), they play rock music so
that her dalliance at the threshold is a rock video. I don't think Chopin is
that bad, but I think that to paint suicide in rosy hues is gross. Almost, I
guess, the same way some Holocaust survivors react badly to fictionaliza-
tion of the Holocaust.

Perhaps because of the constraints of time, no one wrote about specific
conflicts or disturbances experienced while reading *The Awakening*, but
one person speculated on how the story might place some readers at risk:

Surely, issues of engulfment, oppression, marital turmoil, loss, detachment,
romantic failure, and suicide elicit powerful emotions. How could anyone
read deeply and fully without experiencing something of these emotions?
So, if one reads well, and if one has little tolerance for such emotions
(perhaps because of repressed urges?), chances are the experience could be
serious.

Significantly, a number of students remarked that although they had
studied *The Awakening* before, they had never seriously thought about
the implications of Edna's suicide until now. "I had read this novel several times, and I am ashamed to admit I did not consider Edna's suicide

as much as I should have. This seems the most important part of the novel, and sometimes in literature classes it is not discussed as much as it should [be]." Another did not understand how a "feminist-friendly text" could portray a heroine's suicide so affirmatively: "As I responded in a diary entry, I was appalled by the way in which Chopin and her critics (perhaps only her critics) glorify the 'choices' that Edna made which resulted in or rather dignified her emancipation. I was greatly disturbed that any reader could or would accept Edna's actions as emancipatory."

Resuscitating Edna

An empathic reading of *The Awakening* does not require us to romanticize or rationalize Edna's suicide. Nor does an empathic reading force us to choose one form of violence over another. Celebrating her suicide, in the name of female empowerment, is as problematic to late twentieth-century readers as condemning her suicide, in the name of family values, was to late nineteenth-century readers. Reading Chopin's novel with an understanding of the reality (as opposed to the myth) of suicide allows us to appreciate Edna's awakening to the possibilities of life without endorsing her pursuit of death. The power of *The Awakening* lies neither in Edna's final act of desperation nor in the seductive rebirth fantasies she attaches to suicide, but rather in her struggle for a more self-fulfilling life. Edna may not have believed that she had other options at the end of her life; nevertheless, one can imagine other endings, such as Jill McCorkle's revision, appearing in the *New York Times Book Review* in 1987—a revision that my students enjoy hearing as we conclude our discussion of the novel:

> It is as if Edna is now, finally, again, really waking up. She doesn't want to die over those two. What a waste. She starts swimming back toward shore, thinking of all the things her new life will bring: a divorce, a job, birth control, single parenthood, shorter skirts. Edna, swimming with strong steady strokes, is convinced that she's on to something, and she would rather be a pioneer than dead. (qtd. in Toth 405)

CHAPTER 3

Virginia Woolf and the "Embrace of Death"

Septimus Warren Smith bugs me. There really is no other way to put it. In an even stronger way, Clarissa Dalloway bothers me too. Perhaps it is a function of Woolf, her goal in life, to make her reader as uncomfortable as possible. It's hard to tell, I suppose. After spending two weeks with Mrs. Dalloway, *reading what other people thought of her as well, it has become hard for me to separate Septimus/Clarissa/Virginia.*

I think that perhaps what bothers me the most is the description in Clarissa's mind of the act of suicide itself. With Septimus, he goes out the window, and the next thing we are told, he is on the ground, very much dead. But Clarissa is alive, standing by the window in her own house, and her imagination is still very much alive. The dress is in flames, the rusty spikes are coming closer and through her as she hits the ground: it really is a horrifying image. It can't help but make me think, what would it be like on the fall down? To die with intentions, to take one's own life and have that flight downward. . . .

My junior year as an undergraduate, I lived in a tower block, much the same as the towers at SUNY-Albany. Despite protective measures that the university had taken to make sure that our windows didn't open more than about eight inches, a woman still succeeded in breaking a window and jumping from the fifteenth floor. What went through her mind on the way down? They said that the only bones she broke were her shoulders—because her hips went through them when she impacted. I was horrified, but wondered—does time suspend itself on the flight down? Were her clothes on fire, or was her mind completely serene? Did she reconsider, somewhere around the seventh floor?

67

She had chosen to kill herself during the spring break, knowing that there were very few people on campus. Despite this, several people in my tower saw her jump from the tower next door. They were completely shaken, to say the least. Some of them, friends of mine even, will never ever forget what they saw. And yet how much more frightening it must have been for the people in her own tower, sitting in the living room of their suite, drinking tea, enjoying their breakfast, watching a bit of morning television, to see her go flying past the window. What does one do?

In a way, I am confusing the issue here between people who are in the process of suicide and those who are forced by circumstances to watch it. Virginia Woolf drowned herself. Filled her pockets with stone, and purposely jumped into the river. What was going through her mind? Is that death peaceful?

Ironically, as a really strong swimmer, I almost drowned once. I was fifteen years old, and I remember floating toward the bottom of the pool and thinking how peaceful and quiet it was underwater, and how people had been wrong all these years: it really was possible to breathe underwater. Fortunately for me, just as I was going unconscious, somebody pulled me up. I was not scared until I surfaced and realized what happened. Then I was scared. Perhaps that is what it is like when you jump. Maybe you don't realize fully what could be happening unless you survive?

I fear for Clarissa, I really do. If you can form a triangle between Septimus, Clarissa, and Virginia Woolf herself, which I believe you can, two out of the three of them did succeed in ending their own lives. It makes one wonder whether or not Clarissa was able to battle the desire she had to turn inward. To find that center that so many, Septimus and Woolf included, were searching for. If I ever meet Virginia Woolf someday in some other life, I would like to know whether she found the peace she was searching for, and what it is like on the way down. Perhaps it is morbid, in some ways this whole diary is morbid, but like so many other people I have talked to, the question of what really happens when you die perplexes, upsets, and yet somehow intrigues me.

JENNIFER

Nearly everyone who is familiar with Virginia Woolf's writings knows about her suicide, and as Jennifer suggests in her diary, this fact strongly affects readers' responses. No matter how much *The Awakening* romanticizes suicide, there is no biographical evidence to suggest that Kate Chopin was suicidal; the awareness that life did not imitate art is consoling. Yet reading *Mrs. Dalloway* (1925) is disturbing precisely because of Clarissa's and Woolf's intense identification with Septimus Warren Smith, the young man who chooses suicide over psychiatric institutionalization. Septimus's suicide not only haunts *Mrs. Dalloway*—it is the central action in the novel and the one that most profoundly moves its eponymous character—but it also eerily anticipates Woolf's suicide in 1941 when, fearing the return of the mental illness that had periodically darkened her life, she filled her pockets with stones and drowned herself in the river Ouse. Although she never romanticizes suicide in her diaries, letters, or critical writings, Woolf portrays Septimus's embrace of death affirmatively in *Mrs. Dalloway*, leading many readers to conclude that suicide is an act of heroic defiance.

Early Mental Illness and Suicide Attempts

Virginia Woolf struggled against the debilitating effects of mental illness throughout her life. "Five times in her life (four of them between the ages of thirteen and thirty-three) she suffered from major onslaughts of the illness and in almost all (possibly all) of these attacks she attempted to kill herself" (Lee 171). Her first breakdown occurred in 1895 when she was thirteen, shortly after her mother's death from influenza. Virginia attempted suicide by jumping from a window—the method Septimus chooses in *Mrs. Dalloway*. Following the death of her father, the eminent literary critic Leslie Stephen, she suffered her second major breakdown in 1904 and was placed under the care of Sir George Savage, who prescribed, as was the custom in the late nineteenth and early twentieth century, the "rest cure." Based on the principles of S. Weir Mitchell, the leading neurologist of the age, the rest cure involved complete isolation and loss of freedom; force-feeding, when necessary; and the suspension of all activities, including reading and writing. Woolf spent almost three months in convalescence.

A more serious breakdown and suicide attempt came in 1913 when, shortly after marrying Leonard Woolf, she began suffering from severe headaches, heard voices, and could neither sleep nor eat. Years later, when writing *Mrs. Dalloway*, she projected most of these symptoms onto

Septimus, who hears birds singing in Greek and experiences terrifying hallucinations. Woolf's health deteriorated, and she swallowed a potentially lethal dose of veronal. She would have died were it not for the prompt medical treatment she received from a family physician and friend, Geoffrey Keynes, who succeeded in pumping her stomach. Unwilling to have his wife certified and institutionalized, as was customary for a suicide attempt, Leonard had Virginia removed to her stepbrother's country home, where she slowly regained her strength.

The stresses of everyday life often threatened Woolf's health. Whenever she felt herself falling ill, she was required to rest in bed for days or weeks until the symptoms abated. During the most intense moments of her illness, she would sometimes become abusive of those attending her, especially her husband, whom she regarded then as a jailer. As James King has observed, during the breakdown "[s]he wanted to do away with herself and she was violently angry with the person closest to her. She was like an anguished child who is so desperately furious at a parent that she wants to kill them but, at the same time, is so guilt-ridden for harbouring such sentiments that she wants to destroy herself" (224). Both Virginia and Leonard learned to recognize the danger signals of her illness and react appropriately. After her recovery in 1915, she remained generally healthy until the final weeks of her life.

"Great Wits Are Sure to Madness Near Allied, and Thin Partitions Do Their Bounds Divide"

From what did Virginia Woolf suffer? Thomas Caramagno argues persuasively in *The Flight of the Mind* (1992) that throughout her adult life she was afflicted with manic-depressive illness, also known as bipolar affective disorder. Integrating neuroscience, psychobiography, and literary theory, Caramagno demonstrates through an analysis of five novels that Woolf's inner world "oscillated unpredictably between moments when the self seemed magically enhanced and empowered, imposing meaning and value indiscriminately on the outside world, and other moments when the emptiness and badness of the world lay revealed, corrupting (or corrupted by) the sickening self" (3).

There is increasing evidence that manic-depressive illness has a strong genetic component. Kay Redfield Jamison, a leading psychiatric researcher, has shown in *Touched with Fire* (1993) that a much higher percentage of artists suffer from manic-depressive illness than does the general population. She observes that whereas the lifetime rates for manic-depressive and depressive illness in the general population are 1 and 5 percent, respectively, a study of a group of British writers and artists found 38 percent suffering from these affective illnesses (80). Jamison's moving autobiographical memoir *An Unquiet Mind* (1995) chronicles her own lifelong affliction with manic depression.

Leonard Woolf also believed his wife suffered from manic depression, and he quotes in his autobiography John Dryden's famous lines about the relationship between creativity and madness: "Great wits are sure to madness near allied, / And thin partitions do their bounds divide" (*Beginning Again* 32). Several of Woolf's relatives, on both sides of her family, almost certainly suffered from bipolar or unipolar (depressive) illness. (Ernest Hemingway also suffered from manic depression, as did many of his relatives; see chapter 4).

Manic-depressive illness is highly treatable with lithium and newer medication, but in Woolf's time virtually nothing was known about its diagnosis and management. Left untreated, it is often deadly. A higher percentage of untreated manic depressives commit suicide than any other medical risk group. Jamison found in her review of thirty studies that "on the average, one-fifth of manic-depressive patients die by suicide. From a slightly different perspective, at least two-thirds of those people who commit suicide have been found to have suffered from depressive or manic-depressive illness" (*Touched with Fire* 41).

Though literary critics tend to be suspicious of psychiatry in general and biological psychiatry in particular, preferring to see reality as socially constructed rather than as genetically influenced, Caramagno's and Jamison's research on the relationship between manic-depressive illness and creativity cannot be ignored. I agree with Caramagno when he argues that psychobiographers ignore psychobiology at their peril. I also agree with his criticism of scholars who are quick to attribute Woolf's suicide to persons or causes having little if anything to do with the ravages brought on by a deadly genetic disease.

Conspiracy Theorists

For the last two decades "conspiracy theorists" have been determined to prove that Woolf's illness was caused by her family. Many of these critics view her suicide as a sane response to an insane world. Woolf scholarship is now so vast that it would take a lengthy study to chronicle its history, but I cite briefly four books that allege one form of conspiracy or another against the novelist.

Roger Poole asserts in *The Unknown Virginia Woolf* (1978) that the novelist was never mentally ill. Rather, he claims that Woolf was forced by her oppressive physicians and husband to disconfirm her own identity. Poole maintains for existential reasons that Woolf committed suicide because she knew that "history" was about to end with the Nazi invasion of England; when it became apparent to her that suicide was inevitable, Woolf wrote a letter to her husband exonerating him from blame—a letter that Poole calls the "most generous fraud, and the most magnificent deception, in modern literature" (258). In arguing against coercive psychiatric practices, Poole overlooks the fact that patients suffering from severe mental illness may need to be protected against harming themselves. One need not defend the unenlightened psychiatric treatment Woolf received to note that, without it, she might have committed suicide long before she wrote her first novel. It is destructive to disconfirm a person's identity, but it is not wrong to intervene medically if that person is suicidal.

In *"All That Summer She Was Mad": Virginia Woolf and Her Doctors* (1981), Stephen Trombley builds upon Poole's argument and indicts the entire psychiatric community for Woolf's despair. Trombley's book is valuable both for its insights into the treatment Woolf received from her doctors and for uncovering many of the presuppositions of madness that were held at the turn of the century. But Trombley distorts the truth by implicating Woolf's physicians, relatives, and friends in a sinister conspiracy designed to break her will and elicit her compliance. Some of his statements now seem ironic in light of our greater understanding of the genetic nature of manic-depressive illness—as when he condemns Sir George Savage for suspecting that mental illness is a result of heredity rather than environment. Trombley's dismissal of Savage's belief in the efficacy of medication is also ironic. He quotes derisively a statement by Savage that nearly every psychiatrist and psychologist would now endorse: "People nowadays are rather inclined to disparage drugs and drug treatment, but there is no doubt that they are essential in some cases of mental disorder. They may prevent a breakdown, or they may alleviate it in one way or another" (153). Recent breakthroughs in psychopharmacology have confirmed many of Savage's statements, and given the absence of effective medication at the turn of the twentieth century, I doubt that any physician would have been able to cure Virginia Woolf's illness.

An altogether different conspiracy theory appears in Louise DeSalvo's *Virginia Woolf: The Impact of Childhood Sexual Abuse on Her Life and Work* (1989). Since the publication of Woolf's late autobiographical essay "A Sketch of the Past" detailing her stepbrother Gerald Duckworth's sexual abuse of her, biographers have sought to understand the damaging psychological consequences arising from this traumatic experience. It now appears likely that Virginia was also sexually abused by her other stepbrother, George Duckworth. There is evidence to support DeSalvo's view that the novelist "was raised in a household in which incest, sexual violence, and abusive behavior were a common, rather than a singular or rare occurrence" (1). From this one can conclude, as DeSalvo does, that sexual abuse was not only a traumatic experience for Virginia but also a formative one, and that she had few opportunities to work through the disabling fear, guilt, anger, and confusion arising from these experiences.

DeSalvo pushes her conspiracy theory too far, however. Her indignation over sexual abuse leads her to indict others for Woolf's suffering, including Sigmund Freud, who never treated her. DeSalvo tells us that Woolf read Freud's publications toward the end of her life hoping they would verify the link between sexual abuse and depression. But Freud, according to DeSalvo, disconfirmed Woolf's feelings by repudiating his earlier seduction theory and arguing that reports of incest were merely fantasies of wish fulfillment. And so DeSalvo concludes, with no convincing evidence, that Freud "precipitated a crisis" in Woolf, "eroded her sense of self," and "contributed to her suicide" (127–28). Woolf did indeed find Freudian theory upsetting, not primarily because of its abandonment of the seduction theory, but because of its emphasis on instinctual drives and its recognition of the centrality of ambivalence in parent-child relationships.

The sensationalistic title of Alma Halbert Bond's wild psychobiographical speculations, *Who Killed Virginia Woolf?* (1989), reveals her search for scapegoats. She believes the suicide was inevitable because of the ways in which Woolf's relatives had systematically deceived her. Bond proposes to uncover the "true story" of Woolf's life and death, but instead she spends most of her time affixing blame. The major villain in Bond's psychobiography is Leonard Woolf, whom she portrays as cold, duplicitous, and controlling. The following example is representative of Bond's unrelenting attack. She claims that because of her "defect in self-esteem," Virginia was unable to judge her own self-worth or the quality of her writings. Dependent on her husband's evaluation of her novels, Virginia sought his judgment of *The Years* (1937), which she had trouble completing. Bond writes: "Leonard really did not care for it. He feared—correctly—that she would commit suicide if she knew the truth about his opinion. He lied, therefore and told her the book was an 'extraordinary' achievement." Bond conveniently disregards the fact that Leonard was always protective of his wife's health and that spousal love and support were precisely what she needed. Bond next tells us that "on the deepest level, she was *not* deceived" by her husband, and that this lie evoked painful memories of her father's dishonesty to her. A year later, when Leonard expressed misgivings over *The Years*, Virginia was, according to Bond, no less devastated—suggesting that now he had erred in the opposite direction. Notwithstanding Bond's profession of sympathy for Leonard, she asserts that his "dishonesty confused and disoriented Virginia, much as her father's had," and that it was a major precipitating factor in her suicide (159–60).

The central assumptions behind these conspiracy theorists are that Woolf was driven to suicide by sinister or incompetent physicians and relatives and that blame must be assigned for her death. Those who see Woolf as a victim of psychiatric mistreatment or patriarchal society will be inclined to search for scapegoats. And yet clinicians remind us that it is both cruel and unfair to blame others for a person's suicide. As the authors of *Suicide and Its Aftermath* observe, "Of the over 200 families we have seen, we have yet to encounter a family or a family member with anything suggestive of malicious intent or even neglect. We believe that suicide occurs in all types of families: the functional and the dysfunctional; the very good, the not so good, and the just good enough" (Dunne and Dunne-Maxim xvi).

"A Suicide(')s Pathetic Letter"

Woolf's voluminous diaries and letters help us to understand her attitude toward suicide. One of the earliest and most revealing references to suicide appears in a 1903 diary entry based upon a brief newspaper article about a middle-aged woman's drowning in the Serpentine, an artificial lake between Hyde Park and Kensington Gardens in London. Woolf read "A Suicide[']s Pathetic Letter" and could not stop thinking about the victim. Even though bodies in the Serpentine are not uncommon, she is drawn to the story because of a suicide letter pinned to the inside of the woman's clothes: "It was blurred but the writing was still legible. Her last message to the world—whatever its import, was short—so short that I can remember it. 'No father, no mother, no work' she had written 'May God forgive me for what I have done tonight'" (*A Passionate Apprentice* 212).

From these few words, Woolf imagines the emotions of a woman in the moments preceding her suicide. Woolf projects herself into the victim's situation, empathizes with her loneliness and despair, and apprehends the reasons behind the suicide. In writing about an unknown woman, Woolf seems to be writing about herself—in particular, her fear of parental abandonment. She observes that although the woman was old enough to have experienced daughterhood, wifehood, and motherhood, the yearning for her parents was uppermost on her mind. Speculating that the woman's parents died when she was young, leaving her an orphan, Woolf concludes that neither marriage nor children could fulfill the hunger for parental love:

> For the first time in her life perhaps she weeps for her parents & for the first time knows all that they were, & her loneliness without them. That sorrow I say is bitter enough in youth with the world before one & its promise; but in middle age one knows that the loss is one that nothing can heal & no fresh tie renew. Your husband may die & you can marry another—your children may die & others may be born to you, but if your father & mother die you have lost something that the longest life can never bring again. (*A Passionate Apprentice* 212–13)

Woolf intimates in her interpretation of the words "No father, no mother, no work" that parental loss can never be overcome. Not all readers will share Woolf's assumption that the death of one's parents is more devastating than the death of a spouse or a child. We do not know whether the woman was in fact married or had children, but we do know that for Woolf, who was not married at the time and who, to her disappointment, never did have children; maternal loss was one of the central events of her life.

"A Suicide[']s Pathetic Letter" reveals Woolf's compassionate understanding. She is sensitive to the pain that drives a person over the edge, and she is neither judgmental nor accusatory. The author of "A Suicide[']s Pathetic Letter" asks for forgiveness, and the atheistic Woolf, who seldom associated suicide with religious guilt or sin, responds accordingly. Woolf refuses here to stigmatize or romanticize suicide, and while elsewhere her attitude changes, she avoids the temptation in "A Suicide[']s Pathetic Letter" to hold others responsible for what is finally an individual act.

"Why Do I Write All about Suicide and Mad People?"

Woolf's letters are less self-reflective than her diaries but nevertheless contain many references to suicide. Some of these references are casual, others more detailed. A letter written to Lady Robert Cecil in August 1905 records her response to a newspaper article about a charwoman who hanged herself shortly after penning a suicide letter in the form of a melancholy poem. Entitled "An Epitaph for a Tired Housewife," the ten-line poem describes a woman overcome by fatigue. Perhaps because of the doggerel end rhyme (the last lines are "Dont mourn for me now, dont mourn for me never; / I'm going to do nothing for ever and ever"), Woolf's response is sarcastic: "The jury said unanimously that she was mad, which proves once more what it is to be a poet in these days" (*Letters* 1:203). Woolf's next comment is revealing: "Why do I write all about suicide and mad people? — it is not a cheerful way of saying goodbye."

A few of Woolf's letters and diaries reflect sympathy for those whose professional work involved them in suicide prevention. Upon hearing from Jean Thomas (who had nursed Woolf back to health several times at a private rest home in Twickenham) about the necessity to discharge a woman who wished to commit murder and admit another woman who vowed to commit suicide, Woolf wrote to Violet Dickinson on 1 January 1911: "Can you imagine living like that? — always watching the knives, and expecting to find bedroom doors locked, or a corpse in the bath? I said I thought it was too great a strain — but, upheld by Christianity, I believe she will do it" (*Letters* 1:447). In *Mrs. Dalloway*, Lucrezia lives with the constant fear that her husband, Septimus Warren Smith, will kill himself — a fear that comes true.

Sometimes Woolf expressed bemusement or impatience with acquaintances who talked about suicide. She wrote to Lady Ottoline Morrell in

June 1918 about an exasperating conversation with Middleton Murray. "Murray was here too, and such a suicidal conversation I've never listened to in my life. According to Murray we must choose between suicide and indifference, and he vacillates between them. Dora [Carrington] agreed rapturously" (*Letters* 2:249–50). Rather than mocking genuinely suicidal feelings, Woolf derided what she thought were posturings, as when she described, in an October 1921 letter to her sister Vanessa, meeting a woman "who came to tea to discuss her approaching suicide—she's an actress—too large a nose, the managers say; in desperation" (*Letters* 2:486). A facile remark on suicide by Vanessa's husband, Clive Bell, elicited the following indignant diary entry on 23 June 1927:

> Clive walked me round, & standing under the lamp expressed his complete disillusion. "My dear Virginia, life is over. There's no good denying it. We're 45. I'm bored, I'm bored, I'm unspeakably bored. I know my own reactions. I know what I'm going to say. I'm not interested in a thing. Pictures bore me. I take up a book & put it down. No one's interested in what I think any more. I go about thinking about suicide. I admire you for having tried to kill yourself." To think that I should be listening to this in the moonlight from Clive! And he spoke with such dreary good sense too. I could scarcely whip up any ardour of denial. It was all true, it seemed to me. Not, indeed, true of me, but true of him. (*Diary* 3:148)

There were times when Woolf, perhaps unsure of her defenses against suicide, sought help from her friends, as in this letter to Ethel Smyth on 30 October 1930:

> By the way, what are the arguments against suicide? You know what a flibberti-gibbet I am: well there suddenly comes in a thunder clap a sense of the complete uselessness of my life. Its like suddenly running one's head against a wall at the end of a blind alley. Now what are the arguments against that sense—"Oh it would be better to end it"? I need not say that I have no sort of intention of taking any steps: I simply want to know—as you are so masterful and triumphant—catching your train and not running too fast—what are the arguments against it? (*Letters* 4:242)

Woolf later wrote a letter to Beatrice Webb thanking her for her clear philosophical defense of suicide: "I wanted to tell you, but was too shy, how much I was pleased by your views upon the possible justification of suicide. Having made the attempt myself [in 1913], from the best of motives as I thought—not to be a burden on my husband—the conventional accusation of cowardice and sin has always rather rankled. So I was glad of what you said" (*Letters* 4:305).

Dora Carrington's suicide affected Woolf deeply. She did everything she could to persuade the depressed Carrington not to kill herself following the death of Carrington's lover, Lytton Strachey (to whom Virginia had been briefly engaged), in 1932. In a letter written on 2 March 1932, Woolf expresses concern for Carrington's precarious health and affirms the importance of life:

> Oh but Carrington we have to live and be ourselves—and I feel it is more for you to live than for any one; because he loved you so, and loved your oddities and the way you have of being yourself. I cant explain it; but it seems to me that as long as you are there, something we loved in Lytton, something of the best part of his life still goes on. But goodness knows, blind as I am, I know all day long, whatever I'm doing, what you're suffering. And no one can help you. (*Letters* 5:28)

On the night of 10 March, Woolf wrote Carrington a compassionate letter suggesting that Strachey's spirit remained alive through her. The next morning, Carrington shot herself and died in great pain a few hours later, maintaining to the end that the shooting was accidental. Woolf was shaken by the suicide and immediately wrote long letters to Lady Ottoline Morrell and Ethel Smyth reproaching herself for the failure to prevent it. She also irrationally blamed Strachey for Carrington's suicide, perhaps as a way to dispel her own guilt. A 17 March 1932 diary entry records Woolf's grief, anger, and confusion:

> So Carrington killed herself; & again what L. calls "these mausoleum talks" begin again. We were the last to talk to her, & thus might have been summoned to the inquest; but they brought it in an accident. She maintained this, even to [her husband] Ralph. Her foot slipped as she was shooting a rabbit.
> And we discuss suicide; & I feel, as always, ghosts . . . changing. Lytton's affected by this act. I sometimes dislike him for it. He absorbed her[,] made her kill herself. Then the romantic completeness which affects Mary. "a beautiful gesture—her life & her death." Nonsense says Leonard: it was histrionic: the real thing is that we shall never see Lytton again. This is unreal. So we discuss suicide. and the ghosts as I say, change so oddly in my mind; like people who live, & are changed by what one hears of them. (*Diary* 4:83)

Woolf's diaries, letters, and critical writings never portray suicide as a romantic or heroic act. Rather, she depicts suicide as a dark mystery that inexplicably descends upon men and women alike. Woolf captures the shocking and sometimes melodramatic nature of suicide, as when she describes in her essay "Genius" a painter who, after quoting from *King Lear* and writing out a list of his debts and thoughts, "put a pistol to his forehead, gashed a razor across his throat, and spattered his unfinished picture of Alfred and the first British Jury with his blood. He was the faithful servant of genius to the last" (*The Moment and Other Essays* 192). Woolf's essay "Two Parsons" contains another account of a man who shoots himself to death. Beset by tragedy, abandoned by family and friends, and unable to work through the conflict that he recorded in his massive diary, the Rev. John Skinner seems to have exhausted his will to live. Woolf withholds information about Skinner's ending until the last sentence of the essay, when she tells us, nonjudgmentally: "At last, one morning in December 1839, the Rector took his gun, walked into the beech wood near his home, and shot himself dead" (*The Common Reader*, 2d series 96).

"Why Do People Kill Themselves?"

Toward the end of Woolf's first novel, *The Voyage Out* (1915), a brief discussion occurs between St. John Hirst and Helen Ambrose of a letter describing a parlor maid's unexpected suicide. The letter records only the external details of the death. One day she came into the kitchen, stated that she wanted the cook to keep her money for her, then left to buy a hat. Returning shortly later, she announced that she had taken poison and, before the doctor could arrive, died. The dialogue proceeds as follows:

> "Well?" Helen enquired.
> "There'll have to be an inquest," said St. John.
> Why had she done it? He shrugged his shoulders. Why do people kill themselves? Why do the lower orders do any of the things they do do? Nobody knows. They sat in silence. (326)

It is not only the lower orders who commit suicide in Woolf's world; Rachel Vinrace's death also seems self-induced. The daughter of a shipbuilder, the twenty-five-year-old Rachel falls in love with a writer named Terence Hewet, who is interested in writing a novel "about Silence . . . the things people don't say" (*The Voyage Out* 229). Rachel's growing anxiety over love and marriage culminates in a mysterious illness, more psychological than physical; apart from a high fever, her major symptoms include feelings of derealization and disembodiment. The doctors can do nothing for her. A feeling of peace and unity comes over Terence when he realizes that she has stopped breathing: "So much the better — this was death. It was nothing; it was to cease to breathe. It was happiness, it was perfect happiness. They had now what they had always wanted to have, the union which had been impossible while they lived. Unconscious whether he thought the words or spoke them aloud, he said, 'No two people have ever been so happy as we have been. No one has ever loved as we have loved'" (376).

These words uncannily foreshadow Virginia Woolf's suicide note to her husband, but what is most important here is the fantasy of death as a mystical fusion with a lost loved one. The couple are ambivalent toward each other in life, but they now seem joined together in a complete and perfect union, an embrace in death. Though it is death, not suicide, that is romanticized here, we can see Woolf's attraction to "the voyage out." She wrote the novel when she was experiencing the worst breakdown of her life, and perhaps for this reason, *The Voyage Out* dramatizes death as a journey toward a seductive nether world far removed from the pressures of everyday life.

"The Legacy": "Have I the Courage to Do It Too?"

Woolf's late short story "The Legacy" (1940) also dramatizes suicide as a reunion with a lost loved one. The plot focuses on Gilbert Clandon's horrified discovery that the recent death of his wife, Angela, who was struck and killed by a car, may not have been accidental. The story is Jamesian in its technique, filtering everything through Clandon's consciousness. As "The Legacy" opens, Clandon is waiting to give his wife's secretary, Sissy Miller, a pearl brooch that Angela thoughtfully set aside for her. Sissy Miller is also in a state of mourning, having recently lost her brother. Clandon finds it strange that his wife left everything in order, including gifts for her friends, almost as if she had foreseen her death. Angela left to her husband nothing apart from her fifteen-volume diary, which she had kept ever since they were married. Angela sought to preserve the secrecy of her writings throughout her married life; the Clandons' only arguments concerned this issue. "When he came in and found her writing, she always shut it or put her hand over it. 'No, no, no,' he could hear her say, 'After I'm dead—perhaps.' So she had left it him, as her legacy. It was the only thing they had not shared when she was alive" (*The Complete Shorter Fiction of Virginia Woolf* 275).

A self-important politician who regarded his wife as a prized trophy, Clandon reflects contentedly upon his long marriage. With her "genius for sympathy," Angela had been the perfect helpmate to him: faithful, self-sacrificing, anxious to please. But Clandon is jarred by the diary's revelation of her growing involvement with a man mysteriously referred to as B. M. Clandon sees in Angela's entries how agitated she was in her final days. The diary entries intimate that B. M. was forcing her to do something against her will. The narrator captures Clandon's thoughts as he reads his wife's last words: "'No answer to my letter.' Then more blank pages; and then this. 'He has done what he threatened.' After that—what came after that? He turned page after page. All were blank. But there on the very day before her death was this entry: 'Have I the courage to do it too?' That was the end" (280). Only at the end of the story does Clandon discover from Sissy Miller that B. M. was her brother and that he had committed suicide because he was distraught over Angela's refusal to run away with him. The last sentence in the story reveals Clandon's interpretation of the motives behind his wife's suicide. "He had received his legacy. She had told him the truth. She had stepped off the kerb to rejoin her lover. She had stepped off the kerb to escape from him" (281).

Angela's suicide seems motivated by the desire both to rejoin her lover in death and to escape from a loveless marriage. Additionally, she seems to be revenging herself on a husband who has disappointed her. The revenge motive becomes more apparent when we realize that Angela, who has fiercely guarded the privacy of her diary for so many years, makes no effort to destroy her writing following the fateful decision to take her life. Her last diary entry—"Have I the courage to do it too"—is not only a vague suicide note but part of the terrible legacy she bequeaths to her husband, a reminder of his perceived complicity in her death. Angela's imitation of her lover's suicide also demonstrates the contagion theory, in which one person's self-inflicted death "infects" another person.

It is tempting to read "The Legacy" psychobiographically, viewing Angela's motives for suicide as identical with Woolf's. There are a number of parallels between author and character. Both are private, introspective women whose marriages are childless; both turn to their diaries to record their innermost thoughts; both leave suicide notes to their husbands, essentially public men. The differences between author and character outweigh the similarities, however, so we must resist reading too much biography into the story. There is no hint that Angela suffers from serious mental illness or fears the loss of creativity. Angela has little in common, temperamentally, with the novelist who created her. Angela's loveless marriage to a self-preoccupied husband contrasts Woolf's loving marriage to an attentive husband. Despite her commitment to keeping a diary, Angela is not a full-time professional writer, and there is no evidence that writing is central to her psychological health, as it was for Virginia Woolf.

Mrs. Dalloway

If it is unwise to read too much autobiography into "The Legacy," it is impossible to avoid autobiography in Mrs. Dalloway. Septimus Warren Smith's suicide is one of the most haunting in literature, and though Woolf appears to have little in common with her tormented character, whose madness is attributed to his involvement in the Great War, he is among her most autobiographical characters, the one who comes closest to illuminating the wildly fluctuating moods of manic depression.

Septimus is one of the first to enlist in the war, achieves "manliness" in the French trenches, is promoted, and develops a camaraderie with an older officer named Evans, whose death shortly before the Armistice devastates him. Septimus finds himself numbed by the loss, unable to feel. Soon he begins to hallucinate: he hears sparrows singing in Greek, sees a dog turning into a man, and believes that Evans has returned from the dead. Along with hallucinations come headaches, sleeplessness, and fearful dreams. He comes to believe that human nature is a breed of lustful animals: "For the truth is (let her ignore it) that human beings have neither kindness, nor faith, nor charity beyond what serves to increase the pleasure of the moment. They hunt in packs. Their packs scour the desert and vanish screaming into the wilderness. They desert the fallen" (Mrs. Dalloway 78).

As I have argued elsewhere, Woolf's portrait of Septimus Warren Smith anticipates the major characteristics of post-traumatic stress disorder:

[H]is symptoms arise from a traumatic event; the symptoms appear continually and in several forms, including intrusive recollections and recurrent dreams; and he experiences a numbing of emotional responsiveness. He suffers from other symptoms associated with the disorder, such as sleep disturbances, short attention span, and panic attacks. Interestingly, of the three major causes of post-traumatic stress disorder—natural disasters, the taking of hostages, and military combat—Septimus falls into the last category, in that his self-reproaches, feelings of failure, paranoia, and hostility are more prominent in survivors of war than in survivors of natural disasters or hostage situations. (*Narcissism and the Novel* 237)

Septimus's threat to commit suicide terrifies Lucrezia, particularly when he talks about a suicide pact. "Suddenly he said, 'Now we will kill ourselves'" (58). Unable to live with Septimus in his suicidal state, she finds herself almost hoping that he will carry out the threat: "Far rather would she that he were dead! She could not sit beside him when he stared so and did not see her and made everything terrible; sky and tree, children playing, dragging carts, blowing whistles, falling down; all were terrible. And he would not kill himself; and she could tell no one. 'Septimus has been working too hard'—that was all she could say, to her own mother" (19).

Holmes and Bradshaw

Unable to help Septimus, Lucrezia decides reluctantly to enlist the advice of two physicians, Dr. Holmes, a general practitioner with more than forty years' experience, and Sir William Bradshaw, an eminent "nerve doctor." Both embody an authoritarian power associated with "forcing the soul" (163). Controlling, invasive, and patriarchal, they are among Woolf's most sinister creations.

Holmes fails to take seriously Septimus's frightening hallucinations and dispenses platitudinous advice that trivializes his patient's illness. Holmes's refrain—"There's nothing wrong with him"—reveals his incompetency. Woolf depicts him as a boor, a hater of Shakespeare, a man who is more interested in examining antique furniture than his patients' psychological health. His best advice to Septimus is to take two bromides dissolved in a glass of water at bedtime. When that remedy fails, Holmes returns to Septimus's house to lecture him on his "duty" to his wife.

Compared with the bungling Holmes, Sir William is more menacing. Rich, powerful, famous, he is a "priest of science," a man who stands at the pinnacle of his profession. Unlike Holmes, who is dismissive of "nerve symptoms," Sir William acknowledges mental illness; yet he attributes "madness" not to an organic or psychological disorder but to a "lack of proportion": the failure to conform to societal expectations. In one of the most quoted passages in the novel, Woolf characterizes the psychiatrist as the embodiment of evil:

> Worshipping proportion, Sir William not only prospered himself but made England prosper, secluded her lunatics, forbade childbirth, penalised despair, made it impossible for the unfit to propagate their views until they, too, shared his sense of proportion—his, if they were men, Lady Bradshaw's if they were women (she embroidered, knitted, spent four nights out of seven at home with her son), so that not only did his colleagues respect him, his subordinates fear him, but the friends and relations of his patients felt for him the keenest gratitude for insisting that these prophetic Christs and Christesses, who prophesied the end of the world, or the advent of God, should drink milk in bed, as Sir William ordered; Sir William with his thirty years' experience of these kinds of cases, and his infallible instinct, this is madness, this sense; in fact, his sense of proportion. (87–88)

Lest there be any doubt about the novelist's attitude, Woolf describes Sir William as a man who doesn't have time to read, who bears a grudge against educated people, and who is married to a woman who is slowly, silently, inexorably going mad.

There is a degree of truth in Woolf's portrait of Sir William, for, as cultural historians have remarked, medicine was distinctly patriarchal at the turn of the century. Some physicians labeled women "hysterical," "neurasthenic," and a few years later, "narcissistic." These doctors failed to understand that "female maladies" often reflect cultural disorders. Sir William is one of these oppressive physicians, and his rest cure recalls Charlotte Perkins Gilman's semiautobiographical story *The Yellow Wallpaper* (1892). A bitter indictment of the medical establishment, *The Yellow Wallpaper* implies that physicians exert totalitarian control by isolating patients, force feeding them, and depriving them of companionship, communication with the outside world, and the opportunity to read and write. Woolf also felt that she was victimized by the rest cure, and she recreates in the portrait of Sir William her own harrowing experiences with the medical establishment:

> To his patients he gave three-quarters of an hour; and if in this exacting science which has to do with what, after all, we know nothing about—the ner-

vous system, the human brain—a doctor loses his sense of proportion, as a doctor he fails. Health we must have; and health is proportion; so that when a man comes into your room and says he is Christ (a common delusion), and has a message, as they mostly have, and threatens, as they often do, to kill himself, you invoke proportion; order rest in bed; rest in solitude; silence and rest; rest without friends, without books, without messages; six months' rest; until a man who went in weighing seven stone six comes out weighing twelve. (87)

The Rapist/Therapist

Mrs. Dalloway dramatizes Septimus's suicide as a literal and metaphorical flight from psychiatric imprisonment. Holmes is the pursuer, Septimus the pursued. Not only does Holmes provoke the suicide, but in the moments prior to the physician's arrival, Septimus's madness has mercifully passed. Engaged in a calm and rational discussion with Lucrezia, Septimus panics when he hears Holmes downstairs, and despite Lucrezia's efforts to reassure her husband, he concludes that the enemy is now upon him. Lucrezia instantly regrets her decision to bring Septimus to Sir William, who has ordered incarceration in one of his rest homes, but it is too late, for when she tries to prevent Holmes from taking away her husband, the physician roughly pushes her aside and ascends the stairs. Cornered, Septimus desperately searches for an escape and realizes that he has only one option: jumping from the large Bloomsbury lodging-house window.

Mrs. Dalloway asks us to believe that Septimus's suicide is a rejection not of life itself but of the dehumanizing forces antithetical to life. "He did not want to die. Life was good. The sun hot. Only human beings?" (132). Holmes's violent entry into the room conjures up an image of rape, and Septimus's last words—"I'll give it you!" (132)—dramatizes the defiance of a man who prefers death of the body to death of the soul. Anticipating the antipsychiatric novel *Lolita, Mrs. Dalloway* demonstrates Nabokov's assertion that the difference between "the rapist" and "therapist" is a matter of spacing.

Woolf's anger toward Holmes and Bradshaw is as strong as Septimus's, and she holds them responsible for his death. Holmes's response to the suicide conveys his insensitivity. "The coward!" Holmes cries, and then, seconds later, asserts magnanimously that no one could have foretold the suicide. Later he tells Mrs. Filmer, self-servingly, "no one was in the least to blame" (132).

Critical Responses to Septimus's Suicide

Woolf portrays Holmes and Bradshaw so negatively that many critics have accepted the novel's endorsement of Septimus's suicide. In some cases, their affirmation of Septimus's suicide is guarded or qualified, and few if any of them would wish to generalize their comments to all suicides. Nevertheless, the following critics, representing a variety of theoretical perspectives from the 1960s through the 1990s, interpret Septimus's suicide affirmatively:

> At the end of the novel Clarissa's reaction to the disclosure of his suicide gives us a new view of him — and we have learned to trust Clarissa's reactions. What she perceives with shattering clarity is his courage, his defiance, the utter integrity of his commitment against human agencies that would "force the soul," and that have, in part, forced hers. It is the purity and strength of his act that move her so. (Page 123)

> If Clarissa were, like Septimus, to commit suicide, her action would be one of desperation, for she would be acknowledging the basic meaninglessness of her own life and of life in general. In her perception of Septimus' suicide, however, Clarissa comes to realize that although it was a desperate act, it was a desperate act of affirmation and not of negation. Septimus throws himself from the window not because he no longer believes in the value of his own life, but because he believes in it very strongly. Significantly, when Septimus commits suicide he is sane, not insane, but he jumps because Bradshaw and Holmes have made his life intolerable — they have tried to violate the sanctity of the individual and have tried to force his soul. (Shields 85–86)

> But Septimus does not die for his vision in vain; for before the novel ends, it becomes clear that he has died to preserve not only his own vision, but that of Mrs. Dalloway, a woman whose activities in the limited world demand some sacrifice to purify her own sense of unity from insincerity or social lies. (Kelley 100)

> Even in his frantic throwing away of his own life, there is a sanity — that is, a legitimate response to reality — which Clarissa endorses as she retreats to the small room adjoining that in which her party is being held. She can understand why a young man would relinquish his own life to preserve that integrity which the party tends to destroy. (Apter 72)

> Septimus's madness is the madness of an innocence brutally violated by a civilization which cannot understand it, a civilization which sends its young men off to war to be destroyed. His psychopathology — though genuine — is nevertheless infinitely finer than the health possessed by Dr Holmes and Dr Bradshaw, those two apostles of exercise and proportion who hound him to

his death. However aberrant his behavior, he retains a kind of inner purity which makes society and its official guardians of mental and moral stability, like Holmes and Bradshaw, seem far more deranged than he. (Rosenthal 91)

Septimus Smith's suicide anticipates Virginia Woolf's own death. Both deaths are a defiance, an attempt to communicate, a recognition that self-annihilation is the only possible way to embrace that center which evades one as long as one is alive. (Miller 197)

By interpreting Septimus's suicide in her private language of passion and integrity, Clarissa uses the shock of death to probe and resolve her relation to her past, becoming able at last both to admit and to renounce its hold. On the day in June that contains the action of *Mrs. Dalloway*, Clarissa completes the developmental turn initiated thirty years before. (Abel 38–39)

Septimus's death is not primarily a sign of his defeat by Holmes and Bradshaw or a gesture of defiance toward the system their sanctimonious sermons sustain. Rather, it is a tribute to Clarissa, a tribute to the "terror" and "ecstasy" of the personal life over which she rules. (Gilbert and Gubar 26)

Student Responses to Septimus's Suicide

I asked my Literary Suicide students to write brief responses to some of the above critical comments, and they overwhelmingly rejected the view that Septimus's death is heroic, perhaps because, in the weeks prior to reading *Mrs. Dalloway*, we had discussed the constricted logic of suicide, with its reliance upon dichotomous thinking. In what turned out to be a representative point of view, one student wrote: "The feelings that spur on defiance often cloud our judgment. I don't really think that suicide is heroic, but to one so troubled and angry with life, an act of defiance may seem like a heroic exit. I don't think it's right to call it cowardly, though, for the same reason that such confusion clouds us. I don't know how to react really, but I believe there is more bravery or at least something fortunate in being able to seize the survival option."

Other students were less measured in their responses. One wrote sarcastically: "I would agree that Holmes and Bradshaw make life intolerable, but disagree that suicide is a heroic act of defiance, particularly to Septimus. Shoving the doctor out the window—now that would have been an act of defiance." A second observed that Clarissa becomes suicidal upon learning of Septimus's death. "We can see how Clarissa's view of suicide as potentially heroic could assist her suicidal thoughts. Critics do the potentially suicidal reader a disservice by accepting Clarissa's remarks." A third pointed out that it was unfair to blame the two physicians for Septimus's suicide:

It's difficult for me to see Septimus's suicide as heroic/defiant, and I doubt that if there were a real Septimus, Holmes and Bradshaw would have been the primary causes of what made his life intolerable (though it seems that Virginia Woolf thought they were, and that, had Holmes not burst in, Septimus might have been all right). Septimus seemed to me simply the victim of shell shock, and his suicide seemed to me the final implosion of all the feelings he had repressed along with the terrible memories of his friend's death and other horrors of the war that for reasons outside the story he was unequipped to deal with. Critics' perceptions of Holmes's and Bradshaw's attitudes toward suicide seemed apt but not true to Septimus's case.

This comment reflects my own point of view. Woolf captures the repressive nature of Victorian psychiatry, but her caricature of Holmes and Bradshaw is so extreme that it results in scapegoating. Septimus's terrifying symptoms—hallucinations, sleeplessness, loss of appetite, panic attacks, suicidal ideation, and inability to feel—exist long before Holmes's arrival. It is difficult to accept the novel's implication that had the physicians not cruelly intervened, Septimus would have permanently regained his health. Woolf scholars are beginning to reevaluate their interpretation of Septimus's death. Elaine Showalter, for example, has qualified her statement in *The Female Malady* that the suicide is a "heroic act of defiant feeling" (193) and now concedes that "[a]lthough they are tactless, snobbish, patronizing, and obtuse, the doctors of *Mrs. Dalloway* are probably right in recommending rest and seclusion for Septimus" (Introduction to *Mrs. Dalloway* 151).

Mrs. Dalloway implies that Septimus has only two choices: death by psychiatric institutionalization or death by one's own hand. And yet there is a third choice that the novel does not seriously consider: temporary hospitalization until Septimus's suicidal crisis passed. A suicidal crisis is usually temporary, not permanent, and once the crisis passes, it often does not recur. Despite the primitive state of psychiatry a century ago, Victorian physicians were remarkably successful in preventing men and women from killing themselves in state-run asylums and private homes. To accomplish this, physicians employed vigilant surveillance of their patients and, before it became outlawed, mechanical restraints. "Successful suicide attempts within an asylum were extremely rare, thanks to intense vigilance and continual efforts to eliminate all means of suicide" (Anderson 425). As repellent as some of these methods may seem to us today, particularly in light of the psychiatric abuses exposed by Michel Foucault and others, institutionalization did succeed in keeping patients alive until their suicidal crisis passed, after which they were usually discharged. Virginia Woolf was a living example of this.

Clarissa's Interpretation of Suicide

If Woolf asks us to endorse Septimus's suicide as a heroic alternative to psychiatric imprisonment, so, too, does she affirm Clarissa's idealization of suicide. Clarissa once accompanied a friend who was seeking professional advice from Sir William; Clarissa was uneasy in the presence of the great nerve doctor. Like Septimus, with whom she closely identifies, Clarissa viewed the doctor as "obscurely evil, without sex or lust, extremely polite to women, but capable of some indescribable outrage—forcing your soul" (163). Overhearing Sir William tell her husband, Richard, about the suicide of a young man whom she has never met and knows nothing about, Clarissa visualizes all the details of his horrific impact:

> What business had the Bradshaws to talk of death at her party? A young man had killed himself. And they talked of it at her party—the Bradshaws talked of death. He had killed himself—but how? Always her body went through it first, when she was told, suddenly, of an accident; her dress flamed, her body burnt. He had thrown himself from a window. Up had flashed the ground; through him, blundering, bruising, went the rusty spikes. There he lay with a thud, thud, thud in his brain, and then a suffocation of blackness. So she saw it. But why had he done it? And the Bradshaws talked of it at her party! (163)

Clarissa's response is revealing, for she not only visualizes all the details of Septimus's death but also vicariously experiences them. She seems to know the answer to her question, "But why had he done it?": "Death was defiance. Death was an attempt to communicate; people feeling the impossibility of reaching the centre which, mystically, evaded them; closeness drew apart; rapture faded, one was alone. There was an embrace in death" (163).

There is probably no act that has more complex origins and motives than suicide. Clarissa, without knowing anything about Septimus's state of mind prior to his death, constructs the suicide as an act of defiance, revenge, escape, and mystical communication. There is textual evidence to support this reading, but Clarissa does not see the other motives for Septimus's suicide for which there is even more evidence: his hopelessness, fear of permanent insanity, panic, wish for self-punishment, and desire to be reunited with the slain Evans. Nor does she see that what Septimus is chiefly trying to escape from is pain, a motive that Edwin Shneidman sees as the driving force behind all suicides:

> Pain is what the suicidal person is seeking to escape. In any close analysis, suicide is best understood as a combined movement toward cessation of consciousness and as a movement away from intolerable emotion, unendurable pain, unacceptable anguish. Indeed, the wish or need to effect a cessation of consciousness is because of the pain. No one commits suicide out of joy; no suicide is born out of exultation. The enemy to life is pain and when pain does not come from one's soma, then the threat to life is from those who cause the pain or the pain of emotion within one's mind. It is psychological pain of which we are speaking; meta pain; the pain of feeling pain. (*Definition of Suicide* 124).

Nowhere does Clarissa consider whether Septimus's illness might have been preventable or treatable. Nor does she realize that if Septimus's suicide is an attempt to communicate, it forever shatters communication. Curiously, Clarissa blames herself for Septimus's suicide despite the fact that she has never met him: "Somehow it was her disaster—her disgrace. It was her punishment to see sink and disappear here a man, there a woman, in this profound darkness, and she forced to stand here in her evening dress. She had schemed; she had pilfered. She was never wholly admirable. She had wanted success" (164).

We never learn precisely why Clarissa feels complicit in the suicide. Unlike Septimus, she does not seem to have suffered a recent traumatic loss in her life—though at one point she cryptically mentions the accidental death of her sister Sylvia, who was killed by a falling tree. (Among Septimus's agitated writings is the sentence "do not cut down trees.") Without elaborating, Clarissa blames her father for Sylvia's death. It may be that Septimus's suicide reminds Clarissa of her own fears of aging and death. Troubled by her relationship with her daughter Elizabeth, Clarissa remains conspicuously silent about her own mother, whose death occurred years earlier. Whatever the reasons for her self-blame, Clarissa walks toward the window, continues to brood over life and death while watching an elderly woman in the house across from hers prepare for bed, and before returning to the party, reaches her final conclusion about suicide: "She felt somehow very like him—the young man who had killed himself. She felt glad that he had done it; thrown it away while they went on living. The clock was striking. The leaden circles dissolved in the air. But she must go back. She must assemble. She must find Sally and Peter. And she came in from the little room" (165).

While elsewhere in *Mrs. Dalloway* Woolf distances herself from Clarissa, throughout this scene they are essentially one. Identifying with Clarissa, the novelist endorses her celebration of Septimus's suicide. This glorification becomes more apparent in the American edition of the novel. *Mrs. Dalloway* was published simultaneously in London and New York, and when correcting the proofs for the American edition, published by Harcourt Brace, Woolf inserted a sentence, immediately following the image of the leaden circles dissolving in the air, which she omitted from the English edition, published by the Hogarth Press: "He made her feel the beauty; made her feel the fun." Justifying the deletion of this line in the new Definitive Collected Edition of *Mrs. Dalloway*, editor G. Patton Wright notes: "given the serious nature of Clarissa's internal monologue in the room apart, it is gratuitous to have her think that Septimus Smith's suicide 'made her feel the fun'" (*Mrs. Dalloway*, "Textual Notes" 213). And yet there is nothing gratuitous about the deleted line, for the novel consistently romanticizes suicide.

Clarissa endorses Septimus's suicide because in many ways the two characters are identical. Woolf based Clarissa's character on her friend Kitty Maxse, whose accidental death in 1922 Woolf interpreted as suicide. Clarissa, however, has more in common with Septimus than with anyone else. Both Clarissa and Septimus experience rapid alternations of mood, ranging from terror to exaltation; share the same mistrust of doctors; reject heterosexual love; and struggle with feelings of loneliness, isolation, and depression. Both are married to spouses who neither experience nor understand their emotional highs and lows. Septimus's psychological problems parallel Clarissa's heart problems. They physically resemble each other: Septimus is "beak-nosed" while Clarissa's face is "beaked like a bird's." Both strive for the elusive center of life, a flight that results in the literal death of one character and the metaphorical death of the other.

Woolf's acknowledgment of Clarissa's affinity to Septimus Warren Smith confirms their essential oneness. The novelist remarked in the introduction to the 1928 Modern Library edition of *Mrs. Dalloway* that "in the first version Septimus, who later is intended to be her double, had no existence; and . . . Mrs. Dalloway was originally to kill herself, or perhaps merely to die at the end of the party" (Introduction to *Mrs. Dalloway* vi). Woolf viewed the two characters as existing on a continuum, Clarissa representing sane reality, Septimus insane reality. "Mrs Dalloway has branched into a book; & I adumbrate here a study of insanity & suicide: the world seen by the sane & the insane side by side" (*Diary* 2:207).

Woolf was familiar with both realities, and in writing about Septimus's psychotic break, she transmuted her own painful experiences into fiction. Additionally, the novel allowed her to vent her turbulent feelings toward the medical establishment. Her anger over Sir William Bradshaw's insistence on "proportion" has an autobiographical component, as Leonard Woolf notes in *Downhill All the Way:* "At our last interview with the last famous Harley Street specialist to whom we paid our three guineas, the great Dr Saintsbury, as he shook Virginia's hand, said to her: 'Equanimity—equanimity—practise equanimity, Mrs Woolf'" (51). Lyndall Gordon suggests that Woolf may have based the name of her fictional psychiatrist on the Bradshaw Lecture to the Royal College of Physicians given in 1922 by one of her doctors, Maurice Craig (64).

Woolf experienced while writing *Mrs. Dalloway* some of Clarissa's and Septimus's wild emotions. Using an image that recalls Clarissa's reaction to Septimus's death, Woolf admitted in a letter written shortly after completing *Mrs. Dalloway* that his madness and suicide were a "subject that I have kept cooling in my mind until I felt I could touch it without bursting into flame all over. You can't think what a raging furnace it is still to me—madness and doctors and being forced" (*Letters* 3:180).

Suicide As Catharsis?

There is a long mythic, religious, and literary tradition in which sacrificial death is linked to humanity's rebirth, and most critics have assumed that Clarissa experiences cathartic relief from her dark double's death.

Septimus's suicide, Beverly Ann Schlack writes, "has congruences with classical myths of the dying god . . . whose life is offered to redeem humanity. Such rebirth and resurrection motifs suggest analogues to Christ as well as to mythology, but classical rather than Christian parallels seem to be the ones most intricately sustained within the novel" (66). Some of my students felt that Septimus's suicide makes possible Clarissa's rebirth:

She pretends to be indignant that her party has been "besmirched" by the news of an illegal and immoral death, and then she matter-of-factly puts herself through a variety of tortures. Next she turns inward, finding the core of her sympathy, the love of extinction, the soul of the "secret Clarissa." Finally it has sunk in, and she is released. She has experienced in her multi-sided way the pain/torture/humiliation/unity/freedom of death. Suicide is such an enigma, an ambivalence for this woman whose life is so reliant on external (societal) pressures.

Others felt, however, that Clarissa's vulnerability is heightened at the end of the novel:

The first thing that caught my eye was the line "she must assemble." Assemble what? Her defenses. Keep up her pretenses, not let tragedy mar the surface of her party. And as she assembles, she must also dissemble—lie, to herself, that her own thoughts don't often turn to death, that she despises the role she plays; lie to others, that nothing is wrong, that her party, like the show, must go on. Death must not intrude upon the affairs of this imperturbable crowd.

Several students were disturbed by Clarissa's idealization of suicide. "It seems like his tragedy is her salvation," one wrote; "one can almost feel the strength which she must gather and use against what she apparently desires—death." A second objected to the "exhilarating freedom" that Clarissa experiences while contemplating Septimus's suicide, while a third observed, paradoxically, that "for Clarissa, thinking about suicide is one of the ways to keep [on] living." A fourth compared Clarissa with the suicidal characters in Hemingway's, Mishima's, and Chopin's stories: "Clarissa certainly seems to feel some of the visceral attraction to death that Hemingway's characters do, the violence of the act, and then the nothingness. In relation to Mishima there is the idea of duty and an attraction, a glorification of the act. And in relation to *Mrs. Dalloway* there is certainly the aura of distanced fascination with the act, the sort of distanced fascination possessed by Edna Pontellier."

Empathy for Clarissa

Most students felt heightened empathy toward Clarissa when they realized her attraction to death. They were able to identify with her fears without accepting her rationalization of suicide.

Dangerously she circles around, hovers over top, but she won't swoop down and feel emotion. This is as close as she can come, but in her own mind, this is frighteningly close. This is what seeps through when we attempt to seal something out. The images fly up quickly before there is a chance to block them out. And then Clarissa needs to go to her old friends. This is repressed vulnerability that needs distraction. At first I thought her cruel, but now I know that she is scared. The deathly images of flying up to meet her, I've had those too—probably most of us have. I feel for her now more than I did when I read it in the book. She is frail in this.

Two students made particularly interesting observations about *Mrs. Dalloway*. The first remarked on the erotic nature of Clarissa's bodily reactions to Septimus's suicide:

Clarissa's reaction seems really odd. I'm reminded of Mishima's "Patriotism" because of the sexual nature of her reaction—she "flamed" and "burnt." There's sensuality, too, in her recognizing the "embrace" of death, like Edna's embrace by the sea in The Awakening. *Why does suicide have a sexual/sensual tone in these works? It's puzzling; I never thought of it like that. Clarissa's reaction makes her a warmer creature than I'd thought.*

The second student commented that Clarissa's "horror is not in the actual suicide itself but in the discussion of it [at her party]. It is as if the Bradshaws have debased Septimus's suicide by talking casually about it."

The Talking Cure

I find this insight intriguing because it reminds us of the novel's suspicion of public discourse. Woolf's characters have surprisingly little to say to each other; their conversations are either woefully inadequate or misunderstood. Clarissa values the world of feeling but not its overt expression. She literally has nothing to say to Sally Seton when she shows up unexpectedly at the party, despite the fact that the two friends have not seen each other for several years. Clarissa's mistrust of language makes it unlikely that she will ever disclose her convoluted feelings about Septimus's suicide—there is no person in her life who is capable of understanding her thoughts on the subject. Nor does Clarissa wish to learn more about suicide. She remains indifferent to Sir William's discussion of a bill being considered in the House of Commons regarding the deferred effects of shell shock. Neither she nor Virginia Woolf, as Jan Ellen Goldstein has pointed out, seems interested in the idea of repressed conflict.

Nor was Woolf curious about the talking cure despite the fact that she and Leonard owned the Hogarth Press, which published Freud's writings in English. Rather than working through her feelings about Septimus's suicide, Clarissa is left to brood over it. So, too, will Lucrezia. Like *The Awakening*, *Mrs. Dalloway* omits the aftermath of suicide. Dr. Holmes forbids Lucrezia from lingering upon her husband's mangled body and immediately sedates her. The story ends before we can see her anguish, guilt, and anger. If Lucrezia resembles the students who watched in horror as a classmate jumped to her death from the fifteenth floor of a college dormitory, as Jennifer observes in the diary at the beginning of this chapter, then she will never forget what she sees. Nor is it likely that Clarissa will forget her vision of Septimus's crushed body. Woolf's decision to kill off the dark double may convince some readers that Clarissa has now exorcised her suicidal feelings, but other readers will believe that despite her movement away from the window, she desires to hurl herself into space in imitation of Septimus's flight. Perhaps it was for this reason that "when E. M. Forster first read the novel he thought that Clarissa did in fact die at the end" (Hussey 172).

Woolf's Suicide: "It Is This Madness"

Mrs. Dalloway expresses Virginia Woolf's outrage toward physicians who make life unbearable for sensitive individuals like Septimus Warren Smith. And yet, though it is impossible to defend the actions of brutish characters who are identified with the death of the soul, there is unexpected truth in Holmes's observation that no one is responsible for Septimus's death, apart from Septimus himself. If we read Septimus's suicide in the context of Woolf's, we may be less inclined to find scapegoats. Woolf's suicide note to her husband reveals her wish to exonerate him from any wrong doing:

> Dearest,
>   I want to tell you that you have given me complete happiness. No one could have done more than you have done. Please believe that.
>   But I know that I shall never get over this: and I am wasting your life. It is this madness. Nothing anyone says can persuade me. You can work, and you will be much better without me. You see I cant write this even, which shows I am right. All I want to say is that until this disease came on we were perfectly happy. It was all due to you. No one could have been so good as you have been, from the very first day till now. Everyone knows that. (*Letters* 6:486–87)

Woolf could not have known that she had written one of the world's most poignant suicide letters, one whose meaning would be debated by scores of scholars. Despite the fear that she had lost the ability to write, the letter is powerfully written, evidence of her continuing talent. Indeed, she wrote two other suicide letters in the final week of her life, one to her sister and another to her husband, expressing clearly and succinctly her abiding love and gratitude. What is striking about the above letter, apart from its unmistakable echo of Terence Hewet's words to his deceased beloved in *The Voyage Out*, is its effort to absolve her husband of any responsibility for her unhappiness. Perhaps remembering how she had blamed Lytton Strachey for Dora Carrington's suicide, she wished to spare Leonard from anguished self-recriminations. Though some biographers have viewed her idealization of Leonard here as proof of her inability to be honest about her feelings toward him, I believe her protectiveness was genuine. She did not want to blame anyone for her suicide. Nor did she heroicize the act.

The loss was immense for Leonard. "It is no good trying to delude oneself that one can escape the consequences of a great catastrophe. Virginia's suicide and the horrible days which followed between her disappearance and the inquest had the effect of a blow upon the head and the heart. For weeks thought and emotion were numbed" (*The Journey Not the Arrival Matters* 127). Whether he felt that, in killing herself, she was also symbolically killing him is unknown: he does not dwell on the darker emotions arising from suicide. A tough-minded realist, Leonard had no wish to romanticize the act or to view it as inevitable. It would have been out of character for him to interpret suicide as an act of defiance.

Many scholars, however, have heroicized Woolf's suicide, either because they see her as a victim of patriarchal or psychiatric oppression, or because they wish to endow her final act with the conscious control and free will befitting a supreme creator. Roger Poole ends *The Unknown Virginia Woolf* by personifying the river into which she threw herself as a faithful ally. In language reminiscent of Edna Pontellier's hypnotic immersion into the sea, he writes: "The water was her friend, and had been her friend ever since she was a child in Cornwall. The water could be trusted. The water was peace. The water would receive her with the dignity that she felt she needed, and indeed, deserved" (279).

Nigel Nicolson, in his introduction to the final volume of Woolf's letters, confidently rules out the possibility that she was mad when she committed suicide. Instead, he prefers to see her as searching for novelistic closure. "To end her life at this point was like ending a book. It had a certain artistic integrity." Agreeing with Susan Kenney's interpretation of Woolf's suicide, Nicolson concludes: "Many people who take their own lives do not choose to die, but are impelled to it by their mental illness. Virginia Woolf chose to die. It was not an insane or impulsive act, but premeditated. She died courageously on her own terms" (*Letters* 6:xvi–xvii).

I agree with Nicolson that it was probably a "combination of fantasy and fear" that influenced Woolf's decision, along with many other factors that he rules out, including genetically inherited manic depression. We do Woolf a disservice by underestimating the severity of the illness against which she struggled for much of her life. It was her life that was courageous, not her death. Nicolson's celebration of her death as a rational act neglects the unconscious dynamics of suicide, especially the wish to be rescued. Woolf had attempted suicide earlier in her life, and it appears likely that she made another suicide attempt a week before her death. Leonard reports that she came back from a walk in the rain and, "looking ill and shaken," said that she had "slipped and fallen into one of the dykes" (*The Journey Not the Arrival Matters* 90–91).

"Melancholy Diminishes As I Write"

Fortunately, Leonard did not carry out Virginia's instructions in her suicide letter to destroy her unpublished writings, for they indicate, along
with her published ones, the centrality of writing to her life. She affirmed
repeatedly from her first diary entries to the last the necessity for writing.
She extolled the many benefits of writing, even when the words came
painfully slowly. She loved the ability to investigate depths that could not
be approached in any other way. "My writing now delights me solely
because I love writing & dont, honestly, care a hang what anyone says,"
she writes on 16 January 1915; "What seas of horror one dives through in
order to pick up these pearls—however they are worth it" (*Diary* 1:20).
She returns to the same theme on 10 September 1921 when she observes, reflecting upon a recent conversation with Lytton Strachey: "Writing is an agony, we both agreed. Yet we live by it. We attach ourselves to
the breath of life by our pens" (*Diary* 2:135).

Among Woolf's major objections to the rest cure was that she was
forbidden to write, a deprivation as serious as the loss of companionship.
"Melancholy diminishes as I write," she declares on 25 October 1920
(*Diary* 2:72). Writing enabled Woolf to transmute suffering into art. She
records in a diary entry written three weeks before her death: "I mark
Henry James's sentence: Observe perpetually. Observe the oncome of
age. Observe greed. Observe my own despondency. By that means it
becomes serviceable. Or so I hope. I insist upon spending this time to the
best advantage. I will go down with my colours flying" (*Diary* 5:357–58).
In going down with her colors flying, Woolf did not imply that writing
put her at risk. On the contrary. Writing was her life's work, necessary for
her survival. "What a born melancholiac I am!" she confesses to her diary
on 23 June 1929. "The only way I keep afloat is by working" (*Diary* 3:235).
She viewed work as the best antidote to depression or despair, and her
recommendation to those who were unable to emerge from gloom was
to immerse themselves in work, a remedy upon which she herself relied.

Woolf affirmed the cathartic nature of writing, and though she was not
a Freudian, at times she sounded like one. She admits in "A Sketch of the
Past" that until she was in her forties the invisible presence of her mother
obsessed her, despite the fact that the death occurred more than a quarter of a century earlier. She maintained that she ceased to be obsessed by
her mother as a result of writing *To the Lighthouse:*

I suppose that I did for myself what psycho-analysts do for their patients. I expressed some very long felt and deeply felt emotion. And in expressing it I explained it and then laid it to rest. But what is the meaning of "explained" it? Why, because I described her and my feeling for her in that book, should my vision of her and my feeling for her become so much dimmer and weaker? Perhaps one of these days I shall hit on the reason; and if so, I will give it. (*Moments of Being* 81)

Writing allowed Woolf to express and work through feelings that might otherwise have overwhelmed her. Writing was not a perfect therapy, but there is little doubt that it extended her life and gave her a reason to live. If, as a result of chemotherapy or radiation therapy, a patient's cancer goes into remission for several years but then returns, we do not question the value of the treatment that has prolonged life. The same is true for Woolf.

Nevertheless, three of Virginia Woolf's relatives have implied that writing imperiled her health. For example, even as Clive Bell tried to dispel the myth that Woolf was an unhappy person, he created another myth, namely, that she was a martyr to art:

More often than not the diary was written in moments of agitation, depression or nervous irritation; also the published extracts are concerned almost entirely with her work, a subject about which she never felt calmly. Indeed, creating a work of art, as the diary shows, was for Virginia a cause, not only of moral but of physical exasperation—exasperation so intense that often it made her positively ill. I should not be surprised if some lively journalist has dubbed the book "Screams from the torture-chamber," for truly much of it must have been written when the author felt much as one feels at the worst moments of tooth-ache. (qtd. in Stape 96)

Leonard Woolf also believed that writing was psychologically risky for his wife. He implies several times in his autobiography that the creation of fiction weakened Virginia's already shaky sanity. "Thus the connection between her madness and her writing was close and complicated, and it is significant that, whenever she finished a book, she was in a state of mental exhaustion and for weeks in danger of a breakdown" (*Beginning Again* 81). So too does Quentin Bell, her nephew and first biographer, maintain that writing was psychologically damaging to her. "In the final chapters of *The Voyage Out* she had been playing with fire. She had succeeded in bringing some of the devils who dwelt within her mind hugely and gruesomely from the depths, and she had gone too far for comfort" (*Virginia Woolf* 2:42).

Rather than viewing her as an extremist artist, hovering like a moth over a flame, I think it is more accurate to view Woolf as an escape artist. Creating fictional characters did not make her psychotic; there is no evidence to suggest that she lost "reality" when she immersed herself in fiction. For all its agonizing difficulties, writing was a stabilizing influence on her, giving her a structure, identity, and purpose. If the ending of a book left her psychologically adrift, susceptible to the fear that her creativity may have been permanently exhausted, she was always able to begin another writing project. "It was not writing that unhinged her, but having to stop," Peter Alexander suggests (98). That she intuitively recognized the need to write in order to maintain her sanity may be seen in a statement she makes in her biography of Roger Fry. Writing about Fry's situation—living with a spouse who periodically was very ill and finally was admitted to an asylum—Woolf expresses her own darkest fears: "Worst of all, the doctors could give him no certainty as to the future—the illness might be permanent, or again it might pass as suddenly as it had come. . . . It was best, he found, to live as far as he could in the country, and he found, as he was often to find in the future, that the only way of facing the ruin of private happiness was to work" (*Roger Fry* 104).

If novels like *Mrs. Dalloway* and Woolf's brooding masterpiece *The Waves* (1931) reveal her attraction to suicide—the latter ends with the passionate apostrophe, "Against you I will fling myself, unvanquished and unyielding, O Death!"—it was life and art that held Virginia Woolf's greater interest. However difficult it is to separate the novelist from her suicidal characters, we must remember that Woolf endowed all her characters with life. A statement from her essay on Montaigne (1925) is relevant here: "Communication is health; communication is truth; communication is happiness. To share is our duty; to go down boldly and bring to light those hidden thoughts which are the most diseased; to conceal nothing; to pretend nothing" (*The Common Reader*, 1st series 66). Woolf chose to be a novelist, a recorder of truth, and she never shrank from exploring psychic realms that most novelists prudently avoid. This is the type of communication to which Virginia Woolf was committed, a heroic embrace of life.

CHAPTER 4

Ernest Hemingway's Suicideophobia

With all the phobias about heights and open spaces, it surprises me that there isn't a suicideophobia, fear of committing suicide. It's one of my major fears. Although the word "suicideophobia" sounds a little silly, it will suffice until someone comes along with a more arcane word.

MARK

Mark's neologism is unlikely to find its way into future editions of the *Diagnostic and Statistical Manual of Mental Disorders*, the American Psychiatric Association's classification of psychological disorders, but suicideophobia accurately describes Ernest Hemingway's lifelong preoccupation with self-inflicted death. In no other major American writer do we see a stronger ambivalence toward suicide, a subject that haunted Hemingway and his fictional characters. His protagonists are among the most suicideophobic in literature, and while they do not all succumb to this fear, many initiate events leading to predictable deaths. Hemingway was the most famous writer of his age, a larger-than-life figure whose greatest fictional creation was his own public persona of heroic invincibility and disdain of death. His suicide in 1961 was, as Norman Mailer observed, "the most difficult death in America since Roosevelt" (qtd. in Raeburn 171).

"Judgment of Manitou"

Hemingway's fascination with suicide appears in his earliest short stories, including his juvenilia. Peter Griffin reports that of the three stories

101

Hemingway published in his high school literary magazine, his favorite was "Judgment of Manitou." The story is about two trappers in northern Michigan whose mistrust and misunderstanding of each other culminate in a homicide and suicide. Pierre is convinced that his partner, Dick Haywood, has stolen his wallet and sets a trap to murder him. "De tief will tink it a blame sight cooler when he's swingin' by one leg in the air like Wah-boy, the rabbit; he would steal my money, would he!" (qtd. in Griffin 26–27). When Pierre returns to his cabin and sees a squirrel gnawing away at the leather of the missing wallet, he realizes he has made a terrible mistake. He seizes his rifle and rushes madly out to warn his friend before it is too late. Pierre finds the remains of his friend's body, which has been devoured first by a wolf and then by two ravens. As the horrified Pierre takes a step forward, he is ensnared in the crushing bear trap that Dick had come to tend. Pierre's decision to commit suicide seems to be motivated as much by the need for self-punishment—the stern judgment of Manitou, the chief Indian god—as by the wish to avoid slow torture. "He fell forward, and as he lay on the snow he said, 'It is the judgment of Manitou; I will save My-in-gau, the wolf, the trouble.' And he reached for the rifle" (qtd. in Griffin 27).

"Indian Camp": "Why Did He Kill Himself, Daddy?"

The motives behind suicide remain more enigmatic in "Indian Camp," the opening work in the celebrated collection *In Our Time* (1925). As young Nick Adams watches his physician-father attend to a woman who has been in protracted labor, her husband lies in the bunk above, disabled by a severe ax cut on his foot received three days earlier. The husband impassively smokes a cigar and never utters a word while his wife screams in pain. Unnerved, Nick asks his father: "Oh, Daddy, can't you give her something to make her stop screaming?" Dr. Adams responds: "No. I haven't any anaesthetic. . . . But her screams are not important. I don't hear them because they are not important" (*Short Stories* 92). Performing the Caesarean only with a jackknife and nine-foot, tapered gut leaders as thread, Dr. Adams feels euphoric after the delivery. His postoperative exhilaration suddenly gives way to horror, however, when he glances at the father. "The Indian lay with his face toward the wall. His throat had been cut from ear to ear. The blood had flowed down into a pool where his body sagged the bunk. His head rested on his left arm. The open razor lay, edge up, in the blankets" (94).

The reasons for the Indian's suicide remain obscure. Is the thought of fatherhood so distressing that he cannot imagine continued existence? If he is not the child's biological father, is his suicide an act of revenge against a wife who has dishonored him? Critics have offered these and other speculations. The only detail in "Indian Camp" that may offer a clue to his suicide is his mysterious wound, which critics have interpreted as a castration symbol, a subtle indication that he has been rendered impotent by a physical or psychic injury. Whatever the reasons for his death, a few insights into the story's attitude toward suicide emerge from Nick's dialogue with his father:

> "Why did he kill himself, Daddy?"
> "I don't know, Nick. He couldn't stand things, I guess."
> "Do many men kill themselves, Daddy?"
> "Not very many, Nick."
> "Do many women?"
> "Hardly ever." (95)

Dr. Adams is right about actual statistics, though many men commit suicide in Hemingway's world—so many, in fact, that it is rare to find a major Hemingway hero who does not reveal tell-tale signs of self-destructiveness. Perhaps the woman's screams are not important to Nick's father because in Hemingway's stories men are far more vulnerable to suicide than women. The Hemingway hero is invariably wounded, and the wound has created a vulnerability to suicidal thinking. Following this dialogue, Nick asks his father whether dying is hard. Dr. Adams's answer is ambiguous. "No, I think it's pretty easy, Nick. It all depends" (95). The story concludes with Nick seated in a boat and watching the sun rise, feeling "quite sure that he would never die" (95), a statement at odds with his disturbing insight into the suicidality of men.

"Indian Camp" remains, after more than seventy years, one of Hemingway's most enigmatic explorations of suicide. Its mysteries lie precisely in what the author has omitted from the story: the Indian's motivation for killing himself, the precise meaning of his wound, the timing of the act, and the impact of suicide on Nick. These mysteries enact Hemingway's theory of omission, in which a story's meaning remains almost entirely submerged, like an iceberg. Hemingway suggests additionally that suicide cannot be understood either intellectually or emotionally. By the end of the story, Nick has been initiated into a world in which suffering and violent death seem both inexplicable and inevitable, and in which suicide seems to be in the "nature of things." By viewing suicide as an existential rather than a cultural or psychiatric crisis, Dr. Adams suggests that little can be done to avert it.

"The Doctor and the Doctor's Wife": "He Sat with the Gun on His Knees"

The next story in *In Our Time*, "The Doctor and the Doctor's Wife," casts a different image of Nick's father. In "Indian Camp" he is generally self-confident and authoritative, prepared for most emergencies; in "The Doctor and the Doctor's Wife" he appears weak, cowardly, depressed. As the story opens, Dr. Adams is speaking with Dick Bolton, whom he has paid to cut up logs that have been lost from the big log booms. Bolton desires to provoke a fight to avoid paying a debt and accuses Dr. Adams of stealing the timber. When Dr. Adams makes the mistake of uttering an idle threat—"If you call me Doc once again, I'll knock your eye teeth down your throat," Bolton replies tauntingly: "Oh, no, you won't, Doc" (*Short Stories* 101). Dr. Adams walks away in defeat, seething with impotent rage, and then he encounters his wife, who humiliates him in a different way. Pious ("Remember, that he who ruleth his spirit is greater than he that taketh a city" [101]), hypochondriacal, and smothering, she is one of a long list of unsympathetic female characters in Hemingway's stories. The word "dear" that she uses repeatedly to address her husband has an infantilizing effect on him.

The most unsettling detail in "The Doctor and the Doctor's Wife" is the shotgun that Dr. Adams methodically cleans and loads. Resting on his knees, the shotgun becomes both an ironic phallic symbol and a reminder of the explosive force that threatens to turn inward. The gun seems to be his only real companion, the object to which he pays the most attention. "The doctor wiped his gun carefully with a rag. He pushed the shells back in against the spring of the magazine. He sat with the gun on his knees. He was very fond of it" (102). And yet Dr. Adams's mind is elsewhere, for when he stands and places the gun in the corner behind the dresser, he fails to unload it—a clear violation of basic gunmanship.

The violence underlying Hemingway's story is palpable; as Dr. Adams walks out of his house, the screen door slams behind him, causing his wife to gasp. His flight from confining civilization to the openness of nature recalls Huck's journey into the wilderness. "The Doctor and the Doctor's Wife" ends ominously, eerily foreshadowing Dr. Clarence Hemingway's suicide a few years later, when he shot himself in the head with his father's Civil War Smith and Wesson revolver.

"She Forced My Father to Suicide"

Indeed, in light of Hemingway's father's suicide in 1928, it is impossible not to read "The Doctor and the Doctor's Wife" as a chilling autobiographical premonition. The story becomes doubly prophetic in light of Ernest Hemingway's own suicide thirty-three years later.

Biographers have struggled to determine the precise relationship between Hemingway's life and art. The difficulty lies not in establishing the facts of Hemingway's life, which is one of the most exhaustively documented lives of any writer, but in understanding the different points of view of those who exerted a formative influence on his life. Hemingway offered in "The Doctor and the Doctor's Wife" and elsewhere a highly subjective portrait of his parents, and if they were narrating the same story, no doubt it would have been very different.

More self-justifying than most writers, Hemingway needed to find reasons for his own disappointments and failures; more often than not, he found convenient targets. It is well documented that he thoroughly disliked his mother and blamed her for both his eviction from home in the summer of 1920 and his father's suicide. He never forgave her for either event. In many letters written throughout his life, Hemingway described his hatred for her and cast her in the role of scapegoat. In a 1949 letter to Charles Scribner, for example, Hemingway accused his mother of destroying his father and intimated that she felt no remorse: "I hate her guts and she hates mine. She forced my father to suicide and, one time, later, when I ordered her to sell certain worthless properties that were eating her up with taxes, she wrote: 'Never threaten me with what to do. Your father tried that once when we were first married and he lived to regret it'" (*Selected Letters* 670).

Buck Lanham, one of Hemingway's oldest friends, reported that

Hemingway "always referred to his mother as 'that bitch.' He must have told me a thousand times how much he hated her and in how many ways" (Donaldson 293). Hemingway made a similar observation in 1939 to his friend Lloyd Arnold, who, upon reading the manuscript of *For Whom the Bell Tolls*, correctly inferred the autobiographical nature of the hero's reference to his father's suicide:

> [S]ensing the question in our minds, he told us of his father's suicide—in detail—of illness not too serious at his age; of a minor financial problem, magnified in his mind, and already solved had he taken the trouble to open his morning mail. But, he said that the basis of his father's dilemmas was domination, ". . . by my mother, she had to rule everything, have it all her own way, and she was a bitch!"
> Horrified, Tillie [a friend] gasped, regained her breath, burst out:
> "Why, Ernest Hemingway, how dare you! How can you say that about your own mother?"
> "Daughter, I can, and I do, because it's true . . . and I say it at the risk of losing your respect."
> He went on: "True, it was a cowardly thing for my father to do, but then, if you don't live behind the eyes you can't expect to see all of the view. I know that part of his view, and I suppose he was mixing it up some . . . and you do such a thing only when you are tortured beyond endurance, like in war, from an incurable disease, or when you hasten a drowning because you can't swim all of the sea." (Arnold 79)

In Hemingway's view, his mother used his father's suicide as a grim warning of what might befall her son. A. E. Hotchner recounts a story Hemingway told him about receiving a Christmas package from his mother several years after his father's death. "It contained the revolver with which my father had killed himself. There was a card that said she thought I'd like to have it; I didn't know whether it was an omen or a prophecy" (116). Anyone reading Hotchner's memoir would infer that by gratuitously sending Ernest the suicide gun, Grace Hemingway demonstrated shocking insensitivity and perhaps initiated a self-fulfilling prophecy. The truth, however, is that Hemingway requested the gun from his mother, a request she faithfully carried out.

Biographers have offered compelling evidence that Grace Hemingway inadvertently damaged her son's psyche. Michael Reynolds remarks that as Clarence Hemingway withdrew from his wife and children, Grace Hemingway exerted an increasingly dominant role in the household that

Ernest could neither understand nor accept (*The Young Hemingway* 11). Kenneth Lynn stresses in his 1987 biography that for the first several years of Ernest's childhood, Grace dressed him in girl's clothes and treated him as if he were the identical twin of his sister Marcelline, who was a year and a half older. "Thus, she took early action to assert her authority over even the sexuality of her son" (40). According to Lynn, this produced in Hemingway lifelong anger, confused gender identity, and an exaggerated need to affirm his own masculinity.

Yet at the same time there was a more positive side of Grace Hemingway that scholars have acknowledged only recently. The "Adams-Hemingway association is so established, so automatic, that it is almost impossible to read the words *the doctor's wife* and not see in our imagination Grace Hemingway as Destroyer, rather than Grace as she actually was or Mrs. Adams, the literary character" (Westbrook 77). Mrs. Hemingway was a gifted musician and lecturer whose major problem, it now seems clear, was that she was a feminist living in an antifeminist age. As much as Ernest later satirized and scorned his mother's qualities, especially her devotion to art, he was his mother's son. "Grace's problems, in a general sense, were comparable to her son's problems. Both wanted to create and thus needed solitude, both wanted a home and family yet found domestic and family responsibilities an interference, and both tried to compromise between the two" (Westbrook 87).

Ernest Hemingway was also his father's son, and Clarence's self-inflicted death was one of the most important sources of his son's suicideophobia. Their close father-son relationship slowly eroded during Ernest's early teen years as Dr. Hemingway became increasingly despondent and self-absorbed. Unable to verbalize his growing fears or to avail himself of psychological help, he withdrew from his wife and six children, none of whom could understand his depression. Dr. Hemingway's suicide came as a shock to the family, and although it was not hushed up, his wife and children were left stunned and disbelieving, forced to find an explanation for an otherwise inscrutable act. They convinced themselves that heart illness and diabetes compelled Dr. Hemingway to commit euthanasia. "None of the children," Reynolds writes, "least of all Ernest, was ready to admit that long-standing and deadly genetic problems were the invisible cause of their father's death" (*Hemingway* 212). Associating his father with depression, disillusionment, and defeat,

Hemingway vowed never to be like him. For the rest of his life he sought to create in himself an idealized father who would be able to triumph over the fears and insecurities to which Clarence Hemingway had succumbed.

"Mechanic's Depressive"

There was a strong genetic predisposition to "nervousness" on both sides of Ernest Hemingway's family, as with Virginia Woolf. Kay Redfield Jamison notes in *Touched with Fire* that three generations of Hemingways suffered from either depression or manic depression. Left untreated, both illnesses can lead to suicide, as the Hemingway family history demonstrates. In addition to Dr. Hemingway's suicide, three of his children later died by their own hand: Ernest, Ursula, and Leicester. Two of Ernest Hemingway's sons have also suffered from serious mental illness, and recently his granddaughter Margaux Hemingway committed suicide at the age of forty-one. Many of the physical and psychological problems from which Clarence Hemingway suffered during the final months of his life also plagued Ernest. "When Ernest Hemingway put the muzzle of his double-barreled shotgun to his forehead the morning of a much later July, he suffered from all of his father's ills: erratic high blood pressure, insomnia, hypertension, mild diabetes, paranoia, and severe depression" (Reynolds, "Hemingway's Home" 16).

Hemingway's awareness of manic-depressive illness can be seen in the posthumous novel *Islands in the Stream* (1970), which contains a curious discussion of an alcoholic who talks incessantly about killing himself. A barman named Bobby relates the story of a man aptly called "Suicides" who tells Big Harry that he "wanted to take somebody with him" (157). "I'm your man," Big Harry exclaims and then proposes that they travel to New York City and "really pitch one and stay drunk until they couldn't stand it and then jump off of the highest part of the city straight into oblivion." The other inebriated characters are amused by the suicide pact and volunteer to "form an excursion of death seekers." Suicides decides while Harry is away fishing that he can no longer postpone the inevitable and plunges to his death. Big Harry later declares that "old Suicides was crazy," a judgment that is confirmed when a relative of the deceased reveals that he suffered from "a thing called Mechanic's Depressive" (158)—a disease that Hemingway seems to equate with the impulse toward oblivion.

The facetious tone of Hemingway's portrayal of "Suicides" is not the first time the novelist satirized the wish for self-destruction. In his 1937 novel *To Have and Have Not*, Hemingway mocks those who obligatorily withdraw from existence on losing their fortunes in the stock market:

> Some made the long drop from the apartment or the office window; some took it quietly in two-car garages with the motor running; some used the native tradition of the Colt or Smith and Wesson; those well-constructed implements that end insomnia, terminate remorse, cure cancer, avoid bankruptcy, and blast an exit from intolerable positions by the pressure of a finger; those admirable American instruments so easily carried, so sure of effect, so well designed to end the American dream when it becomes a nightmare, their only drawback the mess they leave for relatives to clean up. (237–38)

The reference to the "native tradition of the Colt or Smith and Wesson" suggests that while writing this passage Hemingway may have been thinking about his father. This passage, like so many others in Hemingway's stories, reveals a stunning prophetic quality, an example of life following art. Twenty-four years after the publication of *To Have and Have Not*, Mary Hemingway found herself in the same nightmarish situation of cleaning up the mess of her husband's suicide.

"My Father Was a Coward"

Unable to understand his father's death or mourn it adequately, Hemingway concluded that it was an act of cowardice. Clarence Hemingway's suicide seemed to destroy any possibility that his son would keep alive the "good father" within him. Hemingway resolved that he would never break down as his father had done. Nor would he allow himself to express sadness over his father's death. Leicester Hemingway later reported that his brother prohibited his family from emotional displays during the burial service. "At the funeral, I want no crying. You understand, kid? There will be some others who will weep, and let them. But not in our family" (111). By not allowing himself to grieve, Hemingway thus precluded the possibility of confronting and working through the agonizing emotions that arise from a loved one's suicide: sorrow, guilt, anger, and confusion.

Hemingway made conflicting statements about his father's death, a subject he was loath to discuss yet could never banish from his thoughts. Seldom religious, he told his sister Marcelline during the funeral that his father's soul was condemned to everlasting hellfire, a statement that visibly distressed her. Hemingway observed three years after the death: "To commit suicide except as a means of ending unbearable pain may be compared to cheating at solitaire, but a man making such a comparison is a confident fool" (Reynolds, *Hemingway* 212). Sometimes he resorted to irony when discussing suicide, as when he wrote to Ezra Pound about how his father's untimely act interrupted the completion of *A Farewell to Arms*. "I would have been glad to pay my esteemed father a good sum or give him a share in the profits to postpone shooting himself until the book was completed—Such things have a tendency to distract a man" (Mellow 372–73). Occasionally he was able to hint at the interpersonal consequences of suicide, as the following exchange with Robert Manning in *Conversations with Ernest Hemingway* indicates:

> "You know," he said, "my father shot himself."
> There was silence. It had frequently been said that Hemingway never cared to talk about his father's suicide.
> "Do you think it took courage?" I asked.
> Hemingway pursued [sic] his lips and shook his head. "No. It's every body's right, but there's a certain amount of egotism in it and a certain disregard of others." He turned off that conversation. (qtd. in Bruccoli, 183–84)

One of the most revealing statements about Hemingway's attitude toward his father's suicide appears in a canceled passage of *The Green Hills of Africa* (1935). "My father was a coward. He shot himself without necessity. At least I thought so. I had gone through it myself until I figured it in my head. I knew what it was to be a coward and what it was to cease being a coward. Now, truly, in actual danger I felt a clean feeling as in a shower" (Baker 809). If Hemingway could identify with his father to some extent, it was mainly a counteridentification that he consciously cultivated. He implied repeatedly that he had come to terms with his father's suicide and that he was consequently a stronger person for it.

And yet, though he spent a lifetime trying to exorcise his father's haunting memory and wrote about suicide in several stories, Hemingway could not bring himself to confront, in all its intricacies, his father's situation. Anger prevented him from empathizing with Clarence or Grace, whose suffering he did not want to imagine. Nor did he wish future biographers to intrude upon his privacy. "The suicide of my father," he stated sardonically, "is the best story I never wrote" (Mellow 570).

"A Clean, Well-Lighted Place": "He Was in Despair"

Hemingway's insight into the pain that drives people to suicide appears in "A Clean, Well-Lighted Place" (1933), one of his most empathic stories. It opens with two waiters discussing an old man's recent suicide attempt:

> "Last week he tried to commit suicide," one waiter said.
> "Why?"
> "He was in despair."
> "What about?"
> "Nothing."
> "How do you know it was nothing?"
> "He has plenty of money." (*Short Stories* 379)

The two waiters—the younger one, who matter-of-factly announces the old man's suicide attempt and the older one, whose preoccupation with suicide reveals itself in his incessant questions—differ in their understanding of "nothing." The younger waiter is superficial and arrogant, unable to understand why a person with enough money would commit suicide. He sees the old man merely as a drunk and regrets that he did not succeed in killing himself. The older waiter, however, intuitively grasps the old man's despair over "nothing," a word that is invested with the most profound existential, spiritual, and psychological implications. "Nothing" refers, existentially, to the lack of perceivable meaning and order in the universe; spiritually, to "nada," the loss of both God and the hope of redemption; and psychologically, to the paralyzing fear, depression, loneliness, and insomnia against which Hemingway's protagonists stoically battle. Obsessed with every detail of the old man's suicide attempt, the older waiter disagrees with the younger waiter's conclusion that "An old man is a nasty thing" and replies: "Not always. This old man is clean. He drinks without spilling. Even now, drunk," a judgment the narrator endorses by telling us that the old man walks away "unsteadily but with dignity" (381).

As in "Indian Camp," Hemingway refuses to explore the reasons behind self-destruction, but he does offer a few clues. The older waiter lacks not only youth but "confidence"—a quality he says he has never had. Hemingway feels enormous sympathy in this story for all those who lack self-esteem and self-confidence. The older waiter allies himself with those "who like to stay late at the cafe. . . . With all those who do not want to go to bed. With all those who need a light for the night" (382). He thus expresses solidarity with those solitary individuals who brood over the nothingness of life and whose daily existence remains precarious. Not exactly a therapist, the older waiter is a caretaker of sorts; and though there is no permanent cure to suicidal thinking in Hemingway's world, one can hope for a clean, well-lighted place to escape from private horrors.

A masterpiece of compression—it is only five pages long—"A Clean, Well-Lighted Place" may be Hemingway's greatest short story. In addition to its complex interpretive issues, the story contains textual ambiguities that have baffled readers. Since Hemingway seldom identifies who is speaking in the story, we cannot be sure during key moments of the dialogue whether the older or younger waiter is speaking. It is not entirely clear, for example, whether the older or younger waiter knows about the old man's suicide attempt.

Curiously, despite the vast critical commentary on "A Clean, Well-Lighted Place," its vision of suicide has remained largely unexplored. The story has important implications for suicide prevention. "A Clean, Well-Lighted Place" reveals that although suicide is an increasingly attractive option for the elderly, they can overcome a suicidal crisis through the love and concern of relatives and friends. Rescued by his niece, whose timely intervention thwarted his suicide, the old man does not regret being alive. The fact that he "failed" in his suicide attempt does not diminish Hemingway's sympathy for him. In identifying with the old man, the older waiter demonstrates that one can endure life's indignities through courage and commitment. Although some contemporary readers may be disturbed by the story's emphasis upon drinking—contrary to what Hemingway thought in the 1920s and 1930s, alcohol makes people more rather than less suicidal—"A Clean, Well-Lighted Place" affirms human connection. The "No man is an island, entire of itself" theme is more compelling in "A Clean, Well-Lighted Place" than in any other Hemingway story. The old man's continued survival strengthens the older waiter's purpose in life. "Each night I am reluctant to close up because there may be some one who needs the cafe" (382), he tells the younger waiter, expressing unsentimental kindness. Befriending others, he befriends himself, thus making it easier to survive the Dark Night of the Soul.

For Whom the Bell Tolls: "I Don't Want to Do That Business That My Father Did"

Hemingway's most extended discussion of suicide occurs in *For Whom the Bell Tolls* (1940), his sprawling Spanish Civil War novel set in the 1930s. Less experimental than *The Sun Also Rises* and less economical than his other story of war and love, *A Farewell to Arms*, *For Whom the Bell Tolls* remains fascinating for its autobiographical insights into Hemingway's suicideophobia. Robert Jordan, the novel's code hero, is a Spanish instructor at the University of Montana who travels to Spain to write a book and then volunteers to aid the Loyalist struggle. He joins a hopelessly outnumbered band of guerrillas who are waging a valiant struggle against the Fascists. Unlike Frederic Henry, whose shaky commitment to the Allied cause in *A Farewell to Arms* is never convincing, Jordan's devotion to democracy helps to explain his presence in Spain. He also appears to be running away from the past, specifically, from the memory of his father, whose death continues to trouble him.

Early in *For Whom the Bell Tolls* there is a revealing exchange among Jordan, Maria, the young Spanish woman with whom he immediately falls in love, and Pilar, the outspoken Gypsy who is Maria's guardian and surrogate mother. After Pilar and Maria declare that their fathers were both republicans, meaning that they were anti-Fascists, Jordan observes that his father and grandfather were also republicans. Of his two relatives, Jordan is more eager to talk about his grandfather, who, he notes, was on the "Republican national committee." When Pilar asks him whether his father is still active in the Republic, Jordan replies, "No. He is dead." He then tries to change the subject despite Maria's continuing questions:

> "Can one ask how he died?"
> "He shot himself."
> "To avoid being tortured?" the woman asked.
> "Yes," Robert Jordan said. "To avoid being tortured." (66–67)

Hearing this, Maria, whose father was tortured and killed by the Fascists and who, unlike Jordan's father, was not able to obtain a gun to shoot himself, tells him, "Oh, I am very glad that your father had the good fortune to obtain a weapon." Jordan responds tersely: "Yes. It was pretty lucky. . . . Should we talk about something else?" (67).

We learn nearly three hundred pages later that Jordan does not wish to discuss the past because he still feels anger and contempt toward his father for taking his own life. Hemingway uses a long interior monologue to replay the details of the father's death. The coroner gives the suicide gun to Robert after the inquest and says: "Bob, I guess you might want to keep the gun. I'm supposed to hold it, but I know your dad set a lot of store by it because his dad packed it all through the War" (337). There is no indication that Jordan interprets receipt of the suicide gun as an omen or prophecy, and the coroner's motives seem devoid of malice. The following day, Jordan rides with a friend to the top of a mountain overlooking a lake, climbs out on a rock, leans over until he sees his reflection in the water, then drops the gun and watches until it fades out of sight. The friend later tells Jordan, "I know why you did that with the old gun." Jordan responds with characteristic evasiveness: "Well, then, we don't have to talk about it" (337). He drops the subject, much as he had dropped the gun.

Robert Jordan's glimpse of his own reflection in a pool of water evokes the image of Narcissus, transformed by his own spectral shadow. Yet for Jordan, transfixed by the image of holding his father's suicide weapon, it is not self-love but self-hate that compels his stare. The legacy or illegacy of his father's suicide has been traumatic to the son, forcing him to call into question both his father's and his own manhood. Edwin Shneidman has remarked that the "person who commits suicide puts his psychological skeleton in the survivor's closet—he sentences the survivor to a complex of negative feelings and, most importantly, to obsessing about the reasons for the suicide death" (*On the Nature of Suicide* 22). Nowhere is this statement more true than in *For Whom the Bell Tolls*. Unable to empathize with his father's suffering or to examine the underlying causes of his death, Jordan cannot see beyond his own anger. In one of the most autobiographically significant passages in Hemingway's writings, Jordan reflects on his father's death and, searching for an explanation, indicts his mother:

I'll never forget how sick it made me the first time I knew he was a *cobarde*.
Go on, say it in English. Coward. It's easier when you have it said and there is
never any point in referring to a son of a bitch by some foreign term. He
wasn't any son of a bitch, though. He was just a coward and that was the worst
luck any man could have. Because if he wasn't a coward he would have stood
up to that woman and not let her bully him. I wonder what I would have
been like if he had married a different woman? That's something you'll never
know, he thought, and grinned. Maybe the bully in her helped to supply
what was missing in the other. And you. (338–39)

Although he says later that he understands and forgives his father's
suicide, Robert Jordan cannot work through his confused feelings. His
characteristic response, like those of Hemingway's other suicidal protagonists, is to avoid thinking about the subject. Associating his father with
fear, cowardice, and defeat, Robert is obsessed with proving he will never
repeat his father's fate. Hemingway's plot guarantees that this will not
happen. Jordan suffers a disabling injury to his knee immediately after
dynamiting the bridge. Rather than escaping with the surviving members of his group, he chooses to stay behind—despite the fact that he has
successfully completed his mission and is therefore under no military
injunction to continue fighting. Jordan lies wounded on the ground as
the novel ends, awaiting the anticipated death that will obviate the need
to repeat his father's fate. "Oh, let them come," he thinks to himself,
moments before the Fascist lieutenant Berrendo arrives, "I don't want to
do that business that my father did. I will do it all right but I'd much
prefer not to have to. I'm against that. Don't think about that. Don't think
at all. I wish the bastards would come" (469).

Robert Jordan's fear of self-inflicted death is exceeded only by that of
Kashkin, Hemingway's most suicideophobic character. The Russian free-
dom-fighter, who is instrumental in blowing up an enemy train prior to
Jordan's arrival, is portrayed as irritable and unstable. Long before he is
wounded in battle, Kashkin makes Pablo, the leader of the group, promise to shoot him in the event he becomes disabled. Kashkin talks so much
about his own death that he demoralizes his comrades: "Poor old Kashkin,
Robert Jordan thought. He must have been doing more harm than good
around here. I wish I would have known he was that jumpy as far back as
then. They should have pulled him out. You can't have people around
doing this sort of work and talking like that. That is no way to talk. Even

if they accomplish their mission they are doing more harm than good, talking that sort of stuff" (21).

The parallels between Kashkin and Robert Jordan are striking. Both are jumpy and nervous despite their bravery; both are morally opposed to suicide while being psychologically obsessed by it; both suffer greatly from physical and psychic injuries and are drawn to dangerous situations for counterphobic motives; and both are convinced that they will not survive their missions. Kashkin would agree with Jordan's statement at the end of the novel that "[d]ying is only bad when it takes a long time and hurts so much that it humiliates you" (468). The two men even resemble each other physically; Augustin tells Jordan, "You look like the other one" (45). Appropriately, it is Jordan who fulfills Kashkin's promise to end his suffering. By shooting his psychological double, Jordan seeks to exorcise his own private demons.

The tragedy of Hemingway's suicidal characters is that they rarely proceed from acting out to working through. Shooting Kashkin does not release Robert Jordan from brooding over his own death. Nor does counteridentification with his father liberate him from suicidal thinking. Unable to empathize with his father or to understand the complex reasons for his decision to terminate his life, Jordan cannot tolerate his own dread of breaking down. Instead of acknowledging that everyone has limits beyond which he or she cannot go, Hemingway constructs an ideal code of heroism that only a handful of men (and even fewer women) can follow.

Hemingway sought to show in Robert Jordan's selfless sacrifice at the end of *For Whom the Bell Tolls* that the sins of the father could be redeemed by the son. For both Jordan and Hemingway, this redemption is made possible by the absolute commitment to work: blowing bridges, for the former, and creating art, for the latter. Significantly, on a number of occasions Jordan expresses interest in writing, telling himself that when he returns to the United States he will write a "true book" about his war experiences (163). Sensitive to the ways in which language both reveals and conceals, he wonders whether he will be able to capture the rich experiences he has lived through and, if so, whether writing the book will enable him to make sense of everything that has happened. "But my guess is you will get rid of all that by writing about it, he said. Once you write it down it is all gone" (165). Several years after completing his Spanish novel, Hemingway reiterated Jordan's affirmation of writing as rescue. "There's a paragraph in *For Whom the Bell Tolls* that . . . well . . . took me twenty years to face his suicide and put it down and catharsize it" (Hotchner 115). Jordan thus views writing as his creator did, as a form of venting in which one is magically unburdened of poisonous thoughts. It is not the talking cure but the writing cure that Hemingway affirms, a cure that worked remarkably well until the end of his life.

"Fathers and Sons": "If He Wrote It He Could Get Rid of It"

The same cathartic vision of art appears in "Fathers and Sons" (1935), the last of the forty-nine collected stories. Nick Adams is now himself a father and reflects upon his own father, who died many years ago. "He had died in a trap that he had helped only a little to set, and they had all betrayed him in their various ways before he died" (*Short Stories* 489–90). It is not clear whether Nick includes himself among his father's betrayers. Nick recalls a childhood incident in which he was punished for lying and describes how he later felt: "Afterwards he had sat inside the watershed with the door open, his shotgun loaded and cocked, looking across at his father sitting on the screen porch reading the paper, and thought, 'I can blow him to hell. I can kill him.' Finally he felt his anger go out of him and he felt a little sick about it being the gun that his father had given him" (496–97).

Nick's patricidal feelings eventually pass but not without a residue of remorse and sadness. Like Robert Jordan, Nick cannot come to terms with his father's death. Pamela Boker infers from the patricidal imagery in "Fathers and Sons" that "Nick perhaps felt as guilty as if he had pulled the trigger himself when his father shot himself many years later, and that it was this guilt that rendered grieving for his father's death difficult if not impossible" (204). Older than Jordan—Nick is thirty-eight in "Fathers and Sons"—he, too, expresses the wish to become a writer, and for the same reason: to partake of the therapeutic benefits of writing. Declaring that his father, like all sentimental people, was betrayed repeatedly, Nick vows to write about him—though not just yet. "If he wrote it he could get rid of it. He had gotten rid of many things by writing them. But it was still too early for that. There were still too many people" (491).

"I Tried to Remember What It Was That Seemed Just Out of My Remembering"

Hemingway's inability to mourn his father's death may be seen obliquely in *Death in the Afternoon* (1932), his extended meditation on the art of bullfighting. The book was published only four years after his father's suicide, and the memory of that event hovers over several passages. Hemingway observes early in the book that the challenge of writing about the violent deaths that occur in the bullring is not to shut one's eyes, despite one's inclination to do so. And yet he cannot seem to decide whether to confront the specter of his father's violent death; as Carl Eby observes (personal communication, 10 July 1997), Hemingway's inability to distinguish between how he should feel about his father's death and how he actually feels identifies him as a suicide survivor. Hemingway acknowledges in *Death in the Afternoon* that at first he had not been able to study violent deaths "as a man might, for instance, study the death of his father or the hanging of some one, say, that he did not know" (3). A few pages later, he describes a cowardly matador and notes that "[t]o show his nervousness was not shameful; only to admit it" (20). He then describes the crowd's response to the cowardly matador and his own feelings:

> When, lacking the technique and thereby admitting his inability to control his feet, the matador went down on both knees before the bull the crowd had no more sympathy with him than with a suicide.
> For myself, not being a bullfighter, and being much interested in suicides, the problem was one of depiction and waking in the night I tried to remember what it was that seemed just out of my remembering. (20)

Death in the Afternoon abounds in other statements about suicide, as when he says, "There is no lonelier man in death, except the suicide, than that man who has lived many years with a good wife and then outlived her" (122). Another passage hints at the matador's feeling of omnipotent control during a bullfight, a feeling that has counterphobic implications: "But when a man is still in rebellion against death he has pleasure in taking to himself one of the Godlike attributes: that of giving it" (233).

"To a Tragic Poetess": "Nothing in Her Life Became Her Like Her Almost Leaving of It"

Hemingway waited several years before he wrote about his father's suicide, but he felt no obligation to spare a living friend, Dorothy Parker, from his disdain over her failed suicide attempts. His 1926 poem "To a Tragic Poetess" is a scathing attack on her personal misfortunes. Parker, whose witty and clever stories appeared in the *New Yorker*, had antagonized Hemingway by talking openly about her bouts of depression, abortion, sexual infidelities, and ambivalence over her Jewish heritage. In one of her best-known poems, "Résumé," Parker poked fun at her numerous suicide attempts and offered a wry affirmation of life:

Razors pain you;
Rivers are damp;
Acids stain you;
And drugs cause cramp.
Guns aren't lawful;
Nooses give;
Gas smells awful;
You might as well live. (99)

Hemingway wrote an eighty-two-line poem pouring out his contempt for every aspect of Parker's life. He was particularly irritated by her adulation of him, her criticism of his beloved Spain, which she had visited with her friend Gilbert Seldes and his wife, and her failure to return a typewriter she had borrowed from him. The opening lines establish the mood of the poem:

Oh thou who with a safety razor blade
a new one to avoid infection
Slit both thy wrists
the scars defy detection
Who over-veronaled to try and peek
into the shade
Of that undistant country from whose bourne
no traveller returns who hasn't been there.
But always vomited in time
And bound your wrists up
To tell how you could see his little hands
already formed
You'd waited months too long

That was the trouble.
But you loved dogs and other people's children
and hated Spain where they are cruel to donkeys.
Hoping the bulls would kill the matadors.
The national tune of Spain was Tea for Two
you said and don't let anyone say Spain to you—
You'd seen it with the Seldes
One Jew, his wife and a consumptive
you sneered your way around
Through Aragon, Castille, and Andalucia.
Spaniards pinched
the Jewish cheeks of your plump ass
in holy week in Seville
forgetful of our Lord and of His passion.
Returned, your ass intact, to Paris
to write more poems for the New Yorker.
                    (*Complete Poems* 87)

Hemingway contrasts Parker's failed suicide attempts with a long list of successful suicides committed by desperate Spanish men whose cries of despair he takes fully seriously. He describes a young boy named Litri (the matador Manuel Baez, whom Hemingway writes about in *Death in the Afternoon*) who, "returning from death's other kingdom" (an allusion to T. S. Eliot's poem "The Hollow Men"), discovers that his leg has been amputated without permission and dies in his bed. Other examples of heroic suffering and death include the matador Maera, who, slipping from his bed, dies upon the floor, drowning in his own mucous; an old man named Valentin Magarza (the source of the suicidal old man in "A Clean, Well-Lighted Place"), who, in his eightieth year, jumped to his death from a tower; and a boy called Jaime Noain, who "exploded in his mouth for love / a three inch stick of dynamite" and then inexplicably survived, living to become the "chief attraction of a troupe of horrors / who visit all the fairs of Catalonia." The poem ends with the bitter assertion that fifteen people a day commit suicide in Spain, all desperate men whose suffering can never be understood by tragic poetesses.

Aggression Masquerading as Art

Friends who heard Hemingway read "To a Tragic Poetess" at a party given by Archibald MacLeish in October 1926 were horrified by its venom.

According to Hemingway biographer Jeffrey Meyers, Parker's friends never mentioned the poem to her (189), an assertion at odds with Parker biographer John Keats (113). Whatever the truth, "To a Tragic Poetess" is nothing less than aggression masquerading as art. The poem reflects and reinforces three dangerous myths of suicide, namely, that those who talk about suicide do not actually go through with it, that unsuccessful suicide attempts should not be taken seriously, and that those who succeed in committing suicide are somehow more heroic than those who fail.

"To a Tragic Poetess" defines Dorothy Parker's identity as a failed suicide attempter. The poem also defines Hemingway's intolerance for female suffering. Dividing the world into female suicide attempters and male suicide completers, he reveals two different voices in the poem, one cruel, the other compassionate. Neither voice is aware of the other's existence.

My first reading of "To a Tragic Poetess" filled me with anger and indignation over Hemingway's insensitivity to Dorothy Parker. Subsequent rereadings have not changed my feelings. Every time I read the poem I shake my head in disbelief at its suicideophobia, misogyny, and anti-Semitism. Curious about how Hemingway's critics have interpreted and evaluated "To a Tragic Poetess," I discovered that, apart from a few passing biographical references, the poem seems to have received only one noteworthy comment, by the editor of Hemingway's *Complete Poems*, who defends his artistic intentions:

> Hemingway publicly ridiculed Parker's affairs, abortion, and suicide attempts. Further, the poem is an attack on a writer who failed, in Hemingway's estimation, to see, to feel. It is an attack on sham self-destructiveness, especially when it is coupled with a lack of sympathy for others. Hemingway was particularly disgusted with Parker's histrionics. After offering such a sketch of this "tragic poetess," he recounted the tragedies of a few truly desperate men. Parker's self-described, and self-defeating, tragic qualities are diminished by comparison. (Gerogiannis xviii)

There is no mention in this brief critical comment of Hemingway's failure to see, to feel. Nor is there the recognition that Hemingway engages in a familiar tactic: scapegoating. To read "To a Tragic Poetess" as Hemingway intended it, one needs to privilege male suffering over female suffering, ignore his prejudice against minorities, and remain oblivious not only to his own mordant portrayals of suicides in *To Have and*

Have Not and *Islands in the Stream* but also to the many suicide threats that he himself expressed at various times in his life to relatives and friends.

Biographers have noticed that even before his father's suicide, Hemingway threatened suicide on a number of occasions. "When I feel low," he wrote in 1926, sounding like Dorothy Parker,

> I like to think about death and the various ways of dying. And I think about probably the best way, unless you could arrange to die some way while asleep, would be to go off a liner at night. That way there could be no doubt about the thing going through and it does not seem a nasty death. There would be only the moment of taking the jump and it is very easy for me to take almost any sort of jump. Also it would never be definitely known what had happened and there would be no post mortems and no expenses left for any one to pay and there would always be the chance that you might be given credit for an accident. (Baker 215–16)

Nor was this an idle meditation. "On the eve of his wedding to Hadley Richardson in 1921," Scott Donaldson writes, "he suffered one of the recurrent attacks of depression (or 'black ass,' as he later called it) that plagued his final years. 'What's this?' Hadley wrote her fiancé. 'Not truly so low as to crave mortage [death] are you?'" (286). A few years later, when he was in the process of divorcing Hadley and marrying his second wife, Pauline Pfeiffer, Hemingway confided to both women, as well as to F. Scott Fitzgerald, that he had been having many thoughts of death and that he might actually kill himself if his marital situation did not improve. As the crisis eased, he wrote to Fitzgerald in November 1926, using language almost identical to that of "To a Tragic Poetess": "Anyway I'm now all through with the general bumping off phase and will only bump off now under certain special circumstances which I don't think will arise. Have refrained from any half turnings on of the gas or slitting of the wrists with sterilized safety razor blades" (*Selected Letters* 232). Hemingway would have almost surely agreed with Nietzsche's caustic observation that "[t]he thought of suicide is a great consolation: by means of it, one gets successfully through many a bad night" (*Philosophy* 468).

The Reader's Countertransference

I must remind myself while reading "To a Tragic Poetess" that Hemingway projected his darkest suicideophobia onto Parker, using her to exorcise his own lifelong preoccupation with the specter of self-inflicted death.

Written two years before his father's suicide, the poem reveals many of the fears expressed in "Indian Camp." By lashing out at Parker, Hemingway not only expressed his own ambivalence about suicide but also heroicized those manly individuals who, victims of love, war, or simply old age, chose to exert supreme control over their own destiny. Only by understanding this can I feel a degree of empathy for the creator of "To a Tragic Poetess."

Yet I still find myself inclined to withdraw in horror and condemnation from "To a Tragic Poetess." I counteridentify with the poem, feeling sympathy for Parker and anger toward Hemingway. I feel contaminated by his violence: his rage toward Parker awakens my own rage toward him. Hemingway's reliance upon defense mechanisms, including denial, projection, displacement, and splitting, mobilizes my own defenses. "How dare Hemingway criticize Parker for his own weaknesses and fears," I mutter to myself while reading the poem; "it is Hemingway who is not fit to live!" By succumbing to the temptation to spurn Hemingway, as he himself spurns Parker, I repeat the pattern of rejecting a fellow human being in distress. His intolerance of female suffering diminishes my own tolerance of his narrow vision of male suffering, in which the tight-lipped code hero, unable to express emotion or mourn painful loss, remains superior to those of us who cannot suffer in silence. Hemingway's poem impairs my empathic stance and undercuts my competence as a reader.

In short, my reaction to Hemingway's "To a Tragic Poetess" reflects the countertransference feelings of malice and aversion that are typical of analysts' responses to suicidal patients. I experience these emotions during many of Hemingway's stories, especially those in which he attacks characters with whom I identify, such as Robert Cohn in *The Sun Also Rises*, who, like Dorothy Parker, is mercilessly caricatured as a Jewish scapegoat. My students tell me that when I teach these stories my voice hardens in anger. Sometimes my denunciations of Hemingway's cruelty and prejudice have the unintended effect of compelling my students to rush to the defense of the beleaguered novelist.

It is not likely that "To a Tragic Poetess" will ever gain popularity: apart from appearing in Hemingway's *Collected Poems*, it is not anthologized. Nevertheless, I wondered how my Literary Suicide students would react to the poem before hearing my own interpretation. Would the poem awaken as much violence in them as it does in me?

Student Responses to "To a Tragic Poetess"

To explore these questions, I distributed copies of both Parker's "Résumé" and Hemingway's "To a Tragic Poetess" to my Literary Suicide students and asked them to read the two poems carefully for the following week. At the beginning of the next class, I gave the students the following in-class assignment:

> I would like you to write two paragraphs on Hemingway's poem "To a Tragic Poetess." In the first paragraph, please describe your responses to the poem: whether you like or dislike it, the feelings it awakens in you toward both Hemingway and Parker, and whatever literary or extraliterary issues you find interesting about the poem. After finishing this paragraph, please look on the next sheet and write a one-paragraph response to it.

On the second sheet was the following question:

> To what extent do your feelings toward "To a Tragic Poetess," as reflected in your first paragraph, demonstrate any of the observations that psychoanalysts John Maltsberger and Dan Buie make in their article "Countertransference Hate in the Treatment of Suicidal Patients"? Their thesis, you will recall, is that the countertransference hatred (feelings of malice and aversion) that suicidal patients arouse in the psychotherapist is a major obstacle in treatment, and that its management through full awareness and self-restraint is essential for successful results. The therapist's repression, reaction formation, projection, distortion, and denial of countertransference hatred increase the danger of suicide.

The students' first paragraphs tended to be less self-reflexive than their second paragraphs. This was especially true of the six students who said they liked the poem. I doubt whether the six had ever analyzed their feelings toward literature in terms of countertransference, and they found themselves wondering why they admired a poem that mocked a female poet's suicidal feelings. One student began the first paragraph by expressing admiration for Hemingway's poem but then noted being troubled by its bitter tone:

First Paragraph: *I liked the poem. I had read "Résumé" before, but I didn't know Hemingway's poem was related either to that poem or Dorothy Parker when I read it. I'm uncertain about much of the poem (but I am often confused about poetry until I have read it over many, many times). It seems weird—the thought of acknowledging suicides in a paper. It seems that most of the time people want to hide it or cover it up. I like the way Hemingway is not afraid to describe suicide acts—he gives names and a bit of information about the people he describes—but the bitter tone makes me wonder—why? Why did he write this? I just don't get it.*

Second Paragraph: *I'm not sure I understand the question. I read and understood the "Countertransference" article, but I can't make a connection here between the psychiatrists' thesis and my response in the first paragraph. Maybe my bitterness at Hemingway's seemingly bitter tone would be a place to start. I don't think I have the time to do this now!*

The other students who enjoyed "To a Tragic Poetess" accepted Hemingway's condemnation of Dorothy Parker's "faked" suicide attempts. They were relatively untroubled, at least in their first paragraphs, by his (and their own) lack of empathy for her. They noted the poem's angry tone and believed it was appropriate, aesthetically and psychologically. None of the six knew much about Parker—perhaps this allowed them to accept Hemingway's acidic portrait of her.

In contrast, the twelve students who disliked "To a Tragic Poetess" could not accept Hemingway's treatment of Parker. Reading oppositionally, they identified not with Hemingway but with Parker. Many were sensitive not only to Hemingway's countertransference in the poem but to their own as well. Their second paragraphs acknowledged, in tones ranging from chagrin to astonished self-revelation, that the anger and malice for which they criticized Hemingway were precisely the emotions that "To a Tragic Poetess" awakened within them. One student used an arresting Hemingwayesque simile in the first paragraph and admitted in the second paragraph to being contaminated by the poem's hatred.

First Paragraph: *My responses to this poem by Hemingway would have to be the same as my responses to any of Hemingway's fiction: a sense of horrors revealed to the world, like turning over a log and finding thousands of insects and insect eggs, and knowing that the forest is this way everywhere. Yet buckling up and walking through it anyway. Hemingway's tired stoicism tottling on rickety legs. I don't like the poem, but it doesn't have anything necessarily to do with the topic. But maybe it does.*

Second Paragraph: *JOY BUZZER EFFECT. This is a point well taken. I feel like it should say GOTCHA! I feel like a sucker, but the point is well taken. Anything repulsive or ugly is likely to create hatred of the object in the observer.*

A second student expressed rage toward Hemingway in the first paragraph and then embarrassment in the second paragraph:

First Paragraph: *Hemingway, you dear, you are such an exquisite hate-filled bastard. You hate weak Jewish princesses who find safe passion. You hate fat-assed women who refuse to live, to suffer, to fuck as you might say swilling, smarting, spitting. You bring out all my countertransference. I want to hurt you right back. I want to abandon you. I want to remind you that you know really nothing more about the "funeral passing in the rain" in Luticia than your poetess does. They are not your dead, not your rain days, not your mattas. I hate you because you are a coward.*

Second Paragraph: *Good lord, what do I do now? I did not know, as I rambled on in my first response, that you would ask this question. How uncanny.*

Many students used the countertransference question to explore why they disliked "To a Tragic Poetess," concluding that just as Hemingway attacked Parker for qualities existing within himself, so did they view him as a dark reflection of themselves. Their analysis of the poem contained cultural and psychological insights:

First Paragraph: *This poem is extraordinarily cruel and full of hatred, but in another respect, I've gotta wonder if this honesty of feeling is what makes a writer great. I know Hemingway read this poem publicly at a party at the MacLeishes and that a lot of people got up and walked out. I think it was a tasteless act, but at some point or another, rationally or irrationally, don't we all secretly hate like this? Even if it passes later? Anyway, I don't think that's a justification. The poem is terribly sexist—as if only a man can really commit suicide properly. What a horse's ass Hemingway is. Parker could have drunk him under the table any night of the week. Also, I think Hemingway hates Parker because she is a mirror of him: full of bravado but scared shitless underneath it all. And Hemingway has all those twins and mirror hangups. I think Parker represented a mirror in which he didn't want to look.*

Second Paragraph: *I'm not sure I'm answering this correctly, but I think, for me, the reason I hate Hemingway for hating Parker so much is because of transference. Hemingway hates in a cruel, below the belt cheap shot way in this poem. It's a hatred I think we have all felt but are afraid to recognize in ourselves (unless there are only two assholes in the world, Hemingway and myself). In hating Hemingway I can deny ever feeling cruel about myself. Also, Parker is so on the money about women and the most intimate feelings that they don't speak about. I hate to admit how much I feel and have felt like some of these women. I totally, well, not totally, but I empathize a lot with her, so I get mad at Hemingway. Also, I guess I hate Parker sometimes because I don't want to admit feeling like her at her worst or some of her fictional women.*

Gendered Readings of "To a Tragic Poetess"

Do male and female readers react differently to a poem like "To a Tragic Poetess"? Are countertransference responses to suicidal literature gendered? I don't know to what extent my response to Hemingway's poem is typical of other men, nor do I know how I would have responded to the poem had I read it when I was a graduate student in the 1960s, when the women's movement was beginning. I suspect that I would have accepted many of Hemingway's patriarchal judgments about suicide. But how do male and female readers react to Hemingway's poem in the 1990s?

Since fourteen of the eighteen students in my graduate Literary Suicide class were female, there was little point in asking respondents to indicate their gender when writing the reader-response paragraphs to Hemingway's poem. An opportunity to explore this question arose the following summer, when I taught a combined undergraduate/graduate course on Hemingway. The twenty-four undergraduates and ten graduates were divided almost equally between males and females. I gave each student a copy of "To a Tragic Poetess" and, without providing a context for the poem, issued the following instructions for a brief in-class assignment: "'To a Tragic Poetess' records Hemingway's feelings toward Dorothy Parker, a well-known writer who attempted suicide several times. Would you please describe in one paragraph whether you like or dislike the poem and characterize the feelings it awakens within you toward both Hemingway and Parker. Do not sign the paragraph, but please indicate whether you are male or female."

After I collected the reader-response paragraphs, I randomly selected sixteen of them, divided equally by gender. I typed the sixteen responses, photocopied them, and then distributed them to the students the following week. To make the discussion more interesting, I asked the students to see if they could correctly guess on a separate note card the gender of each of the sixteen respondents.

Despite my prediction that gender differences would emerge in the reader-response paragraphs, I was astonished by the consistency of these patterns. A large majority of the students were able to predict correctly the writer's gender in twelve of the sixteen paragraphs. The students were evenly split in their responses to two paragraphs and incorrect, by a wide margin, in their responses to the remaining two paragraphs. Here are the eight paragraphs written by males, with the percentage of students who correctly guessed the writer's gender.

Male Readings of "To a Tragic Poetess"

1

"To a Tragic Poetess" is a bitter assertion of power, and I suppose that's why I like it. Hemingway is aware of the power of his words. He relishes the power and enjoys wielding it with a "vengeful giddiness." The poem is a stab back at Dorothy Parker, who, we are told, has crossed Hemingway. With the deft hands of a master, he thrusts his sword directly for what is certainly a most sensitive area for Ms. Parker: her suicide attempts. Since Hemingway sees suicide as an act of cowardice, he destroys and belittles her powerfully. Hell hath no fury like an effective writer scorned. (82 percent)

2

The difficulty that Hemingway had with Parker is quite evident. He seems to feel her to be self-satisfying and is angry with her. Parker, due to multiple suicide attempts, appears incapable of dealing with the situations that arise. I did like this poem: it pissed me off. (82 percent)

3

I like the poem. In it, Hemingway shows to me almost a respect for suicide. It is not an act to be taken or entered into lightly. I agree. Slit your wrists, jump out the window or overdose on those pills, only if you mean it. If you don't mean it, and your intentions are not true, then there is no dignity in the act. It is to be an act of finality, your last deed, your last statement. Don't make it a false one. Be brave in your cowardice. (91 percent)

4

Hemingway seems to dismiss Parker's suicide because it is neither macho nor successful. I dislike his macho imagery and, almost, his sneers at Parker's attempts, with his obsession with suicide. I find it amazing that he could react thus to a friend and fellow writer. The poem could be more aptly titled "Proper Suicides I Have Known." I'm not sure how much it reveals about Parker, but it speaks volumes about Hemingway's feelings toward her. (15 percent)

5

I dislike the poem, both for its literary as well as its biographical value. It seems cruel. Not knowing anything about Dorothy Parker, I can't comment on the "validity" of her suicide attempts, but it seems in poor taste for Hemingway to mock such a serious event in anyone's life. Hemingway shows us his bullying, unforgiving, blind side here. It's painful to see this in one who could be so serious, thoughtful, and sensitive. (50 percent)

6

The poem is satirical but also powerful. Although it is aimed at Parker and her unsuccessful suicide attempt, I sense a deeper meaning. First, I sense fear by Hemingway. The description of Spain is morbid, therefore, leading to a high suicide rate. Hemingway seems to be caught, or even trapped, in this suicidal environment. Due to his family's personal history, I think he fears his own desire to commit suicide. This gives the poem its power. In addition, I can see Hemingway's portrait of a coward in Parker. He mocks her unsuccessful attempt at suicide as if, in competition, he could do better. Eventually, he succeeds. Again, this is why I feel he has written the poem in fear. (65 percent)

7

Suicide always leaves me with a disturbing mixture of repugnance and compassion. It seems Hemingway viewed Parker's attempts as ridiculous charades done to elicit sympathy or attention, neither of which seems honorable to the Hemingway code. His glorification of the deaths and/or sui-

cides of the males in the poem denies any correlation or similarity and seems to me to be overromanticized or idealized. I wonder what his final observations on suicide and death were, as he was pointing the gun at his own face. Did he feel sympathy for himself, or was it a last ditch effort at the ultimate tough guy ending? (53 percent)

8

The poem is good. Better if I knew that incident which changed their relationship. The tragedy of Parker is her cowardice. For this, Hemingway is criminal, cold, and calculating. He writes to kill, and as we know, ultimately shames her by accomplishing what she could not. (85 percent)

Four of the eight men (1, 2, 3, and 8) express approval and admiration of "To a Tragic Poetess," endorsing Hemingway's attitude toward Parker and praising, implicitly or explicitly, his vision of courage and manhood. The word "power" dominates two paragraphs (1 and 6), indicating the students' appreciation of the poem's aesthetic impact on them. They also seem to identify with Hemingway's aggression toward Parker. Student 1 seems to take vicarious pleasure in Hemingway's rhetorical dismemberment of Parker, while student 3 urges Parker to act on her suicidal threats if she is serious. And student 8, noticing that Hemingway writes to kill, accepts the need to humiliate her artistically.

None of the men who esteem the poem questions whether Parker deserved the scorn Hemingway casts upon her. They agree with his judgment that she is a coward and therefore unworthy of sympathy. They also accept Hemingway's vision of suicide; as student 3 observes, sounding like Hemingway himself, if you are seriously contemplating suicide, don't simply talk about it—do it.

Of the remaining four males, two disapprove (4 and 5) of "To a Tragic Poetess," while the other two (6 and 7) seem to be ambivalent toward it. Students 4 and 5 read the poem oppositionally, distressed by Hemingway's cruelty toward Parker. A large majority of the class (85 percent) assumed that student 4 was female—and only half were able to guess the gender of students 5 and 7, indicating that these two students' responses did not seem stereotypically male.

Female Readings of "To a Tragic Poetess"

The female responses to "To a Tragic Poetess" were strikingly different.

9

I'm finding it very difficult to decide whether I like the poem or not; I am certainly moved by it, which in itself is a form of success. It is obviously sarcastic and hateful, to the point of causing nausea in this reader. Regardless of Hemingway's opinion of Parker, I feel his complete lack of sympathy is unforgivable (particularly considering his destiny!). His callous reference to abortion was almost too cynical to even begin to relate to. In conclusion, his opinion that a successful suicide makes a person more heroic is ludicrous. (94 percent)

10

The poem works out in an odd way Hemingway's tendency toward absolutes: everything or nothing. Parker's suicide attempts are reduced to black comedy, allusion-laced, because their purpose may not have been an easy death. The poem awakens in me sympathy for Parker and an uneasy feeling that Hemingway's vision is limited here not by sexism but by a failure of imagination. For a writer, I think that might be much, much worse. Like or dislike? Well, I do not like it, but I'm not sure that equals disliking it. I am put off by its gratuitous cruelty. (76 percent)

11

I found the poem and, of course, the author to be particularly invasive, voyeuristic, and sadistic. While I do not profess to understand with confidence this or any other poem, I gleaned from "To a Tragic Poetess" a sense of my own disgust and discomfort. As Hemingway himself has stated, some things are better left unsaid. (71 percent)

12

I admire Hemingway's well-crafted poem, but I find his audacious criticism of a woman's life and attempts at suicide deplorable. Life is filled with tragedies, and he above many should know better than to set himself in judgment as if he is a God and can determine what is more tragic. (76 percent)

13

I appreciate Hemingway's imagery, cadence, and language; however, the poem appears to diminish Dorothy Parker's suicide attempts as real or important. Perhaps it is Hemingway's pervasive machismo again. For him, it seems, the loss of a bullfighter or, in general, a man is more tragic than the loss of a woman. This may be colored by Hemingway's dislike of Parker, but he appears to denigrate not only her feelings but her talent as well. (85 percent)

14

I do not like Hemingway's taunting in the poem. The poem itself, without looking at the meaning, only the style, is outstanding. The meaning is another thing. I feel angry and disappointed when reading Hemingway poking fun at a former friend's suicide attempts. What could possess a person to dislike someone so much that they taunt his or her unhappiness? (61 percent)

15

This is definitely a very powerful poem: it seems as though Hemingway is totally mocking Parker's attempt to take her life, and yet making it sound acceptable for the other people who succeeded. Knowing what we have discussed thus far, Hemingway is pro-suicide for whatever reason. I find this to be extremely depressing and a cowardly way of looking at life. He makes the people who attempt suicide seem heroic. That's really sad. (35 percent)

16

I enjoyed the poem because it flowed nicely and kept my interest as a crossword puzzle does. It seems that Hemingway does not understand tragedy or suffering and attempts to acquire empathy by mocking others' efforts. I believe in the realness of Parker's despair and do not condemn her for continuing to live. (65 percent)

All eight women read "To a Tragic Poetess" oppositionally, including those who otherwise like the poem, and all protest Hemingway's caricature of Parker. In identifying with Parker and counteridentifying with Hemingway, they imply that the poem is an attack on women in general, not simply on one woman poet. They conclude that despite the ironic title of the poem, Parker's life was indeed tragic and that therefore Hemingway's satire is inappropriate.

Reading the poem is a painful experience for several of the women: it awakens nausea in student 10, disgust and discomfort in student 11, anger and disappointment in student 14, depression and sadness in student 15. Student 11 actually feels violated while reading the poem, experiencing it as "invasive, voyeuristic, and sadistic." Whereas the male readers interpret "To a Tragic Poetess" as an indictment of Parker's cowardice, the female readers remark upon Hemingway's cowardice, or at least his gratuitous cruelty and unfairness.

What is perhaps most striking about the female reader-response paragraphs is that they are more empathic than the male responses, more sensitive to the assaultive nature of Hemingway's poem. And yet it would be wrong to conclude from the reader-response paragraphs on "To a Tragic Poetess" that all the male students condoned Hemingway's attack on Dorothy Parker. A male student came to my office after the Hemingway class and proudly confided that he was the author of paragraph 4, which most of his classmates misidentified as having been written by a woman. Students 5 and 7 also protested Hemingway's bullying tactics. Although Hemingway's macho view of heroism continues to have great appeal to men, there is growing awareness of the limitations of his heroic code. If men are still taught to believe they should embrace Hemingwayesque suffering, they can learn to appreciate Parkeresque pain.

Hemingway's Suicide and Its Aftermath

Years of traumatic injuries and heavy drinking took a terrible toll on Hemingway's physical and mental health, and toward the end of his life he became paranoid and delusional. The electroshock treatments he received at the Mayo Clinic resulted in a terrifying loss of memory and the complete inability to write. The use of lithium for the treatment of manic depression was still in its infancy, and like many writers, he was suspicious of any drug that might harm his creativity, despite the fact that he spent his entire adult life self-medicating with alcohol. He rejected help offered by well-meaning relatives, friends, and physicians, and he came to believe, as did many of them, that his situation was hopeless.

A. E. Hotchner's moving account of his last meeting with Hemingway captures the helplessness and sadness that both men felt:

"Papa, why do you want to kill yourself?"

He hesitated only a moment; then he spoke in his old, deliberate way. "What do you think happens to a man going on sixty-two when he realizes that he can never write the books and stories he promised himself? Or do any of the other things he promised himself in the good days?"

"But how can you say that? You have written a beautiful book about Paris [*A Moveable Feast*], as beautiful as anyone can hope to write. How can you overlook that?"

"The best of that I wrote before. And now I can't finish it."

"But perhaps it is finished and it is just reluctance . . ."

"Hotch, if I can't exist on my own terms, then existence is impossible. Do you understand? That is how I've lived, and that is how I *must* live — or not live." (Hotchner 297)

The accuracy of many of Hotchner's assertions has been challenged, but the emotions at the close of *Papa Hemingway* seem genuine. Unable to convince the depressed novelist that he had written a lifetime's work of great stories and that he could still pursue other passions, Hotchner recalls how Hemingway suddenly turned against him, accusing him of exploitation and persecution. Hotchner was stung by the criticisms and left shortly thereafter, overcome with pain and anger, never to see Hemingway again.

So, too, were Hemingway's relatives and friends overwhelmed by grief and guilt, the harsh legacy of suicide. The opening sentence of Gregory Hemingway's 1976 memoir *Papa* underscores the suicide survivor's unique plight. "I never got over a sense of responsibility for my father's death and the recollection of it sometimes made me act in strange ways" (1). A physician, like his grandfather, Gregory Hemingway describes his intense ambivalence toward his father, an ambivalence that made mourning his suicide more problematic. He admitted that he "felt profound relief when they lowered my father's body into the ground and I realized that he was really dead, that I couldn't disappoint him, couldn't hurt him anymore" (118). Nor was he the only family member who felt implicated in the suicide. Mary Hemingway had locked her husband's guns in their storeroom, fearing the worst, but she did not conceal the key because she felt that he had the right of access to his possessions. According to Jeffrey Meyers, even as she denied for five years that her husband had deliberately shot himself, she felt gnawing guilt that she had not hidden the key to the gun cabinet. Other relatives attempted to justify Hemingway's death.

Leicester Hemingway described his brother's suicide as the "final positive action of his life": "Like a samurai who felt dishonored by the word or deed of another, Ernest felt his own body had betrayed him" (283). His conclusion was that Ernest Hemingway acted heroically, a view shared by Gregory Hemingway. "I think he showed courage in accepting the only option left" (16).

To what extent did Ernest Hemingway's suicide contribute to the suicides of his siblings Leicester and Ursula? Given the genetic predisposition toward manic-depressive illness in the Hemingway family, it is likely that both nature and nurture combined to produce a deadly outcome. It is well known that suicide heightens the risk of other suicides in a family (Pfeffer). Quite apart from genetic factors, suicide is a learned act, and the death of one relative may teach another that suicide is an acceptable solution to the pain of living. Hemingway intuitively knew this. Upon hearing of his father's suicide, John Hemingway recalled a promise the novelist had obliged him to make several years earlier, when John was confronting a personal crisis:

> After I left the army and was married, I was very depressed about what I was going to do, very gloomy. And Papa said, "You must promise me never, never . . . we'll both promise each other never to shoot ourselves." He said, "Don't do it. It's stupid." This was after quite a few martinis. I hadn't said anything about shooting myself, but I was obviously very depressed. He said, "It's one thing you must promise me never to do, and I'll promise the same to you." (Brian 262)

Hemingway's antisuicide pact with his son testifies poignantly to his recognition of the shattering impact of suicide upon the survivors and the fear that suicide was an intergenerational curse. Did he sense that, decades earlier, his father's suicide would have a formative, perhaps even fatal, influence on his own life? This is the interpretation that John Berryman, whose life also ended in suicide (as did *his* father's life), reached in his haunting stanzas on Hemingway in *The Dream Songs:*

> Save us from shotguns & fathers' suicides.
> It all depends on who you're the father *of*
> if you want to kill yourself—
> a bad example, murder of oneself,
> the final death, in a paroxysm, of love
> for which good mercy hides?

. . . .
But to return, to return to Hemingway
that cruel & gifted man.
Mercy! my father; do not pull the trigger
or all my life I'll suffer from your anger
killing what you began. (254)

Copycat suicides followed Hemingway's death. Upon being told of Hemingway's death, the great Spanish bullfighter Juan Belmonte responded, in carefully chosen words, "Well done," and not long afterward shot himself in the same way (Meyers 564). A hint of romanticization appears in Meyers's own attitude toward Hemingway: "His suicide had elements of self-pity and revenge, but was not inspired by desperation and derangement. It was a careful and courageous act" (559).

Deromanticizing Suicide

In light of the growing number of students who have seriously contemplated suicide and who may be at risk when reading a writer whose stories abound in fantasies of heroic death, it is essential to avoid celebrating suicide. This is especially true of a writer like Hemingway, whose stories have great appeal to youth. "Teenagers are probably more affected by media coverage of suicide than other age groups; they also may be affected by mystic, romantic, and glorified treatment of suicide in the literature and movies" (Poland 52). Suicide is not about courage or cowardice but about pain and hopelessness, and Hemingway's writings deserve honest and informed discussions, including awareness of the gender implications of reading suicidal literature. Contrary to the mythology of suicide that Hemingway perpetuates in a poem like "To a Tragic Poetess," empathy for male suicidal depression does not preclude empathy for female suicidal depression. Hemingway's greatest stories, like "A Clean, Well-Lighted Place," affirm knowledge through suffering, and though he did not always express compassion for others' pain, he sought to conquer his demons and live life to the fullest. What I find genuinely heroic about Hemingway is not his death but the extent to which he was able, until the end of his life, to transmute his deepest fears into great art, thereby triumphing over his suicideophobia.

CHAPTER 5

Sylvia Plath and the Charge of Art

Reading Sylvia Plath tempts me back, back into the gray and burnt red stone buildings, back, back to the giant old oaks and its purple and yellow crocuses, back, back to the puddled brick walks of my college days. In The Bell Jar *Plath makes fun of her friends who answer the question, "Where do you go to college?" with a flippant, "In Boston." She writes that she has decided to say, "In Northampton." I remember reading that novel for the first time in ninth grade, and I remember being enthralled: suicide, Smith, free thought, poetry: it all seemed just perfect. I remember lying on my bed and shaking my head as I read how Plath looked at a handwoven rug that a woman had labored over only to use as a mat for her husband to wipe his feet. Such a waste of a woman's handiwork, I concluded, along with young Plath.*

And her poems were so raw, so bloody, so cutting, so real to me then. A thumb stump, a woman-cow, a pair of dead moles, a murderous father: so many painful and tragic images. Take something ugly, truly hideous, and display it well: give it juxtaposition; give it duality; give it texture; give it angst, and my young self beat its angel wings. I want to cry when I remember how innocence apprehends danger.

Elizabeth

Sylvia Plath remains the most haunting twentieth-century literary suicide, the counterpart to the romantic English poet Thomas Chatterton, whose suicide in 1770 at the age of eighteen symbolized artistic martyrdom for writers of the next century. Unlike Hemingway, whose self-shooting was motivated partly by the fear that his creativity was irretrievably lost, Plath wrote the best poems of her life in the days preceding her death. She was only thirty when she killed herself on 11 February 1963, less than half Hemingway's age, with a dazzling future ahead of her. Whereas Hemingway spent a lifetime battling the specter of suicide, unwilling to seek psychotherapy for a problem he considered too private to discuss with anyone other than his "Portable Corona Number 3," Plath received valuable psychiatric help following her 1953 suicide attempt. She remained in touch with her psychiatrist, transmuting the personal material of her analysis into wildly original poems that continue to astonish readers. A perfectionist, she was proud of her recovery and looked forward to a long creative life as a poet, wife, and mother.

Hemingway's suicide signaled the passing of one era and Plath's the beginning of another. Neither Hemingway's wife, Mary, nor Plath's mother, Aurelia Schober Plath, could bear to admit that the deaths were suicides. Newspapers and magazines around the world immediately reported Hemingway's shooting as accidental. A larger-than-life figure, Papa Hemingway appeared invincible to millions of men. It seemed inconceivable that the man who successfully defied death so many times, and who dismissed suicide as an act of cowardice, would eventually perish by his own hand. Mrs. Plath was similarly horrified by her daughter's suicide; the grieving mother told the newspapers that Sylvia died from a respiratory infection. The details of the suicide emerged only after the family's shock subsided. Though she had achieved recognition in poetry circles at the time of her death, Plath was relatively unknown to the general reading public. Her only novel, *The Bell Jar*, appeared in England in January 1963 under the pseudonym "Victoria Lucas." Within a few years, Plath became a cult figure whose self-asphyxiation in a stove came to be interpreted by early feminists as an act of martyrdom.

Anyone who has taught Sylvia Plath's writings knows that female students identify with her portrayal of victimization. *The Bell Jar*, Plath's thinly fictionalized account of her frenetic life at Smith College in the early 1950s, mercilessly exposes the hypocritical double standards of a patriarchal society. The novel reveals a claustrophobic bell jar vision descending upon a woman, distorting her sense of self, snuffing out her self-esteem, and culminating in suicidal depression.

As Elizabeth's diary entry reveals, many readers of *The Bell Jar* are dismayed upon discovering that Plath committed suicide shortly after its publication. Edna Pontellier's suicide may enthrall readers, yet they can remind themselves that *The Awakening* is, finally, a work of fiction. No such reassurance is possible for readers of *The Bell Jar*. The reality of Plath's tragic death exposes the fictionality of the heroine's recovery in *The Bell Jar*.

"Dying Is an Art"

The Bell Jar and two of Plath's most celebrated poems, "Daddy" and "Lady Lazarus," portray suicide as a prelude to rebirth. They dramatize in autobiographical and mythic terms the 1953 suicide attempt that, methodically executed, should have been successful. Even Hemingway would have been forced to acknowledge the seriousness of her actions. Plath wrote a note saying she was going on a long walk, swallowed a potentially fatal dose of sleeping pills, and then buried herself in the crawl space of her parents' home. Buried alive for three days before she was rescued, she later compared her near-miraculous recovery to a resurrection. She regarded herself as a Lady Lazarus and viewed suicide as part of a process of death and rebirth. The speakers in *The Bell Jar*, "Daddy," and "Lady Lazarus" symbolically die, only to be reborn. This is not to imply that Plath's speakers are not serious about killing themselves. They attempt suicide for many reasons: to punish themselves, to revenge themselves on others, to escape from intolerable pain, and to be reunited with lost loved ones. But they almost always come back to life, rejecting the role of victim and triumphing over their oppressors. "Lady Lazarus" dramatizes suicide as a ritualized performance or striptease that Plath simultaneously affirms and mocks. The speaker observes, with wry, self-deprecating irony: "Dying / Is an art, like everything else. / I do it exceptionally well" (*Collected Poems* 245).

Plath's belief that suicide leads to rebirth allows readers of *The Bell Jar*, "Daddy," and "Lady Lazarus" to appreciate the ways in which she transmuted personal suffering into potent art. These texts invigorate as well as shock readers, and although they involve us in the protagonists' self-destructive world, they celebrate renewal. But it is more difficult to find consolation in Plath's last poem, "Edge," written only two or three days before her death. "Edge" is, without doubt, Plath's most unsettling poem, largely because, instead of looking backward to her failed suicide attempt a decade earlier, it startlingly foreshadows her death and the near-death of her two young children, whom she imagined killing. "Edge" raises vexing questions about the relationship between madness and creativity and the boundary between healthy and unhealthy art.

Extremist Art

These questions have long disturbed critics. A. Alvarez argues in his influential 1971 book *The Savage God* that Plath committed suicide in an attempt "to get herself out of a desperate corner which her own poetry had boxed herself into" (xii). Believing that, in the end, "she was beyond the reach of anyone" (31), that she was, in short, doomed, Alvarez postulates a theory of art in which the dredging up of gloomy personal material may heighten "extremist" writers' vulnerability to suicide and undermine their will to live: "[F]or the artist himself art is not necessarily therapeutic; he is not automatically relieved of his fantasies by expressing them. Instead, by some perverse logic of creation, the act of formal expression may simply make the dredged-up material more readily available to him. The result of handling it in his work may well be that he finds himself living it out" (36–37).

Alvarez is correct in saying that art is "not necessarily" therapeutic, yet if we go by the statements of writers themselves, including those who later commit suicide, the creation of art nearly always has a cathartic impact on the artist. As I suggest in *The Talking Cure*, Plath invariably spoke about poetry as a release, and there is no reason to disbelieve her. Art is a necessary but not always sufficient part of an artist's support system. It was not writing or, as in Hemingway's case, the inability to write that killed Plath; rather, it was, as Alvarez himself movingly chronicles, the breakdown of her personal life. She felt abandoned and betrayed when her husband, Ted Hughes, left her for another woman. Plath's vulnerability was heightened by the personal mythology she constructed around suicide. She came to view herself as an escape artist, compelled to commit suicide so that she could be magically reborn—a mythology that works better in literature than it does in life.

Five major biographers—Edward Butscher, Linda Wagner-Martin, Anne Stevenson, Paul Alexander, and Ronald Hayman—have described in elaborate detail Plath's preoccupation with suicide. None has investigated, however, the impact of her suicidal art upon readers. Nor has this question been explored by Jacqueline Rose or Janet Malcolm, the latest critics to write comprehensive studies on Plath. The poet herself raises this question in "Lady Lazarus" when the speaker exclaims sardonically, after describing her death-defying acts, "There is a charge / For the eyeing of my scars, there is a charge / For the hearing of my heart— / It really goes" (*Collected Poems* 246). She never tells us, however, the nature of this charge either to herself or to her readers.

The Charge of Art

What is the charge, or price of admission, for witnessing Plath's speakers as they exhibit their scars to us? What is the charge, in the form of guilty pleasure, for observing her speakers as they are violated by sadistic, Nazi-like men? What is the psychic charge, in terms of heightened liability or vulnerability, as we find ourselves implicated in a world of murderous violence that always threatens to turn against the self? And what is the charge, or responsibility, of teachers who read Plath's suicidal literature with their students? Is there the danger, when entering Plath's world, of being overcharged?

Suicidal writers do not necessarily write more authentically about suicide than nonsuicidal writers, but we read them differently. We scrutinize their writings for clues to their death, and when we find them, we cannot avoid attaching psychobiographical significance to them. If the writer is highly autobiographical, as Plath was, then we may find ourselves implicated in her suicidal art. A suicidal poem, no less than an act of suicide, may be a cry for help, and for some readers it is difficult to avoid the urge to intervene. Plath's poems are distressing to readers precisely because she goes out of her way to make us feel like accomplices to her characters' attempted and completed suicides.

The Bell Jar and the Fear of Insanity

To understand Plath's portrayal of suicide and the complex interrelationship of her biography and art, we may begin with *The Bell Jar*, the story of the events leading to her 1953 depression, near-fatal drug overdose, hospitalization, and recovery. Early in the novel Esther Greenwood reflects upon a conversation with Buddy Willard several years earlier. Buddy, now a medical student, had asked: "Do you know what a poem is, Esther?" Unable to answer his question, Esther hears his smug reply: "A piece of dust" (*The Bell Jar* 61–62). She broods over the exchange for a whole year, unhappy with her failure to challenge his bias against art. Finally she imagines a more satisfactory response. "So are the cadavers you cut up. So are the people you think you're curing. They're dust as dust as dust. I reckon a good poem lasts a whole lot longer than a hundred of those people put together." Esther concludes her imaginary conversation by declaring that "[p]eople were made of nothing so much as dust, and I couldn't see that doctoring all that dust was a bit better than writing poems people would remember and repeat to themselves when they were unhappy or sick and couldn't sleep" (62).

As her depression intensifies, Esther finds that she cannot read, much less write, poetry. Writer's block seems to be a cause and effect of her developing panic. She can read only the scandal sheets, "full of the local murders and suicides and beatings and robbings" (*The Bell Jar* 153), and the abnormal psychology textbooks she buys in an effort to analyze and heal herself. Esther's writer's block takes on added significance because she defines herself as a poet and, until the onslaught of depression, has been remarkably successful in making her artistic dream come true. Winning a scholarship to a prestigious all-women's college outside Boston, Esther has been a straight-A student, college correspondent for the town newspaper, editor of the literary magazine, and secretary of Honor Board. The goal of becoming a professor and poet appears within her grasp. She has attracted the attention of Philomena Guinea, a wealthy novelist who attended the same college in the early 1900s. As a result of winning a contest, Esther spends an exciting month in New York City where she serves as a guest junior editor on a famous magazine, *Ladies Day*. Esther's life in *The Bell Jar*, which closely parallels Sylvia Plath's experiences at Smith College and her guest editorship on *Mademoiselle*, seems to be an excellent preparation for a writer—and yet, like her creator, she finds her mind growing blank during the summer of 1953.

Esther's growing fear of insanity compels her to scan the newspapers, where she reads in lurid prose about others who succumb to acts of madness and despair. Riveted by the headline "SUICIDE SAVED FROM 7-STORY LEDGE!" Esther reads about a man named George Pollucci who allowed himself to be helped to safety by a police officer. Peering at the face of the would-be suicide, Esther "felt he had something important to tell me, and whatever it was might just be written on his face" (*The Bell Jar* 153). But the newspaper article can tell Esther nothing about the man's suicidal crisis. Instead, "the smudgy crags of George Pollucci's features melted away as I peered at them, and resolved themselves into a regular pattern of dark and light and medium-gray dots" (153). Nor does Esther discover anything about the mystery of suicide from another headline: "STARLET SUCCUMBS AFTER 68-HOUR COMA" (163).

The Bell Jar offers several insights into Esther's suicidal crisis. Esther's perfectionism seems to be a defense against feelings of insecurity caused, in large part, by her intense ambivalence toward her parents. Her father, a professor of entomology, died when she was a child, and his death has affected her profoundly. She tells us, in a revealing sentence, "My German-speaking father, dead since I was nine, came from some manic-depressive hamlet in the black heart of Prussia" (*The Bell Jar* 36), thus linking her paternal origins to mental illness. Esther, who has difficulty learning German, intimates that her mother was angry at him "for dying and leaving no money because he didn't trust life insurance salesmen" (43). Although she claims that the last time she had felt "purely happy" was when she was nine years old, running along the hot white beach with her father the summer before he died, Esther presents elsewhere a less positive portrait of her father. Esther's cynicism about marriage seems to be a reflection of her parents' troubled marriage: "Hadn't my own mother told me that as soon as she and my father left Reno on their honeymoon — my father had been married before, so he needed a divorce — my father said to her, 'Whew, that's a relief, now we can stop pretending and be ourselves'? — and from that day on my mother never had a minute's peace" (94).

Esther blames her mother for not allowing her to attend her father's funeral — surprisingly, no one in the family has visited his grave. She notes that her father's death has always seemed unreal to her and vows to make amends for the past. "I had a great yearning, lately, to pay my father back for all the years of neglect, and start tending his grave. I had always been my father's favorite, and it seemed fitting I should take on a mourning my mother had never bothered with" (*The Bell Jar* 186). She breaks down in tears and grieves for the first time when she finally locates his gravestone. "I laid my face to the smooth face of the marble and howled my loss into the cold salt rain" (189). She begins plotting her suicide in the next scene.

Esther's incomplete mourning over her father's death is a major cause of her suicide attempt. Experiencing the death as an abandonment, she attempts suicide both to atone for her ambivalent feelings toward her father and to be reunited with him in death.

Esther is no less ambivalent toward her mother. Mrs. Greenwood is a hardworking woman who has single-mindedly devoted herself to her children's welfare. She has succeeded in raising a family and having a career and thus would appear to be an excellent role model for her daughter. Yet Esther fears becoming like her pragmatic mother, and nearly every reference to Mrs. Greenwood is unsympathetic. Esther's announcement that she will not continue electroshock treatments with Dr. Gordon elicits a disturbing response from her mother:

> "You can call him up and tell him I'm not coming next week."
> My mother smiled. "I knew my baby wasn't like that."
> I looked at her. "Like what?"
> "Like those awful people. Those awful dead people at that hospital." She paused. "I knew you'd decide to be all right again." (163)

From the dialogue we infer that Mrs. Greenwood cannot understand her daughter's frightening situation and that she blames Esther for becoming mentally ill. Indeed, Mrs. Greenwood experiences her daughter's depression as an indictment of her own parenting.

Mrs. Greenwood's disapproval becomes more evident when she visits Esther in the hospital immediately following the suicide attempt. "My mother perched on the edge of the bed and laid a hand on my leg. She looked loving and reproachful, and I wanted her to go away" (*The Bell Jar* 194). Toward the end of the novel, when she is almost ready to be released from the hospital, Esther reflects upon a statement made to her by her second psychiatrist:

> Doctor Nolan had said, quite bluntly, that a lot of people would treat me gingerly, or even avoid me, like a leper with a warning bell. My mother's face floated to mind, a pale, reproachful moon, at her last and first visit to the asylum since my twentieth birthday. A daughter in an asylum! I had done that to her. Still, she had obviously decided to forgive me.
> "We'll take up where we left off, Esther," she had said, with her sweet, martyr's smile. "We'll act as if all this were a bad dream." (267)

Mrs. Greenwood may forgive her daughter, but Esther cannot reciprocate. The daughter perceives her mother as hard and wounding, and when

Esther sees her climbing into bed earlier in the story, the pin curls on Mrs. Greenwood's head seem to be "glittering like a row of little bayonets." Esther's description of her snoring mother is chilling in its matricidal imagery. "The piggish noise irritated me, and for a while it seemed to me that the only way to stop it would be to take the column of skin and sinew from which it rose and twist it to silence between my hands" (*The Bell Jar* 137–38). The turning point in Esther's psychotherapy occurs when she vents her rage to Dr. Nolan: "'I hate her,' I said, and waited for the blow to fall. But Doctor Nolan only smiled at me as if something had pleased her very, very much, and said, 'I suppose you do'" (229).

Letters Home and the Journals

The story of Esther Greenwood's convoluted feelings toward her parents appears in far greater detail in Sylvia Plath's two posthumously published autobiographical works, *Letters Home* (1975), the five-hundred-page edition of her correspondence, edited by Aurelia Schober Plath, and *The Journals of Sylvia Plath* (1982), selected and edited by Frances McCullough and Ted Hughes. The letters and journals are indispensable for an understanding of the continuities and discontinuities in Plath's life, illuminating not only the interrelationship of her biography and art but also the psychological conflicts she sought to work through and transform into art. She wrote 696 letters to her family, mainly to her mother. As Mrs. Plath observes in the introduction to *Letters Home,* "Throughout her prose and poetry, Sylvia fused parts of my life with hers from time to time" (3).

Letters Home demonstrates that Plath told her mother mainly what the latter wished to hear. In light of Esther's bitter resentment toward Mrs. Greenwood in *The Bell Jar,* the absence of any criticism toward Mrs. Plath in *Letters Home* is startling. Mrs. Plath acknowledges the lack of boundaries in their relationship: "Between Sylvia and me there existed — as between my own mother and me — a sort of psychic osmosis which, at times, was very wonderful and comforting; at other times an unwelcome invasion of privacy" (*Letters* 32). Mrs. Plath disregards the irony of publishing her daughter's private correspondence, an act that Sylvia would have regarded as another unwelcome invasion of privacy.

Plath's preoccupation with suicide appears in the earliest letters that she wrote as a college freshman. The first references seem casual enough. In a letter written on 10 October 1950, Sylvia asks her mother how she should take the medication prescribed to her for a cold. "By the way, do you suck those buffered penicillins or swallow with water? . . . I don't want to kill myself by taking them the wrong way!" (*Letters* 52). A month later she tells her mother about unexpectedly receiving a phone call from a girlfriend inviting her to go out with a group of boys who had just dropped over. "So I threw on my clothes, all the time ranting . . . on how *never* to commit suicide, because something unexpected always happens" (58). A more ominous reference to suicide appears in a 10 December 1950 letter in which Sylvia tells her mother about fearing for a friend whose "usual gaiety has been getting brighter and more artificial as the days go by" (*Letters* 64). The friend has been depressed since Thanksgiving, unable to sleep or concentrate, obsessed with the feeling that "she was not intelligent enough for Smith." In Plath's view, the friend believes that her parents have either deceived her about her academic capability or are simply unaware of how incapable she really is. "I got scared," Sylvia confides to her mother, "when she told me how she had been saving sleeping pills and razor blades and could think of nothing better than to commit suicide" (64).

Sylvia's narration of the story reveals her own fear and inadequacy. It is as if her friend's suicidal crisis has dissolved the boundary between self and other, inducing a similar crisis within Sylvia. Mrs. Plath's footnote lends support to this interpretation. "Actually, the girl in question was not suicidal; perhaps Sylvia's earlier Thanksgiving depression was influencing her words here. Yet when Sylvia found herself in a similar state two years later, razor blades and sleeping pills were her first thoughts" (*Letters* 64).

The 1952 crisis to which Mrs. Plath refers conveys Sylvia's highly charged emotional state, reflecting the intense academic pressures that had been building. "The crux of the matter is my attitude toward life—hinging on my science course. I have practically considered suicide to get out of it, it's like having my nose rubbed in my own slime" (*Letters* 97). Unable to explain her "irrevocable futility," she declares gloomily that when "one feels like leaving college and killing oneself over one course which actually nauseates me, it is a rather serious thing" (97). The crisis apparently passed, for there are no additional references to it, but in a letter to her brother Warren written in the spring of 1953 she returns to the possibility of suicide—not her own but their mother's. "You know, as I do, and it is a frightening thing, that mother would actually Kill herself for us if we calmly accepted all she wanted to do for us. She is an abnormally altruistic person, and I have realized lately that we have to fight against her selflessness as we would fight against a deadly disease" (112). The expression "kill herself" often means "overwork herself," but Sylvia's capitalization suggests a more literal meaning.

To understand Plath's reference to her mother's "abnormally altruistic" nature, we must turn to the *Journals*, where she explores in great detail her convoluted feelings toward her parents. Despite the fact that the edition is riddled with mysterious "omissions" and gaps that have exasperated Plath scholars, the journals are extraordinarily candid and relentlessly self-analytic. Plath expresses here many of the feelings she omitted from her letters: anger toward her mother's conditional love and resentment over the extreme dependence upon her mother, rage over her father's death, idealization and devaluation of friends and mentors, and intense jealousy of and competitiveness toward friends. Plath's perfectionism concealed feelings of unworthiness, and she learned to wear multiple masks, particularly the veil of innocence. Only by disguising the conflicting sides of her personality could she hold together her disparate selves.

"I Give You Permission to Be Happy"

Many of Plath's most important insights arose from her therapy with Dr. Ruth Beuscher (now the Reverend Ruth Tiffany Barnhouse, M.D.), the gifted psychiatrist who treated her at McLean Hospital in Belmont, Massachusetts, shortly after the 1953 suicide attempt and with whom she secretly reentered therapy in late 1958 after marrying Ted Hughes. Dr. Beuscher is the model for Dr. Nolan in *The Bell Jar* and one of the few people about whom Plath never spoke unkindly.

Some critics have suggested that Plath's treatment with Dr. Beuscher resulted in the adoption of a new mask, a "Freudian" one, but it seems more likely that she made real breakthroughs in her self-understanding. She analyzed her tormented feelings toward her mother and found ways to break out of the symbiotic union that seemed part of the bell jar vision.

The relationship with her mother was so close, Sylvia observes, speaking about herself in second person, that "you were frightened when you heard yourself stop talking and felt the echo of her voice, as if she had spoken in you, as if you weren't quite you, but were growing and continuing in her wake" (*Journals* 26). In one of her most self-revealing entries, she remarks on 12 December 1958 that she felt unloved by her mother despite overwhelming evidence to the contrary: "I felt cheated: I wasn't loved, but all the signs said I was loved: the world said I was loved: the powers-that-were said I was loved. My mother had sacrificed her life for me. A sacrifice I didn't want. . . . I made her sign a promise she'd never marry. When [I was nine]. Too bad she didn't break it" (*Journals* 268). Four days later Sylvia observes, anticipating Esther's conversation with Dr. Nolan in *The Bell Jar*, "Have been happier this week than for six months. It is as if R. B., saying 'I give you permission to hate your mother,' also said, 'I give you permission to be happy'" (*Journals* 275). A 27 December 1958 entry illustrates Sylvia's fear that her mother will appropriate everything in her life, including her writing:

> [Omission.] WHAT DO I EXPECT BY "LOVE" FROM HER? WHAT IS IT I DON'T GET THAT MAKES ME CRY? I think I have always felt she uses me as an extension of herself; that when I commit suicide, or try to, it is a "shame" to her, an accusation: which it was, of course. An accusation that her love was defective. Feeling, too, of competing with Warren: the looming image of Harvard is equated with him. How, by the way, does Mother understand my committing suicide? As a result of my not writing, no doubt. I felt I couldn't write because she would appropriate it. Is that all? I felt if I didn't write nobody would accept me as a human being. Writing, then, was a substitute for myself: if you don't love me, love my writing and love me for my writing. It is also much more: a way of ordering and reordering the chaos of experience. (279–80)

Her journals help us understand the rage Plath later expresses toward her father in "Daddy" and "Lady Lazarus." In *The Bell Jar* we see only glimmerings of Esther's hostility toward her father, but in the *Journals* Sylvia probes her relationship with Otto Plath and reaches several conclusions. She records in the 12 December 1958 journal entry, the first since returning to analysis with Dr. Beuscher, that she "hated men because they didn't stay around and love me like a father: I could prick holes in them & show they were no father-material" (267). Sylvia then relates one of her mother's terrifying dreams:

It was her daughter's fault partly. She had a dream: her daughter was all gaudy-dressed about to go out and be a chorus girl, a prostitute too, probably. [Omission.] The husband, brought alive in dream to relive the curse of his old angers, slammed out of the house in rage that the daughter was going to be a chorus girl. The poor Mother runs along the sand beach, her feet sinking in the sand of life, her money bag open and the money and coins falling into the sand, turning to sand. The father had driven, in a fury, to spite her, off the road bridge and was floating dead, face down and bloated, in the slosh of ocean water by the pillars of the country club. Everybody was looking down from the pier at them. Everyone knew everything. (267–68)

The mother's dream is rich in psychoanalytic meaning. From an Oedipal point of view, the father's anger seems to arise over his daughter's promiscuity: she is a "prostitute" selling herself to other men. The mother, unable to defuse his rage, runs along the beach with her money bag open, perhaps suggesting the waning of her own sexuality or her unsuccessful efforts to placate her husband. From a pre-Oedipal point of view, the dream reveals a fused or symbiotic mother-daughter relationship, the mother sacrificing her own life for her daughter's. The father's violence is directed toward both wife and daughter, and his suicide—driving off the pier—is a revenge against both of them. Plath's own interpretation of the dream appears in a 27 December 1958 journal entry, where she expresses the fear that her mother held her responsible for Otto Plath's death. "I have lost a father and his love early; feel angry at her because of this and feel she feels I killed him (her dream about me being a chorus girl and his driving off and drowning himself). I dreamed often of losing her, and these childhood nightmares stand out" (*Journals* 278). She writes in the same entry about the shock of recognition while reading Freud's essay "Mourning and Melancholia":

Read Freud's *Mourning and Melancholia* this morning after Ted left for the library. An almost exact description of my feelings and reasons for suicide: a transferred murderous impulse from my mother onto myself: the "vampire" metaphor Freud uses, "draining the ego": that is exactly the feeling I have getting in the way of my writing: Mother's clutch. I mask my self-abasement (a transferred hate of her) and weave it with my own real dissatisfactions in myself until it becomes very difficult to distinguish what is really bogus criticism from what is really a changeable liability. How can I get rid of this depression: by refusing to believe she has any power over me, like the old witches for whom one sets out plates of milk and honey. This is not easily done. How is it done? Talking and becoming aware of what is what and studying it is a help. (279)

"My Temptation to Dig Him Up"

Plath visited her father's grave, with the encouragement of Dr. Beuscher, on 9 March 1959. "I found the flat stone, 'Otto E. Plath: 1885–1940,' right beside the path, where it would be walked over. Felt cheated. My temptation to dig him up. To prove he existed and really was dead" (*Journals* 298). A few days later she acknowledges for the first time the fear that she (rather than her mother) may have contributed to her father's death: "Got at some deep things with R. B.: facing dark and terrible things: those dreams of deformity and death. If I really think I killed and castrated my father may all my dreams of deformed and tortured people be my guilty visions of him or fears of punishment for me? And how to lay them? To stop them operating through the rest of my life?" (299).

Plath confided her patricidal fantasies to her college roommate, Nancy Hunter Steiner: "He was an autocrat. . . . I adored and despised him, and I probably wished many times that he were dead. When he obliged me and died, I imagined that I had killed him" (Steiner 62–63). Plath's guilt was complicated by the fear that her father had committed a kind of suicide in that his refusal to consult a physician for symptoms that turned out to be caused by diabetes mellitus resulted in a needless death. The surgeon who examined Otto Plath privately murmured to Mrs. Plath, "How could such a brilliant man be so stupid?" (*Letters* 23). Plath describes herself in the poem "Electra on Azalea Path," written immediately after the visit to her father's grave, as "the ghost of an infamous suicide, / My own blue razor rusting in my throat." She ends the poem with the observation, "It was my love that did us both to death" (*Collected Poems* 117).

Plath explored with the aid of Dr. Beuscher the psychological dynamics of writer's block, particularly the extent to which her unconscious wish to hurt her mother was hurting herself:

Dr. B.: You are trying to do two mutually incompatible things this year. 1) spite your mother. 2) write. To spite your mother, you don't write because you feel you have to give the stories to her, or that she will appropriate them. (As I was afraid of having her around to appropriate my baby, because I didn't want it to be hers.) So I can't write. And I hate her because my not writing plays into her hands and argues that she is right, I was foolish not to teach, or do something secure, when what I have renounced security for is nonexistent. (*Journals* 279)

The upsurge of rage that had culminated in her 1953 suicide attempt now became the driving force in Sylvia Plath's art. By creating what Susan Van Dyne has called a "poetics of rage" (63), Plath was able to write fiercely angry poems and stories while simultaneously thwarting her mother's desire to appropriate her writings. Surely Mrs. Plath would not wish to claim a novel like *The Bell Jar*, which contained such an acidic portrait of motherhood. Sylvia could thus play the role of the "bad" daughter in both *The Bell Jar* and her poetry, exulting in her aggression toward parents and patrons.

"Writing As Therapy?"

Plath's aggressive vision of art can be seen in *The Bell Jar* when Esther decides to spend the summer writing a novel. "That would fix a lot of people" (133). Naming her heroine Elaine—"I counted the letters on my fingers. There were six letters in Esther, too" (134)—Esther is an autobiographical novelist, like her creator. Plath's depictions of the characters in *The Bell Jar*, including Esther's literary patron Philomena Guinea, based upon the popular novelist Olive Higgins Prouty who provided Plath with a scholarship to Smith and later paid for her medical expenses, were so caustic that she decided to publish the novel in England under a pseudonym. Mrs. Plath later tried unsuccessfully to block the publication of *The Bell Jar* in the United States, correctly anticipating that Sylvia's friends and mentors would be devastated by her portrayal of them. It is a novelist's prerogative to shape reality in whatever way she sees fit; in Plath's case, the expression of anger toward the people on whom she was dependent seemed to have a liberating effect.

Central to Plath's emerging vision of art was the expression of rage, which allowed her to vent the murderous feelings she had long repressed. Her most affirmative statement appears in a 27 August 1958 journal entry. "Fury jams the gullet and spreads poison, but, as soon as I start to write, dissipates, flows out into the figure of the letters: writing as therapy?" (*Journals* 255). Her view of art as a purgation of toxic emotions is strikingly similar to Woolf's and Hemingway's; for all three artists, as well as for Sexton and Styron, writing is essential to psychic health. "If I could once see how to write a story, a novel, to get something of my feeling over," Plath records on 10 January 1959, "I would not despair. If writing is not an outlet, what is?" (290).

Yet Plath may also have realized that the creation of art neither solves all the writer's personal problems nor guarantees psychological health. She did, after all, place a question mark after the phrase, "writing as therapy," and she must have known that fury is a doubled-edged sword. An aesthetics based primarily upon rage is risky for several reasons. Rage may turn against the self, as Freud describes in "Mourning and Melancholia"; rage may not be discharged when the artist suffers writer's block; and the venting of rage may lead to inner depletion. In addition, the expression of rage may alienate those people who are part of the artist's support system, including the audience. Most artists seek not merely discharge of emotion but their audience's approval and validation. Plath was not one of the artists who could create only for herself: she needed an admiring audience, and her letters and journals indicate her devastation over rejection slips and negative reviews. There is also the risk that a writer who returns obsessively to certain subjects such as suicide may not be working through inner conflicts so much as acting them out in print. In certain cases, "writing does not serve the functions of catharsis and release; rather, it is a reiteration of an idea until it becomes a creed. . . . The writings take on a power of their own; they become fatal self-fulfilling prophecies" (Shneidman, "Risk Writing" 577).

Plath survived the Russian roulette of her 1953 suicide attempt and came to view herself as an escape artist. "I feel like Lazarus," she remarks in her journals, "that story has such a fascination. Being dead, I rose up again, and even resort to the mere sensation value of being suicidal, of getting so close, of coming out of the grave with the scars and the marring mark on my cheek which (is it my imagination?) grows more prominent: paling like a death-spot in the red, windblown skin, browning darkly in photographs, against my grave winter-pallor" (100). Nancy Hunter Steiner also saw Plath as an escape artist, constantly flirting with death. "[S]he was driven, periodically, to stage a symbolic salvation with herself as the suffering victim and me as the deliverer, almost as though only by being snatched from the brink of death could she confirm her worth" (101). Plath described her "Mental Hospital Stories" as containing the "Lazarus theme. Come back from the dead. Kicking off thermometers. Violent ward. LAZARUS MY LOVE" (*Journals* 308). She similarly structured *The Bell Jar*, "Daddy," and "Lady Lazarus" around the pattern of death and rebirth. But there are problems with viewing suicide in this way, as we can see in *The Bell Jar*.

The Double

Esther's recovery seems to be based not mainly upon the insights she reaches in her life but upon the suicide of her "evil double," Joan Gilling. Introduced early in *The Bell Jar* as a big, horsey girl who comes from Esther's hometown and who is a year ahead of her in college, Joan is a formidable rival: "president of her class and a physics major and the college hockey champion" (65). Esther is "cold with envy" upon hearing that Joan has been dating Buddy Willard. We learn nothing more about Joan until 150 pages later, when she reappears at Esther's psychiatric hospital, not as a visitor but as a patient.

Joan's room is a mirror image of Esther's, and the two women are doppelgangers, each mirroring the other's failed perfectionism. The parallels between Esther and Joan are striking. Both are brilliant students who are involved in similar extracurricular activities, date the same man, read the same newspapers, appear in the same hospital for the same problem, and form close relationships with female psychiatrists. When Esther asks how she arrived at the hospital, Joan answers, "I read about you" (220), then she relates a series of improbable events that pique Esther's interest. Joan shows Esther several newspaper clippings sensationalizing the latter's suicide attempt. The headlines—"SCHOLARSHIP GIRL MISSING. MOTHER WORRIED," "SLEEPING PILLS FEARED MISSING WITH GIRL," "GIRL FOUND ALIVE!"—record Esther's (and Plath's) suicide attempt in tabloid prose.

Esther, we recall, found herself irresistibly drawn to similarly lurid headlines immediately prior to her own suicide attempt. Significantly, the effect of reading these newspaper accounts of Esther's suicide attempt is to heighten Joan's own suicidality. Joan then travels to New York City, where Esther has been living while working on *Ladies Day*, shoves her fists through her roommate's window, and is then brought back to Boston and hospitalized by her father.

Joan Gilling's copycat suicide attempt underscores Plath's belief that reading about suicide in sensationalistic publications can indeed encourage others to imitate the act. Sylvia Plath's suicide heightened Anne Sexton's wish to die, just as Sexton's *own* suicide was an impetus behind Elizabeth Wurtzel's suicide attempt. Though Plath does not allow us to take Joan's suffering seriously—she is never developed as a character—Joan does demonstrate the danger of heroicizing suicide. There is no distance between Plath's protagonist and antagonist; each seems to threaten and be threatened by the other. "Joan was the beaming double of my old best self, specially designed to follow and torment me" (*The Bell Jar* 231). Plath uses a revealing oral image a few pages later to describe how Joan impedes Esther's recovery. "Joan hung about me like a large and breathless fruitfly—as if the sweetness of recovery were something she could suck up by mere nearness" (243).

Plath's biographers have noted that while Joan Gilling was based upon a real character, her suicide is entirely invented, suggesting that Joan mirrors Esther's—and Sylvia's—dark self. Esther intuits their mirror relationship: "Sometimes I wondered if I had made Joan up. Other times I wondered if she would continue to pop in at every crisis of my life to remind me of what I had been, and what I had been through, and carry on her own separate but similar crisis under my nose" (246).

Joan's death by hanging seems to exorcise Esther's remaining doubts about her own recovery, and *The Bell Jar* ends ten pages later, with Esther guiding herself, "as if by a magical thread" (275), into a room full of physicians who will presumably allow her to leave the hospital. The reader may feel, in light of Plath's suicide one month after the publication of the novel, that Esther is left hanging by a thread. Esther's recovery would be more convincing if Plath allowed the protagonist's dark double to remain alive. Coexistence would imply that Esther had come to terms with her former nemesis. The juxtaposition of Esther's rebirth with Joan's death reveals the all-or-nothing thinking that is symptomatic of suicidal ideation. Plath's vision of psychological recovery depended, as Murray Schwartz and Christopher Bollas have suggested, not on heightened self-analysis but on a "magical emptying out of unbearable inner conflict" (184). And yet Esther learns something valuable from Joan's death, namely, that the person who commits suicide must accept major responsibility for the act. Disagreeing with Buddy Willard's statement that he has caused Joan's death, Esther relates a recent conversation with Dr. Nolan: "'Of course you didn't do it!' I heard Doctor Nolan say. I had come to her about Joan, and it was the only time I remember her sounding angry. 'Nobody did it. *She* did it.' And then Doctor Nolan told me how the best of psychiatrists have suicides among their patients, and how they, if anybody, should be held responsible, but how they, on the contrary, do not hold themselves responsible" (270).

"Lady Lazarus": "What a Trash / To Annihilate Each Decade"

The psychiatrist's injunction to avoid blaming suicide on others does not seem to be borne out in "Daddy" and "Lady Lazarus." Both poems, written shortly after Ted Hughes had left her and their two young children, reflect Plath's belief that her husband's abandonment was a repetition of her father's abandonment twenty-two years earlier.

In contrast to *The Bell Jar*, where Esther's anger seethes below the surface of the narrative, rising only occasionally in the form of a cynical or ironic comment, the speaker's rage in "Lady Lazarus" explodes everywhere. The poem is a cauldron of violent emotion stoked by the fire of indignation. The speaker begins by asserting that "I have done it again. / One year in every ten / I manage it" (*Collected Poems* 244). She describes herself in concentration camp imagery: her skin resembles a Nazi lampshade, her foot a paperweight, her face a "Jew linen." She reveals that she is only thirty, "And like the cat I have nine times to die." This is her third suicide attempt, she says, adding, "What a trash / To annihilate each decade."

The first time she attempted suicide occurred when she was ten and was an "accident," but the second time she was deadly serious. She "rocked shut / As a seashell," a reference to Plath's 1953 self-burial in the crawl space of her parents' home. The speaker asserts boldly that "Dying / Is an art," an art form in which she excels, and acknowledges that she attempted suicide to inflict pain upon herself in order to validate her existence. She views suicide as her "calling" and performs her art not in a private cell but in a public setting. After referring to the "charge" for this horror show, the speaker addresses her words to "Herr Doktor," "Herr Enemy": her deceased father. Noting that she is his "opus," his "pure gold baby," she imagines herself melting to a shriek while he callously looks on. He pokes and stirs, finding nothing but ash. Just as her body seems to be consumed by the raging inferno, she mysteriously comes back to life, like Lazarus or the phoenix, only with a vengeance. "Out of the ash / I rise with my red hair / And I eat men like air" (*Collected Poems* 247).

No summary of "Lady Lazarus" can capture its astonishing power and originality. With its incantatory rhythms, juxtaposition of sacred and profane imagery, jarring repetitions, Holocaust allusions, and tragicomic tone, "Lady Lazarus" is a poetic tour de force. It is also profoundly disturbing.

Like "Daddy," with which it has so much in common, "Lady Lazarus" portrays suicide as a heroic form of resistance to patriarchal tyranny and as a grotesque spectator sport. Even as she describes how she meant to "last it out and not come back at all," the speaker confidently believes in her powers of rebirth. As Plath herself noted when introducing the poem for her BBC reading, "The speaker is a woman who has the great and terrible gift of being reborn. The only trouble is, she has to die first. She is the Phoenix, the libertarian spirit, what you will. She is also just a good, plain, very resourceful woman" (*Collected Poems* 294).

"Lady Lazarus" remains one of Plath's most fiercely debated poems. Early critics such as M. L. Rosenthal, who used the word "confessional" to describe the late poems of Robert Lowell, have seen "Lady Lazarus" as an intensely personal reflection of Plath's nightmarish suffering. Later critics reject this view and interpret the poem as mythic, having little to do with Plath's life. Many readers would endorse Margaret Dickie Uroff's contention that "Lady Lazarus" is a self-parody, in which the "poet behind the poem allows Lady Lazarus to caricature herself and thus to demonstrate the way in which the mind turns ritualistic against horror" (162). Mary Lynn Broe interprets "Lady Lazarus" as a "peculiarly futuristic indictment of all those critics, editors, and collectors who promote the Plath legend, guest editor to ghastly suicide" (178). Yet as Jacqueline Rose observes about "Daddy," the problem is that we cannot be sure whether these poems reproduce fantasies of martyrdom or expose them (236). Should we identify or counteridentify with the speakers' victimization? What complicates the question further is that "Lady Lazarus" views the reader as one of the "peanut-crunching crowd," who "Shoves in to see / Them unwrap me hand and foot" (*Collected Poems* 245). We are thus equated with the readers of the "scandal sheets" in *The Bell Jar*, who derive voyeuristic pleasure from seeing the suffering of others. Esther cannot avoid reading these ghastly tabloids, and Joan Gilling's imitative suicide attempt is the by-product of her own reading. Even as we strive to remain empathic readers of serious literature, Plath assumes otherwise.

We may feel, indeed, that we have become accomplices to Plath's self-victimization insofar as she invites not only her enemies but also her readers to participate in the gruesome dismemberment of her speaker's body and soul. "Plath's poems convince us," Joyce Carol Oates remarks, "when they are most troubled, most murderous, most unfair" (220). Addicted to suffering, Lady Lazarus casts us, masochistically, in the role of sadistic audience. It is the same role the author of a recent study of suicide notes tries to impose on us when he observes cynically, on the opening page: "This book of suicide notes is pornography. In reading these, the most intimate documents, you are a sadistic voyeur, transforming someone else's pain into your own pleasure. Suicide notes simply should not be read by strangers" (Etkind viii).

How, then, does one read a poem like "Lady Lazarus"—or suicide notes or diaries—without exploiting or being exploited by its inner violence and pain? How does a reader experience a victim's pain without becoming wounded by it? How does a reader respond to the distancing techniques of caricature and parody that Plath uses in her poem? Nancy Milford observes that in "Lady Lazarus" the "sad joke is that the reader— surrounded by all those other poets in the imaginary museum who can be summoned up in a twinkling for a performance—really doesn't have to pay very much to watch the show" (76). Is the joke, then, on us?

Bearing Witness

Many of the problems encountered with a poem like "Lady Lazarus" are similar to those of bearing witness. Suicidal literature is by implication traumatic literature, and psychoanalyst Dori Laub has commented on the difficulty of bearing witness to another's pain: "By extension, the listener to trauma comes to be a participant and a co-owner of the traumatic event: through his very listening, he comes to partially experience trauma in himself. The relation of the victim to the event of the trauma, therefore, impacts on the relation of the listener to it, and the latter comes to feel the bewilderment, injury, confusion, dread and conflicts that the trauma victim feels" (57–58). Yet Laub reminds us that even as listeners partake of the victim's experience, they also remain separate human beings with their own identity and perspective. Reading empathically enables us to avoid feeling like an accomplice to Plath's self-victimization in "Lady Lazarus" or a "sadistic voyeur" while reading suicide notes. In this way, we can feel the plight of the victim without becoming ourselves a victim or, in some cases, a victimizer. This empathic stance is easier to achieve in theory than in practice, however, as Plath criticism demonstrates.

Student Responses to "Lady Lazarus"

I have taught "Lady Lazarus" for several years, yet I have never before systematically studied students' reactions to the poem. If critics have so much difficulty interpreting and evaluating "Lady Lazarus," how do students read the poem, particularly in the context of a Literary Suicide course? To investigate this question, I asked my students the following question:

> In "Lady Lazarus" Plath observes: "The peanut-crunching crowd / Shoves in to see / Them unwrap me hand and foot— / The big strip tease." If we interpret these lines as an allegory of reading, do readers of suicidal literature in general, and Plath's late poetry in particular, find themselves in the position of the peanut-crunching crowd, voyeuristically watching the artist suffering? If so, when Plath later writes in "Lady Lazarus" that "There is a charge / For the eying of my scars, there is a charge / For the hearing of my heart," what is that charge—or cost—to the reader?

Four students resisted the idea that the reader is complicit in the speaker's suffering. They maintained distance from the poem and viewed it mainly as an aesthetic object. "For the lover of poetry," one person wrote, "as I am, the words 'voyeuristically watching the artist suffer' seem to be quite harsh. Regardless of whether the poet commits suicide later, I look on her poetry as quite a beautiful and artistic form, and I consider myself privileged to be given the opportunity to be able to read it." A second maintained that we can read Plath and other suicidal writers "without being charged or paying a cost I imagine could only be pain. There is more to Plath than her suicide, and more in her poems than her suffering." A third, unsure how to answer the questions, wrote about desiring to learn more about suicidal artists. "Taking the course seems a safe way of exploring these works, and the only charge is tuition and a few papers— so I'm writing all this to say that I don't want there to be a charge to the reader—at least not to me." A fourth distinguished between reading Plath's poetry and studying her biography; only the latter, not the former, produced voyeuristic feelings:

For me the voyeurism comes not when I am reading the work but when I am reading or otherwise hearing about the author's life. It doesn't seem to matter whether the biographical stuff comes first or later (though I feel slightly less prurient if it comes later, I guess, since I can use it perhaps to clarify some elements of the work). When I'm reading the work itself, I am usually

*enough caught in the emotions and images so that I forget about the physi-
cal person who created them and who is now dead. I read for the same
reasons I read any other fiction and poetry: to find out about somebody else
and, in so doing, about myself. As to the cost—for me the cost is facing
difficult issues and feelings, and this is also the benefit, so I don't mind
paying it. The cost of the biographical voyeurism, on the other hand, is
sometimes shame.*

For the other fourteen students, reading "Lady Lazarus" was unsettling
because they felt forced to witness and share the speaker's anguish. One
person compared "Lady Lazarus" to the human melodramas seen daily
on television shows and reached a pessimistic conclusion about the exploitation of suffering:

*If we interpret these lines as an allegory of reading, then I think it is true
that the reader, the public, is the peanut-crunching crowd. Her pain is our
entertainment. It is like the stories on "Geraldo" or "Hard Copy": people
selling their pain for the pleasure or at least the fascination of others. I've
never before considered poetry and "Hard Copy" in the same light, maybe
because poetry is put in a beautiful form whereas tabloid TV is shameless
in its desire to captivate.*

*The charge or cost to readers is that they are drawn into thoughts and
possibilities that they may have never before considered. In some respects,
this could change one's life forever. The price that the poet pays is, I believe, much steeper and more painful.*

Another student felt uneasy about reading "Lady Lazarus" and used a
metaphor that Plath herself would appreciate:

*Yes, I think most readers are attracted to this woman and her poetry in
general because of this reason. We are, in a sense, literary ambulance chasers, horrified yet staring with greedy eyes at the scene of the tragedy.*

*The charge or the cost is the same as the cost of being an ambulance
chaser—nightmares, perhaps, but certainly a changed view of the world.
The reader must share to some extent, and I suppose this is in part up to the
reader and in part determined by the reader's psychological makeup, in
Plath's bitterness and self-hatred. The cost would be a dose of bitterness;
the size of that dosage I'm not sure about.*

If we are literary ambulance chasers while reading "Lady Lazarus," are we also rubberneckers? Although the students did not want to feel this way, preferring to remain involved and concerned onlookers, they were still troubled by the extent to which the poem's violence transfixed them. "I think that a fascination with the incomprehensible does lend itself to a sort of voyeurism," one student wrote, adding, "[a]s for the charge, well, I believe that we're confronted by the very thing which we wish only to see from a safe distance. But there isn't much distance when you read the words, and the meanings register in the mind." A second, unsure whether the reader is a voyeur, acknowledged feeling uneasy while reading "Lady Lazarus":

Yes! I'll buy that—I am a voyeur when I read Plath's work. Or, well, maybe not exactly; in voyeurism, isn't the person being watched unaware of the watcher? Maybe because Plath put herself (oops! I mean her) poems) out there for me to see, maybe then I'm not a voyeur. But as for the charge, for me it's guilt. I, my sane self, feel guilty in the presence of Plath's pain. I am immediately implicated in her pain because I become a witness to it.

For other students, the way to avoid literary ambulance chasing was to empathize with a character's suffering, even if this meant experiencing narrowed distance between self and other:

For those who can relate to her experience, for those who suffer, Plath's poetry may be a vehicle to their own emotion. These people, within the experience, are not the peanut-crunchers. Peanut-crunchers are those without her experience, who cannot relate, who cannot understand, who stand outside her suffering. It is they who ogle, who criticize—Plath's tone in this verse is rather sarcastic, sharp. She's resentful of those who shove in to see her: the pornography of death. So, it depends on how close they are to her experience. That's what distinguishes the peanut-crunchers from the nonpeanut-crunchers.

The reader-response paragraphs on "Lady Lazarus" confirm that most of my students find Plath's poem as disturbing as I do, and for similar reasons. Readers struggle to locate the right distance that will allow them to empathize with the speaker's suffering without feeling too close or too detached from it. Awareness of Plath's biography makes it more difficult to appreciate "Lady Lazarus" as an autonomous work of art. No one regarded the poem as Plath's joke on us. "Lady Lazarus" is charged with violent emotions, and one student indicated that reading it touched off personal conflicts that appeared unrelated to the poem.

These days, I feel like I am trapped and haunted by something: something which might blow up everything and dump shit all over me. In such circumstances, when I read, I feel like the author is watching me crunching peanuts. Books don't help, though they allow me to escape. I feel that everyone is indifferent to me, and that I am accused falsely by some big thing. Evil? God? However, the feeling doesn't usually last long. There are helpers for me, but maybe in Plath's case, she didn't have helpers such as friends or psychiatrists.

Another, venting anger toward those critics (such as myself?) who overanalyze Plath, held them responsible for exploiting and perhaps even destroying her:

To me, the poem "Lady Lazarus" is full of images of fragmentation. Plath is no more than a disparate, "falling apart" compilation of elements, a list of things that comprise her (a wedding ring, a gold tooth). As she breaks down or falls apart, these things are all that are left of her; they are the fossils of Plath, the pieces of her that the psychiatrists greedily study and the academicians greedily snatch up to analyze. These groups, the readers, are the "peanut-crunching crowd" who are eager for Plath's breakdown so they may study it. I picture them fighting over the souvenirs of her demise (the tooth, the ring, a swatch of hair) and forgetting the person who went through the infernal pain. Readers may reify Plath, and the "cost" to them is that they forget to be human, forget that their subject of study was also a person whose life hurt so much that she was forced to end it.

I'm troubled by the cynicism of this comment, yet there is a degree of truth here. We may sometimes forget the terrible human pain of Plath's "fossils" and ignore the violence of her poetic world. Nowhere is this more evident than in "Edge."

"Edge"

Only twenty lines long, "Edge" opens with an image of a lifeless woman who is "perfected." The poem never states explicitly that she has committed suicide, but her body "wears the smile of accomplishment" (*Collected Poems* 272). The "illusion of a Greek necessity / Flows in the scrolls of her toga," suggesting that, like the ancient Greeks, she has been ennobled through death. She appears to be at peace with herself, her journey through life now completed. None of the explosive rage or furious indignation of "Daddy" or "Lady Lazarus" appears in "Edge": the tone is eerie, mysterious, deathly still. Joining the woman in death are her two young children, each coiled like a white serpent at an empty pitcher of milk. The mother has folded both children into her body as a rose closes at night in a garden. The poem ends with an image of the unperturbed moon gazing at the dead mother and children. "She is used to this sort of thing / Her blacks crackle and drag."

The last poem she wrote, "Edge" suggests that Sylvia Plath may have contemplated infanticide as well as suicide. If so, she changed her mind, for before placing her head in the oven of her English flat during the early morning hours of 11 February 1963, she carefully taped the kitchen door so that the gas would not enter her children's bedroom upstairs. She also provided them with cups of milk and bread. "Edge" foretells the poet's death, and before responding to the poem, we may ask why she finally chose to end her life.

Freud believed that suicide arises from aggression that, initially directed toward another, becomes internalized, resulting in the death of both self and the internalized other. As her 28 December 1958 journal entry on "Mourning and Melancholia" indicates, Plath endorsed the psychoanalytic interpretation of suicide as symbolic murder of another. She may have been struck by the following sentence in "Mourning and Melancholia": "The self-tormenting in melancholia, which is without doubt enjoyable, signifies . . . a satisfaction of trends of sadism and hate which relate to an object, and which have been turned round upon the subject's own self" (251).

Plath's suicide was motivated in large part by the rage arising from the breakup of her marriage. Alvarez suggests that she was ambivalent toward suicide at this time and perhaps expected to be saved, an interpretation consistent with her identity as Lady Lazarus. Plath may have seen herself in the end less as an abandoning mother than as an abandoned child. Clarence Hemingway's suicide tormented Ernest Hemingway his entire adult life, forcing him to counteridentify with the man he believed was a coward; Otto Plath's suicidal disregard of his own health similarly haunted Sylvia Plath, preventing her from coming to terms with her convoluted feelings toward him. "Daddy, I have had to kill you. / You died before I had time" (*Collected Poems* 222). Viewing her husband as another version of her heartless father ("If I've killed one man, I've killed two"), and grief-stricken over the loss of both men, she could not pound a stake into the vampire's "fat black heart," as the villagers do in "Daddy." Instead, she internalized the violence, destroying her persecutors together with herself.

Pamela Annas has suggested an important link between "Edge" and a 1955 letter Plath wrote to Richard Sassoon: "At midnight, when the moon makes blue lizard scales of roof shingles . . . the hungry cosmic mother sees the world shrunk to embryo again and her children gathered sleeping back into the dark, huddling in bulbs and pods, pale and distant as the folded bean seed to her full milky love which freezes across the sky in a crucifix of stars" (*Journals* 92). The "hungry cosmic mother" represents, psychoanalytically, Plath's internalized mother, cold and distant. Esther uses similar language to describe her mother's face, which "floated to mind, a pale reproachful moon" (*The Bell Jar* 267). Matricidal and infanticidal imagery pervade Plath's writings. Mrs. Plath reveals in *Letters Home* that shortly before the 1953 suicide attempt Sylvia exclaimed to her, "Oh, Mother, the world is so rotten! I want to die! Let's die together!" (124). Mrs. Plath was understandably horrified by this suicide pact, but this is precisely what the mother in "Edge" has done. Esther herself is a mother—she refers at one point to her child—but most of the references to children in *The Bell Jar* are negative, including the image of babies "pickled in a laboratory jar" (14) and the picture of Dodo Conway as a baby-making machine. "Children made me sick," Esther admits (131). Career and motherhood are not only mutually exclusive in Esther's world, but babies and mothers are locked in a destructive fusion, each depleting the other's energy.

Plath's biography reveals a grim repetition-compulsion principle. Plath criticized her mother for martyring herself for her children, an act her daughter opposed as one would resist a deadly disease, yet she herself committed the ultimate self-sacrifice. The tragic irony is that Plath's identification with the abandoned child prevented her from understanding how her motherless children would later feel. And yet she must have been able to anticipate their future grief, for a few months before her death she wrote a poem called "For a Fatherless Son" in which she imagines the impact of paternal loss on her young child. "You will be aware of an absence, presently, / Growing beside you, like a tree" (*Collected Poems* 205). She could imagine her son growing up with an "utter lack of attention," as she herself felt growing up without a father.

All suicides are unique yet share many characteristics, as Herbert Hendin observes:

> All of the psychodynamic meanings given to death by suicidal patients can be conceptualized as responses to loss, separation, or abandonment. Rebirth and reunion fantasies may be seen as attempts to undo or deny such losses. Becoming the one who leaves is one way to avoid the feeling of having been left. Feelings of rage that are repressed, suppressed, or expressed may derive from the experience of loss. Self-punishment may express guilt at having been responsible for a loss and the fantasy of rapprochement through atonement. ("Psychodynamics of Suicide" 1154)

What I find most distressing about "Edge" is that Plath asks us to affirm infanticide as an act of love and protectiveness. Under extraordinary circumstances, infanticide may be justified or at least understandable, as Toni Morrison dramatizes in her novel *Beloved*. But to portray suicide and infanticide as acts of perfection is to require, for readers such as myself, an impossible suspension of disbelief.

"The Birth of the True Self" in "Edge"

"Edge" remains perhaps the most poetic suicide note ever written, yet despite the fact that the poem holds a prominent position in Plath's art and biography, it has been ignored by most critics. Those who comment on it do so evasively, avoiding the troubling questions it raises about the distinction between healthy and unhealthy art. The best example of this may be seen in Judith Kroll's influential 1976 book *Chapters in a Mythology*, written with the help and approval of Ted Hughes. Kroll views Plath's poetry as part of an elaborate mythic system removed from the artist's daily concerns. From this viewpoint, Plath's suicide is irrelevant to the meaning of her work:

> The image of death in Sylvia Plath's late poetry usually encodes a deeper, hidden wish for rebirth, the birth of the true self. Certain poems contain clear images of rebirth; but even "Edge," "Death & Co.," and "A Birthday Present," which focus on actual or imminent death, envision death in such a way as to make plain that, although the poem does not overtly indicate its achievement, the ultimate motive for death is rebirth or transcendence. . . .
>
> Although "Edge" presents a vision of death, the terms in which it is envisioned contradict the superficial reading that Plath is merely morbidly fascinated with the prospect of personal annihilation—one would not think of calling Cleopatra a morbid suicide. Cleopatra's obstacles were, of course, external, and many of the afflictions in Plath's poetry—and life—are not. It is nevertheless significant that in her poems death so often appears in noble, mythic terms. "Edge" may be a harrowing poem for its note of finality (together with the extraneous knowledge that it was one of the last two poems Plath wrote before she killed herself), but it cannot be called a depressed poem. Its pervasive clarity and calm have been widely acknowledged. Plath's dying heroines, in poems such as "A Birthday Present" and "Edge," have little in common with stereotypes of suicidal women (in whose actions a sense of the *meaning* of death does not even figure), and a great deal in common with tragic heroines who die calmly and nobly. (129, 147–48)

Kroll's mythic interpretation of "Edge" recalls many of the interpretations of suicide in *The Awakening* and *Mrs. Dalloway*. To view a character's suicide as a prelude to rebirth and transcendence is to ignore its catastrophic interpersonal implications. Kroll concedes in a footnote that the children in the poem are dead, "implicitly through the agency of their mother," yet she sees nothing wrong with this; in fact, she rationalizes the infanticide. "The children must be dead in order for the woman's history to be perfected, for she regards them as extensions of herself; that is why she speaks of folding them '*back* into her body'" (260 n. 28). Would Kroll, one wonders, offer the same interpretation had Plath actually committed infanticide? This may be an unfair question; nevertheless, I am disturbed by Kroll's endorsement of the mother's perception of her children as extensions of herself.

I don't mean to suggest that "Edge" is artistically flawed. Unlike psychiatrist Albert Rothenberg, who believes that the poem's imagery is "distinctly unpoetic and uncreative" (71), I find "Edge" to be aesthetically powerful. It is the poem's antihumanistic vision that concerns me, especially its implication that the mother's children have no life of their own and thus no claim to freedom. I agree with David Holbrook that one cannot enjoy the poem "without being troubled by doubt, as to where it might be taking the reader in admiring it" (271). Most critics do not confront the fact that the poem is about suicide and infanticide. For example, Stephen Gould Axelrod's deconstructive interpretation of "Edge" as an allegory of misreading focuses entirely on textual self-creation. "Edge" becomes a less threatening poem if we limit its meaning to textual rather than human suicide.

Ted Hughes has endorsed Kroll's mythic interpretation of Plath's poetry as a struggle between true and false selves. His wish to read Plath's poetry in this way is understandable, for "Edge" is so personally distressing and biographically invasive that it must have been distressing for him to see the poem in print. He may have considered omitting it from Plath's *Collected Poems*. There is no proof of this, but he did delete many of her journals from the published volume. He acknowledges in the foreword to the *Journals* that the published selection contains only about a third of the entire bulk. Two more notebooks, recording Plath's entries from late 1959 to within three days of her death, survived for awhile. "The last of these contained entries for several months, and I destroyed it because I did not want her children to have to read it (in those days I regarded forgetfulness as an essential part of survival). The other disappeared" (xv). A poem like "Edge" makes forgetfulness impossible.

Hughes's refusal to use the first-person pronoun when speaking of his relationship with Sylvia Plath—he refers to "her" children, not "our" children—is also revealing. One would never know from his foreword to the *Journals* or his essay "Sylvia Plath and Her Journals" that they were married or had children together. Hughes's description of Plath's poetic development implies the near-inevitability of her suicide:

> As time went on, she interpreted what was happening to her inwardly, more and more consciously, as a "drama" of some sort. After its introductory overture (everything up to 1953), the drama proper began with a "death," which was followed by a long "gestation" or "regeneration," which in turn would ultimately require a "birth" or a "rebirth," as in Dostoevsky and Lawrence and those other prophets whose works were her sacred books. ("Sylvia Plath and Her Journals" 154)

Hughes's and Kroll's argument that autobiography does not function in Plath's poetry as it does in the confessional poets raises an interesting question: how do a suicidal poet's writings affect her family? What is the charge to Plath's mother, husband, and children? Hughes's desire to protect his children from the contents of Plath's journals led him to destroy one if not both of her notebooks, and he has invoked his children's welfare to deny permission to Plath scholars to quote from her work. Jacqueline Rose reports that Hughes asked her to remove her controversial analysis of the poem "The Rabbit Catcher" from her book *The Haunting of Sylvia Plath*. When she refused, he told her that her analysis, in Rose's words, "would be damaging for Plath's (now adult) children and that speculation of the kind I was seen as engaging in about Sylvia Plath's sexual identity would in some countries be 'grounds for homicide'" (xi). Whatever he meant by these words, it is well known that he believes writings by and about Plath have taken a heavy toll on his family. If Hughes's children would find the destroyed journals or Rose's interpretation of "The Rabbit Catcher" disturbing, then how much more disturbing would they find "Edge," with its vision of their destruction?

Student Responses to "Edge"

How do students respond to "Edge"? Do they remain detached, able to appreciate the poem's imagistic power, or do they feel unwitting accomplices to suicide and infanticide? I asked my students to write a paragraph on these questions. About two-thirds felt they were not accomplices or chose not to address my question; the remaining one-third found themselves unable to locate a safe vantage point when reading the poem.

The following responses are representative of those who were able to appreciate the poem's aesthetic power without being threatened by its violent subject.

I did not feel an accomplice to either the suicide or the infanticide; rather, I felt an outsider to them, a bystander, an observer. I feel that Plath's moon looks over all of us and is black or bright depending on how we see her. I did not feel an accomplice—strangely, perhaps, I found the poem very beautiful and comforting.

I can't say that I felt like an accomplice. You could argue that the beauty of the language mesmerizes you, renders you unable to challenge what she is saying, but I wonder if your question can have meaning only to readers who know the context of the poem. Would you ask the same question about a poem with a similar theme whose writer was not known to be suicidal? Then again, could a nonsuicidal writer have written something like "Edge"?

It seems to me that Plath isn't forcing readers into being "unwitting accomplices" to either suicide or infanticide. I liked this poem and enjoy reading Plath in general, but I don't feel I'm just denying that this happens, either. I like/enjoy all kinds of things, but it's just not the same as being an "accomplice." She wrote this poem for and by herself, it seems to me.

Some students defended the poem's infanticide theme:

I'm not sure I agree that the reader is an accomplice in "Edge": I think this could be a poem written by someone who does not commit suicide. How would we read it if it was by a living author? I see it as a war poem. Mother, dying, enfolds her children, already dead, protectively.

Bizarre, perhaps, this interpretation. But I believe that our foreknowledge of Plath's act prejudices us toward her work. This is true of many writers, not only Plath.

Far from being untypical, this interpretation reflected the belief of a number of students that the mother in "Edge" was acting appropriately in a patriarchal society. As one student observed, "Plath makes me think of the woman in a society that is misogynistic. The woman in the poem 'Edge' is reduced to silence by her own imagination or through a society that would reject her emergence as a creative being. So she must retreat back into her own cocoon, taking with her 'each child' which she must protect from a predatory society."

Some students found the mother's suicide hauntingly evocative, though they felt guilty over their aesthetic pleasure: "Sadness is beautiful here. I'm sorry to say that; I wish I didn't feel it. But the images of the night flower and the moon, and the idea of rebirth are lovely. I feel like a 'sicko' for having this interpretation, knowing that it was much more than a poem written in anger, like so many other Plath poems. There was grief and sadness and hopelessness too."

Two students were angered by "Edge," reacting to the poem as if they were unable to prevent a suicide in progress:

I hope that I am able to answer this question without too much digression—Sylvia Plath's poetry is stuck to my insides in a rather uncomfortable way. I do not read this particular poem in terms of infanticide, and therefore I don't feel that she forces her reader into being an unwitting accomplice in that respect. Suicide, however, is another issue entirely. I felt very manipulated by Plath's poetry, almost as if she were taking me down with her—drowning in her words and images. I felt rage at times toward her and her death and her expressions of suicidal thoughts, especially since she made them so beautiful at times. I cannot help thinking of an image of her death in her home with her children locked in, unable to escape. Perhaps she does force her readers in this poem into being unwitting accomplices to infanticide. Contradiction seems to run rampant when speaking of suicide.

First of all, overall I found all the poetry of Plath that was assigned on the syllabus to be disturbing. It all grated, more so even than Mishima's story of solitary suicide. There seems to be this inexorable, inevitable quality to what Plath writes, as though she is on this suicide trip and nothing will stop her. The examples in "Edge" that I find most troublesome are the comparisons of her children to "white serpent[s]" and the metaphor that her breasts are empty of milk, i.e., that she is out of nourishment and love. Perhaps what bothers me about all this is that I feel like shouting at her, "Don't write all this down: GET HELP!" It is also especially disturbing how she has more or less written off her own two children. Seemingly she does not consider (at least in her poem) how her impending suicide may affect them.

It reminds me of our discussion of The Awakening *and Edna's indifference to her boys, only they were fictional, and how Jeff said something about if he were ever so depressed [as] to consider suicide, the thought of his daughters would stop him. Plath doesn't show this concern about her own children or anyone else.*

Fewer students responded to the dead children in "Edge" than to the dead mother. Of the slightly more than half the class who commented upon the infanticide, most felt they were not implicated. Three were unaware of the poem's allusion to infanticide, one remarking, parenthetically, "actually, until you asked this question, I hadn't taken the infanticide literally—if I take it literally, my reaction becomes confused with a real case of infanticide I'm fairly well acquainted with, and I stop attending to the poem." Another observed, "although we are accomplices to Plath's suicide, I feel less so about infanticide because we know that in the end she didn't take them with her. The ugliest, most unbearable image in this poem relates to the infanticide: 'white serpent.' Thankfully, this was not carried out. I guess I'd prefer not to get too close to that one."

I suspect the main reason several students did not comment on the children's deaths in "Edge" is that Plath finally did not take their lives. Had the children perished with their mother, it would have been impossible for most readers to accept the poem's vision of infanticide as an act of maternal protection. I also suspect that readers would find the poem more disturbing if they realized that its suicide-infanticide theme literally came true for Assia Weevil, the woman with whom Hughes had an affair after leaving Sylvia. In 1969 she gassed herself and her two-year-old child, Shura, who was fathered by Hughes, in the kitchen of her flat. She was severely depressed about her relationship with Hughes, whom she feared would soon leave her, as he had left Plath. There is little doubt among biographers that the suicide imitated Plath's. Whether Assia Weevil actually thought of "Edge" in the moments prior to the suicide-infanticide is not known. The poem was published in *Ariel* in London and New York in 1965, and it is possible she read it and came to believe that, like the mother in "Edge," she was protectively folding her child back into her body, as petals of a rose close at night. One can understand why Hughes wished to protect his children from the contents of Sylvia's writings.

The wide variety of responses to "Edge" goes beyond the usual disagreements over a poem's meaning. "Edge" calls into question age-old humanistic issues, including literature's impact upon readers. For those who can disconnect a poem from its biographical and historical moorings, "Edge" is a poem of haunting peace, resignation, and transcendence. But for readers who cannot ignore the consequences of art, "Edge" remains a profoundly disquieting poem. For even as they appreciate the poem's cold beauty and carefully wrought imagery, they find themselves in the position of the children in the poem, confronting a pitcher of milk, life itself, devoid of nourishment.

Birthday Letters

Ted Hughes was appointed poet laureate of Great Britain in 1984 and has written more than a dozen volumes of poems, but until recently he has refused to comment on the details of his marriage to Sylvia Plath. The publication of *Birthday Letters* in 1998, marking the thirty-fifth anniversary of her death, offers for the first time Hughes's side of the story. The eighty-eight poems in the volume, written over a period of more than twenty-five years, dramatize his relationship with Plath from 1956, when they first met, through her suicide and cover the major events of their life together—their wedding, trip to the United States, Plath's unhappy teaching experience at Smith College, the birth of their daughter and son, and the collapse of their marriage. Many of the poems are written in the form of letters addressed to his wife and record his devastation over her suicide and his helplessness in averting it. The volume contains some of Hughes's most riveting poems and reveals a vulnerability and tenderness absent from his earlier volumes. *Birthday Letters* explores the tangled emotions arising from the harsh legacy of suicide, and while the poems will not silence the criticisms of those who, like the American feminist poet Robin Morgan, hold Hughes directly responsible for Plath's death, they do offer a wrenching account of one of the most controversial literary marriages of the century.

Birthday Letters depicts Plath less as a human being, with mortal strengths and weaknesses, than as a larger-than-life figure whose frenetic energy captivated Hughes and never ceased to haunt his imagination. The poems are both a celebration and dissection of her magnetic power over him. She appears as a volcanic force that erupts periodically, devastating everything in its path, a thunder cloudburst flooding the parched earth. She was a woman who, according to her analyst, had "instant access" to the "core" of her "Inferno" (69). The husband who is portrayed in "Daddy" and "Lady Lazarus" as an obliterating figure seems in *Birthday Letters* to be effaced by his wife's presence. Hughes describes himself in these poems as more acted upon than active, a man who, smitten by his love for the vivacious American, alternately played the role of the swineherd stealing the king's daughter and, when spurned, a discarded Caliban. In "The Blue Flannel Suit" he compares her life with an ocean liner in which he voyages (67). Their momentary happiness inexplicably gives way to torment and despair, and he assigns himself a secondary role in her tragic drama, a witness who, upon becoming the male lead, cannot rewrite the script of her doomed life.

Unable to understand or allay her panic attacks, hysterical outbursts, and nightmares, Hughes confesses in "Fever" that even as he tried to nurse her through her illnesses, he could not prevent himself from thinking she was crying wolf. The feral image changes after her suicide to one of wolves comforting the grief-stricken husband and children. Hughes seems at the beginning of their relationship powerless to resist the artillery of her erotic advances and, at the end of their marriage, as much a victim of her wild mood swings as she is. The scars on Plath's temples from the electroshock treatments following her 1953 suicide attempt seem etched indelibly on the body of Hughes's poetry, and he cannot write about her without recalling her inner violence. *Birthday Letters* intimates that both husband and wife affirmed and negated each other—each the creator and destroyer of the other.

Hughes presents throughout *Birthday Letters* his own point of view, yet he accepts with little revision Plath's own mythic perspective in "Daddy" and "Lady Lazarus." He implies that, at a certain point in their relationship, Plath began to see him as a version of her tyrannical father and that he could not resist the role thrust upon him. Many of the darkest poems in the volume expose the deadly consequences of Plath's perception that her father and husband were monstrous creatures whom she was compelled simultaneously to deify and revile. Hughes reinforces the impression gleaned in Plath's writings that the formative experience in her life was her father's raging death. Hughes sees their relationship as triangular, with the Oedipal father rising from the dead in order to wrest his daughter from her husband. Hughes accepts responsibility for their failed marriage but not for her growing infatuation with extinction. *Birthday Letters* portrays Otto Plath as the antagonist in the story, and Hughes's bitterness toward his rival is palpable.

Hughes mythologizes Otto Plath into a hideous daddy who is seldom absent from his daughter's waking and sleeping life. The poem "Isis" describes Plath's agreement to give up her dead father in order to gain a child, but she later breaks the pact, unable to exorcise her fatal attraction to Otto. In "The Minotaur" Hughes describes the "demented rage" that compelled his wife to smash a mahogany tabletop that had been his mother's heirloom. If Hughes accepts some of the blame here—he was twenty minutes late for baby-sitting—he also accepts much of the credit for encouraging her to sublimate her violence into poetry. The smashing of the tabletop marked not only the symbolic end of their marriage and the orphaning of their children but also the turning point in her artistic career, in which her unleashed fury drives her toward her paternal past. "The Minotaur" is one of many poems that dramatizes Otto Plath as his daughter's demonic muse. *Birthday Letters* suggests repeatedly that the inspiration behind Sylvia Plath's greatest poems was the barbaric resurrection of her father, a demon who stole her life as the price for her art.

In Hughes's view, the creation of poetry required Plath to descend nightly into her father's grave in order to worship, fetishistically, his gangrenous, amputated leg. Hughes paradoxically endorses this Oedipal interpretation even as he suggests that she was destroyed by her belief in it. In "Night Ride on Ariel" he implicates Plath's psychiatrist, Dr. Beuscher (whose name he misspells as "Beutscher," perhaps recalling Plath's first biographer, Edward Butscher), in her death. The analyst's encouragement of Plath to exhume her father's bones helped her to dig her own poetic grave. Hughes's bitterness extends to other persons as well. In the penultimate poem in the volume, "The Dogs Are Eating Your Mother," he insinuates that his wife's remains are being desecrated by those who exploit her for their own purposes, including academics, who regurgitate the body of her poems during their gruesome "symposia" (196).

Hughes makes no reference to A. Alvarez, whose early writings on Plath he has disagreed with sharply, but he does appear to support the theory of extremist art appearing in *The Savage God*. In "Suttee" Hughes contrasts Plath's 1953 suicide attempt, from which she emerges resurrected, with the creation of the searing poems written in the final months of her life, poems that seemed to require the poet to be consumed on a pyre. "Suttee" suggests that Hughes himself could not escape the "torching gusher" of her fiery creativity and that the flames "sucked oxygen out of both of us" (149). A similar image appears in "The Literary Life," in which the suffocating power of Plath's bell jar poems makes readers like Marianne Moore "gasp / For oxygen and cheer" (75).

"Suttee" is one of the most striking poems in *Birthday Letters*, yet Hughes never explores why a female poet, more than her male counterpart, may be at risk. Nor does he intimate anywhere in *Birthday Letters* that his own extraordinary creativity demanded a similar sacrifice. A suttee is the act of a Hindu woman cremating herself on her husband's funeral pyre, but in this case the husband has remained alive and well. Hughes was reported to have said to the British author Blake Morrison several years ago that writing about the death of someone you loved "might give you some control over the demons that were haunting you" (*New York Times,* 27 January 1998), but he seems to reject the possibility that Plath experienced any therapeutic relief while writing her poems. *Birthday Letters* remains silent about the many statements Plath made in her journals regarding writing as a form of release and self-rescue. Nor does Hughes appear to believe that anyone or anything could have deflected her death wish. He implies in "Suttee" and "The Blue Flannel Suit" that her suicide was inevitable and that, like Tiresias, he could foresee the future but not change it.

Hughes dedicates *Birthday Letters* to his children, Frieda and Nicholas, and one senses his protectiveness of them. One of the most moving poems, "Life after Death," seems to be a commentary on "Edge." Hughes's poem describes the children growing up without their mother while their father, who lies awake at night feeling like the Hanged Man, tries to comfort them. Whereas Plath ends "Edge" with the inert children coiled against their lifeless mother, Hughes ends his poem with the two babes, now orphans, lying beside their mother's corpse. Significantly, neither the children nor the husband in "Life after Death" experiences her death as an act of mystical transcendence or ennoblement. If Hughes romanticizes Plath's artistic creativity, he does not glorify the aftermath of her suicide. He suggests in "The Blackbird" that Plath's suicide was also a homicide, an effort to kill the man whom she perceived as her jailer but who was, in reality, a protector condemned to suffer her terrible fate. *Birthday Letters* will doubtlessly provoke endless debate among scholars about the Hughes-Plath marriage, but there is little question that it portrays, perhaps better than any other volume of poetry in English, the devastation wrought upon suicide survivors.

Confronting the Edge of Art and Life

Writing about the edge or abyss of life, Sylvia Plath made a conscious decision to confront the horrors of existence. "Don't talk to me about the world needing cheerful stuff!" she wrote to her mother in October 1962, shortly after her husband left her: "What the person out of Belsen—physical or psychological—wants is nobody saying the birdies still go tweet-tweet, but the full knowledge that somebody else has been there and knows the *worst*, just what it is like. It is much more help for me, for example, to know that people are divorced and go through hell, than to hear about happy marriages" (*Letters* 473).

Paradoxically, Sylvia Plath dramatized in her best poems the worst in life. We come away from her poems with a heightened understanding of how innocence apprehends danger, as Elizabeth observes in her diary at the beginning of this chapter. Poetry was the essence of Plath's life, and she wrote about artistic creativity with a mixture of joy and wonder. "The blood jet is poetry / There is no stopping it," she affirmed in the late poem "Kindness" (*Collected Poems* 270). If we can read Plath's poems without succumbing to the various roles in which she casts us—peanut-crunching crowd, literary ambulance chasers, or the indifferent moon—then we will be able to appreciate her dazzling escape artistry without feeling we have been overcharged.

CHAPTER 6

Anne Sexton and the
Poetics of Suicide

I've thought a lot about Anne Sexton since our class discussion last week. Hearing so much about her life, filtered through the passion with which it was told, made me appreciate her even more. Her poetry is beautiful. Poetry is not my favorite genre, so when I do find some that I like, it is not a half-hearted appreciation.

Maybe this is unfair to say, not nice perhaps, but I enjoy her poetry so much more than Sylvia Plath's poetry. It's OK to like one poet over another, but I feel bad in this case because I feel like they are competing for something. And the fact that they both committed suicide makes me want to soften any of my judgmental edges. And now I wonder about this. Here they are, both young American women poets, struggling with powerful emotions. One goes off to England, the other stays here. They both write, but they both still suffer. And the picture that I hold in my mind of Anne Sexton is the one at the kitchen table enjoying the sunshine. The one of Sylvia Plath that I hold is where she is "squelching" around in her "wellingtons," "squelching through the beautiful red." (Funny that this is the image I have of her, because it's one of her poems that I like best.)

But for some reason, I feel a pang more of something for Anne Sexton because she stayed here in her pain, instead of trying to leave it, and bringing it with her anyway. Whenever I've really been down, I've always thought, "But if only I could go away. Then it would be OK." But I've come to learn that this is not so. So I think that if we face the pain and are able to sit in the same room with it, we can accept it. Not love it. Just accept it. This runaway part of me has always bothered me, and I'm not always sensitive to that part. And that is the way my feelings are divided between Anne Sexton and Sylvia Plath.

RHONDA

Anne Sexton and Sylvia Plath grew up in the same suburban town of Wellesley, Massachusetts, and met for the first time in Robert Lowell's 1958 graduate poetry seminar at Boston University. The two intensely gifted and ambitious young poets regarded each other as friends and competitors. They shared with each other the details of their early suicide attempts and talked about death from the viewpoint of survivors. After the seminar ended, they went their separate ways, Plath to England with her husband, Ted Hughes, Sexton (who was four years older than Plath) to her husband and two young children. They never saw each other again despite a brief exchange of letters. Plath's suicide in 1963 came as a shock to Sexton, who regarded it as an act of abandonment. She felt her rival had stolen something magical and forbidden that she herself had long desired. Sexton's own suicide came in 1974, an event long foreshadowed by her poetry.

Read with Caution

Reading Anne Sexton's poetry after reading Plath's seems pedagogically unwise if not psychologically dangerous. We may feel that a warning label should be placed on their poetry. "Caution: contents are toxic and may undermine your will to live." Sexton acknowledged that Plath's suicide deepened her own fascination with self-extinction. Her poem "Sylvia's Death," written a few days after the event, unabashedly romanticized the suicide. We have already seen how Sexton's poem "Wanting to Die" came to Elizabeth Wurtzel's mind in the moments preceding her own suicide attempt. We have also noted Assia Weevil's imitative suicide. In short, those reading Plath's or Sexton's death poems are bound to be affected deeply—and in ways that may be literally harmful to their health.

No warning labels appear on their poems, nor should there be: such labels would be self-defeating, only heightening readers' fascination with death. Nor should their poems be sold only by prescription, as potent drugs are dispensed. These poems should be read and discussed, for they offer unforgettable accounts of suicidal depression and the longing for death. But given Plath's and Sexton's tendency to glamorize suicide, we may wonder whether a literature teacher should take special precautions when discussing their poems.

Sexton poses a special problem to readers because the impulse that gave rise to her numerous suicide attempts seems to have been closely allied with her creativity. Not that her "madness" is identical with or can be reduced to her art; rather, she began writing poetry in an effort to master the intolerable feelings that brought her repeatedly to the brink of suicide. The frequency and intensity of her psychological breakdowns were devastating to her, and over the years her suffering took its toll on everyone close to her. As Rhonda notes in her diary entry, Sexton lived longer than Plath did, dying shortly before her forty-fifth birthday. She attempted suicide at least nine times and wrote far more poems about the attraction to death than Plath did. Suicide was so much part of Sexton's everyday life and art that she seems to have constructed her personal and artistic identity around it. She referred to suicide in "Wanting to Die" as an "almost unnameable lust" (*Complete Poems* 142), and she came closer to describing this impulse than any other contemporary American poet. She was remarkably successful in transmuting suicidal depression into the stuff of poetry.

Compared with Sylvia Plath's childhood of paternal loss, Anne Sexton's early years seemed relatively uneventful and privileged. She was born on 9 November 1928 to affluent parents, and she attended public schools in Wellesley and a boarding school for girls in nearby Lowell. She enjoyed writing poetry but was not academically motivated. After one year of study at a Boston junior college, she eloped with Alfred Muller II (nicknamed Kayo) in 1948. She lived briefly in Baltimore and San Francisco before returning to Massachusetts, where her first child, Linda Gray Sexton, was born in 1953.

Sexton experienced her first major breakdown in 1954 and was hospitalized in Westwood Lodge, a private sanitarium, where her psychiatrist, Dr. Martha Brunner-Orne, diagnosed her as suffering from postpartum depression. A second daughter, Joyce Ladd Sexton, was born in 1955, and within a year Sexton again broke down and was rehospitalized, this time after threatening to harm herself and her children. Following her discharge from the hospital, Sexton began treatment with Dr. Brunner-Orne's son, Dr. Martin Orne. Her health worsened in the next few months,

and on 8 November 1956—a day before her twenty-eighth birthday—
she swallowed an overdose of barbiturates and was rushed to Newton-
Wellesley Hospital, the same institution to which Plath was taken after
her 1953 suicide attempt. Sexton stayed in treatment with Dr. Orne until
his departure to Philadelphia eight years later.

Martin Orne became a central figure in Sexton's therapeutic and artistic life. As Sexton told an interviewer in 1968, "Until I was twenty-eight I
had a kind of buried self who didn't know she could do anything but
make white sauce and diaper babies. I didn't know I had any creative
depths. I was a victim of the American Dream, the bourgeois, middle-
class dream" (*No Evil Star* 84). Neither marriage nor children brought
an end to her tormenting panic attacks and blackouts, and after her psychotic breakdown and suicide attempt, she told Dr. Orne:

> "I'm no good; I can't do anything; I'm dumb." He suggested I try educating
> myself by listening to Boston's educational TV station. He said I had a per-
> fectly good mind. As a matter of fact, after he gave me a Rorschach test, he
> said I had creative talent that I wasn't using. I protested, but I followed his
> suggestion. One night I saw I. A. Richards on educational television reading
> a sonnet and explaining its form. I thought to myself, "I could do that, maybe;
> I could try." So I sat down and wrote a sonnet. The next day I wrote another
> one, and so forth. My doctor encouraged me to write more. "Don't kill your-
> self," he said. "Your poems might mean something to someone else some-
> day." That gave me a feeling of purpose, a little cause, something to *do* with
> my life, no matter how rotten I was. (*No Evil Star* 84–85)

Sexton's first published poem, "You, Doctor Martin," reveals one of
the major themes that would preoccupy her for the rest of her days: the
need to escape from death-in-life. The speaker in the poem refers to herself sardonically as the "queen of this summer hotel" and describes life in
a "madhouse." More dead than alive, the patients in the psychiatric hospital are broken in spirit and inhabit a wasteland, devoid of hope. The
speaker's life now consists of making rows and rows of moccasins that
wait on the silent shelf.

Early Success

Yet if the speaker in "You, Doctor Martin" can make only moccasins,
Sexton, with her psychiatrist's encouragement, was making poems. She
wrote so many poems that within a period of three years she had achieved

striking results. In 1957 she enrolled in John Holmes's poetry class at Boston University, where she met another aspiring poet, Maxine Kumin, who became her best friend. Unlike most writers, Sexton enjoyed early success, her poems appearing in the *New Yorker, Harper's Magazine,* and the *Saturday Review.* She received a scholarship in 1958 to attend the Antioch Summer Writers' Conference; studied with W. D. Snodgrass, whose poem "Heart's Needle" was to have a decisive impact upon her own work; and enrolled in Lowell's poetry seminar at Boston University, where she met fellow poets Sylvia Plath and George Starbuck. Lowell, who later came to be regarded as the leader of the "confessional poets," was writing *Life Studies* and quickly recognized Sexton's poetic talents. Her first volume of poetry, *To Bedlam and Part Way Back,* was published in 1960 and received generally high praise from the critics, who were struck by the originality of her themes and her poetic voice.

Sexton established herself in the next fourteen years as a major poet, receiving both critical and popular acclaim. She was astonishingly productive despite frequent suicide attempts and hospitalizations. Her second volume, *All My Pretty Ones,* came out in 1962 and a year later was nominated for the National Book Award. She received the first traveling fellowship of the American Academy of Arts and Letters in 1963. Other awards followed, including election to the Royal Society of Literature in 1965. One year later she published *Live or Die,* which won the Pulitzer Prize. Fame brought her additional awards and recognition, including honorary membership to both the Harvard and Radcliffe chapters of Phi Beta Kappa and honorary doctorates of letters from Tufts University, Fairfield University, and Regis College. She taught poetry to patients at McLean Hospital in Belmont, Massachusetts; received an academic appointment at Boston University, rising from lecturer to full professor; and held the Crashaw Chair in Literature at Colgate University. She continued publishing at a brisk pace: *Love Poems* appeared in 1969, followed by *Transformations,* her reworkings of the Grimm Brothers' fairy tales, in 1971, and *The Death Notebooks* in 1974.

Sexton's personal life, always precarious, grew more unstable despite her growing literary success. After Dr. Orne's departure in 1964, she went into therapy with a psychiatrist who, contrary to professional ethics, succumbed to a romantic and sexual involvement with his patient. Sexton appeared at first to benefit from the relationship, but when he terminated both therapy and the affair, she was left more vulnerable than ever. Nor was she helped by her third psychiatrist, pseudonymously referred to as Dr. Constance Chase, who lacked the empathy and patience that Sexton needed. The decision in 1973 to divorce her husband, against the strong advice of her therapist and friends, deprived her of another important part of her support system. She became increasingly addicted to alcohol and a wide variety of sleeping pills and tranquilizers. As her psychological health deteriorated, she began talking openly about killing herself and started making final preparations, including appointing her daughter Linda as her literary executor. The end came on 4 October 1974, when she asphyxiated herself in her automobile.

"The Double Image"

Sexton wrote at least twenty poems about suicide. One of the most important is "The Double Image," written in 1958, shortly before her parents' death. The poem is addressed to Sexton's younger daughter, who spent the first three years of her life in her paternal grandmother's care. "The Double Image" has autobiographical and poetic significance, revealing many of the feelings toward suicide that appear in Sexton's other death poems, and portraying the "almost unnameable lust" in ways that had not been seen previously in American poetry. Consisting of seven parts, each containing between two and six stanzas, "The Double Image" offers profound insights into intergenerational conflicts. The poem opens with the speaker about to turn thirty, trying to explain to her young daughter why she has been unable to care for her:

> I, who chose two times
> to kill myself, had said your nickname
> the mewling months when you first came;
> until a fever rattled
> in your throat and I moved like a pantomime
> above your head.
> (*Complete Poems* 35–36)

Suicidal thoughts in the form of "Ugly angels" haunt the speaker, accusing her of indefinable crimes. She tells her daughter that although she wanted to be with her, the fear of killing herself prevented her from mothering the child. The speaker's violence remains internalized throughout "The Double Image," resulting in the reader's close identification with the suffering poet. There is no evidence in the poem to intimate that the speaker harbors infanticidal feelings, an admission that might weaken the reader's sympathy. But evidence of Sexton's infanticidal feelings during this time appears in Diane Wood Middlebrook's biography as well as in Linda Gray Sexton's *Searching for Mercy Street*, a moving account of her strained relationship with her mother.

"The Double Image" does not describe in detail Sexton's two suicide attempts, but it does reveal the paradoxical dynamics of suicide, including the sense of being simultaneously in and out of control. Although she refers to herself early in the poem as "I, who chose two times / to kill myself," the decision to commit suicide seems to have been made not by the "I" but by demonic inner voices. Suicide thus appears to be less a rational, voluntary decision than one determined by a sinister force over which the self has no control. The guilt is so overpowering that the speaker yearns for death as a release from private torment:

> I pretended I was dead
> until the white men pumped the poison out,
> putting me armless and washed through the rigmarole
> of talking boxes and the electric bed.
> (*Complete Poems* 36)

The speaker's drug overdose reflects Sexton's characteristic method of suicide: ingestion of pills. She depicts suicide not as an active, violent assault on the body but as an eating away from within. Sexton does not romanticize suicide in "The Double Image," as she does in many of her later poems; rather, she views it as an act of desperation arising from the absence of healthy self-love, an insight that has important psychological, cultural, and feminist implications.

Part 2 of "The Double Image" focuses on the most troubling relationship in Sexton's life: the bond with her mother. After recovering from her first suicide attempt, the speaker finds herself unable to return to her husband and children and travels instead to her ancestral house in Gloucester, where she lives with her mother. The mother-daughter connection in "The Double Image" is fraught with guilt, anger, and disappointment, as it is in Plath's *Bell Jar*. Boundaries are problematic in both mother-daughter relationships, and genuine communication is nonexistent. Like Esther Greenwood, Sexton's speaker cannot relate to her mother, who is offended by her daughter's mental illness. "I cannot forgive your suicide, my mother said. / And she never could. She had my portrait / done instead" (*Complete Poems* 37). Sexton's speaker finds herself infantilized and objectified as she lives "like an angry guest" in her mother's house. Unable to love and understand her daughter, the mother takes her to Boston to be reshaped into an acceptable image. The result is a portrait of a young woman who is smiling on the surface but seething underneath. The parents are so enamored of the portrait that they hang it on the wall, preferring to look at the inanimate object rather than at the anguished daughter living in their midst.

Motherhood remains a vexed subject for Sexton, and despite the disappointment she expresses toward her father elsewhere, the sins of the mother predominate in her poems. "The Double Image" suggests that the mother is one of the "witches" who is bearing away the speaker's guilty soul. The speaker's suicide attempt seems to be symbolic murder of her mother and then self-punishment for harboring murderous thoughts. An undercurrent of matricide and infanticide flows through "The Double Image," as it does in Plath's "Edge." Mother and daughter appear to be locked in a symbiotic relationship, each aware of the other's enmity. The hostility is so intense that when the mother develops cancer, she holds her daughter responsible. "She turned from me, as if death were catching, / as if death transferred, / as if my dying had eaten inside of her" (*Complete Poems* 38).

Sexton's letter to W. D. Snodgrass in late 1958, a few months before her parents' deaths, suggests the autobiographical basis of the poem's troubled mother-daughter relationship. The letter also reveals a link between Sexton's guilt and depression: "I have been, in truth, very depressed lately—tho I am adroit at hiding behind the verbal and pretty mask—still, I am depressed. My mother is dying of cancer. My mother says I gave her cancer (as though death were catching—death being the birthday that I tried to kill myself, nov. 9th 1956). Then she got cancer . . . who do we kill, which image in the mirror, the mother, ourself, our daughter????? Am I my mother, or my daughter?" (*Self-Portrait* 40).

In a letter to Snodgrass in February 1959, Sexton returned to her mother's approaching death. "With all these good fine things happening to my poetry (and I haven't told you half of it yet) I'm dropping out of myself. Partly because my mother is dying now and I . . . I know it's crazy, but, I feel like it is my fault. . . . Now don't lecture to me, De, I'm just telling you how it feels" (*Self-Portrait* 51). Diane Wood Middlebrook quotes a statement Sexton made to Dr. Orne indicating her ambivalence toward her mother's impending death. "Part of me would be free if she died. It would also be awful—I would dissolve" (*Anne Sexton* 47).

Sexton also believed she was responsible for the illness of her beloved great-aunt, Anna Ladd Dingley, the "Nana" of Sexton's poems. Middlebrook reports that one of the most traumatic events in Sexton's childhood occurred when Anna Ladd Dingley displayed symptoms of mental illness and shouted to the terrified thirteen-year-old: "You're not Anne!" The incident, according to Middlebrook, had a permanent effect on Sexton:

> After Anne Sexton's own breakdown, she worried about ending up in a mental institution like Nana. More important, she believed that she had personally caused her great-aunt's breakdown, and that Nana, who condemned her as "not Anne" but a "horrible and disgusting" imposter, had sentenced her to break down as well. Nana's rage took root in Sexton as a frightening symptom, which she described as a "tiny voice" in her head "shouting from far away," telling her she was awful, often taunting her to kill herself. (*Anne Sexton* 16)

Sexton's fear that she had caused her Nana's and mother's illnesses recalls Freud's theory of the "omnipotence of thought": the belief that one's hostile thoughts can literally kill another person. It seems likely that a major reason for Sexton's preoccupation with suicide was the need to punish herself for harboring ambivalent feelings toward those closest to her. She felt the same guilt toward her father, stating to an interviewer the fear that her opposition to his remarriage had caused his death (*No Evil Star* 54).

And so we can see how the mother's angry accusations in "The Double Image" have an insidious effect on her daughter's health, undermining her recovery and making her feel unfit to live. The speaker has ingested a toxin that seems to be part of the same cancer ravaging her mother. The daughter's inability to love herself reflects the mother's failure to love her. The speaker recognizes a terrible kinship despite her counteridentification with her mother. The mother temporarily recovers from her illness and has her own smiling portrait painted, to match her

daughter's; nevertheless, there seems to be no hope of family reconcilia-
tion. As in Oscar Wilde's *Picture of Dorian Gray*, the speaker's portrait
begins to rot, mirroring both her mother's and her own disintegration.

Unable to love either her mother or herself, the speaker is ambivalent
over being reunited with her own daughter. Each time the child calls the
speaker *mother*, the speaker thinks of her own mother and becomes depressed again. The poem ends with a disturbing insight into the speaker's
relationship with her daughter:

> . . . We named you Joy.
> I, who was never quite sure
> about being a girl, needed another
> life, another image to remind me.
> And this was my worst guilt; you could not cure
> nor soothe it. I made you to find me.
> (*Complete Poems* 41–42)

Years before psychoanalysts investigated the complex dynamics of narcissism, Sexton explored the subject with extraordinary depth and power
in "The Double Image." Like Ovid's Narcissus, transfixed by his own
spectral image, Sexton's speaker pursues her (m)other only to realize the
impossibility of union. The blurred boundaries between mother and
daughter make it impossible for the child to grow up and become an
autonomous, independent woman. Creating a daughter in her own image in a vain attempt to heal her own psychic wounds, the speaker discovers she cannot mother her "Joy" because she cannot joyfully mother herself. Sexton intuits the wisdom of Blake's observation in "The Marriage
of Heaven and Hell": "Sooner murder an infant in its cradle than nurse
unacted desires" (152). Sexton dramatizes the consequences of internalized rage, which destroys the child within the adult and, if it is not properly understood and worked through, contaminates a parent's relationship to her own children.

Sexton creates in "The Double Image" a brilliant psychological portrait of pathological narcissism. The poem shows that while it may be too
late for the speaker to be reconciled with her mother, it is not too late for
her to forge a relationship with her own daughter. The speaker knows the
value of unconditional love, and therein lies hope for the future. As in
Yeats's "Prayer for My Daughter," she blesses her child and in turn asks to
be blessed. She also expresses the fervent wish that her daughter will

grow up with a healthier sense of self than she has experienced herself. "Today, my small child, Joyce, / love your self's self where it lives" (*Complete Poems* 36). Love may not always be sufficient to restore a damaged self to health, but without love, no real psychological progress is possible.

"The Double Image" arises from the poet's despair and holds out the possibility that one can overcome years of suicidal depression and emerge from darkness. The poem refuses to romanticize madness or suicide and authentically captures the horrors of mental illness while simultaneously pointing the way to partial recovery—hence the appropriateness of the title of the volume in which "The Double Image" appears: *To Bedlam and Part Way Back*.

Poetic Healing

"The Double Image" was painful for Sexton to write and must have been troubling for her daughters to read years later, but she felt that others could benefit from her experiences. Critics like John Holmes advised her against writing such intensely personal poems about illness, yet she received letters from readers who told her how much "The Double Image" had helped them in their own struggle against mental illness. Sexton was convinced of the therapeutic power of her poetry, and there are at least half a dozen statements in her correspondence affirming the relationship between writing and healing. "Poetry has saved my life and I respect it beyond both or any of us," she wrote to W. D. Snodgrass in 1958 (*Self-Portrait* 42). She repeated this idea to John Holmes one year later. "[P]oetry has saved my life; has given me a life and if I had not wandered in off the street and found you and your class . . . I would indeed be lost" (*Self-Portrait* 59).

Sexton turned to art to make sense of the madness of her life. She wrote to Snodgrass in 1959, when she was battling depression and trying to cope with her parents' deaths: "My old gods are tumbled over like bowling pins. All is an emotional chaos. Poetry and poetry alone has saved my life" (*Self-Portrait* 81). She repeated the observation to Snodgrass a year later on two separate occasions, the first time tentatively—"The life of poetry is saving me (I hope) as some things are as bad as I've ever known" (*Self-Portrait* 107)—the second time more emphatically: "Only poetry saves me (and by poetry I don't mean getting famous but the writing of it)" (*Self-Portrait* 111). She told her psychiatrist-friend Anne Clarke in 1964 that she was "working like mad" on the poems that would later be called *Live or Die*. "Maxine says I'm going to exorcise all my death wishes and get rid of them. I think so. I don't mind either! Pretty damn good idea" (*Self-Portrait* 232). She wrote to a student in 1968, while teaching poetry to patients at McLean Hospital: "Poetry led me by the hand out of madness. I am hoping I can show others that route" (*Self-Portrait* 335).

Sexton believed writing was therapeutic because it heightened self-understanding and allowed her to master, if only temporarily, anxieties that might otherwise be overwhelming. She did not generally regard the creative process with anxiety. She eagerly sought publication and craved critical and popular approval. Unlike Virginia Woolf, who was most vulnerable to a breakdown following the publication of a novel, Sexton did not dread the completion of a work. She suffered from many illnesses but never from postartum depression.

Yet Sexton also knew that writing is not always a permanent solution to severe psychological problems. The psychic relief arising from artistic creation is sometimes short-lived; pain may return after the completion of a poem, requiring another poem. Sexton was realistic about what poetry could and could not do. She understood that it was easier to "forgive" a character in literature than in real life. She told an interviewer in 1970, "You don't solve problems in writing. They're still there. I've heard psychiatrists say, 'See, you've forgiven your father. There it is in your poem.' But I haven't forgiven my father. I just wrote that I did" (qtd. in McClatchy 46). She believed that contrary to the popular view, she had not overcome her illness; she had simply become a poet. Poetry did not replace psychotherapy for her; both were necessary for her well-being. Poets and patients enter into dialogic relationships with others, the former with readers, the latter with therapists. The existence of an audience, to whom one can express one's feelings, is crucial. Sexton prided herself on receiving letters from patients in psychiatric institutions thanking her for her courageous poetry. She faithfully answered these letters and told her well-wishers that just as she survived the ordeal of mental illness, so could they, with the proper help: "Yes, you can go far down—but you can come back up . . . you don't need to die down there—and I know it's hell . . . but at least you can reach out to me and to your doctor. That is truly hopeful.

I used to say to my doctor 'You're not crazy if you can find one sane person who you can talk to'" (*Self-Portrait* 324).

Sexton also maintained that reading was therapeutic, largely because it forged a bond between writer and reader that allowed them to feel connected with each other and the world. Sexton believed passionately in the power of literature to expand readers' self-knowledge and to change their lives. She told an interviewer in 1957 that Snodgrass's "Heart's Needle" had an immediate impact upon her life:

> I had written about half of my first book [*To Bedlam and Part Way Back*] when I read that poem, and it moved me to such an extent—it's about a child, and he has to give up his child, which seems to be one of my themes, and I didn't have my own daughter at that time—that I ran up to my mother-in-law's where she was living and got her back. I could only keep her at that time for a week, but the poem moved me *to action*. It so changed me, and undoubtedly it must have influenced my own poetry. (*No Evil Star* 79)

"The Ax for the Frozen Sea within Us"

Sexton was so convinced about the power of literature that she used for the epigraph to *All My Pretty Ones* a quotation from Kafka's 1904 letter to Oskar Pollack, in which he argues that "the books we need are the kind that act upon us like a misfortune, that make us suffer like the death of someone we love more than ourselves, that make us feel as though we were on the verge of suicide, or lost in a forest remote from all human habitation—a book should serve as the ax for the frozen sea within us" (*Complete Poems* 48). When asked by an interviewer in 1965 whether this was the purpose of her own poetry, Sexton exclaimed: "Absolutely. I feel it should do that. I think it should be a shock to the senses. It should almost hurt" (*No Evil Star* 72). Years later, when another interviewer asked her to apply the Kafka quotation to her new book, *Love Poems*, Sexton responded: "Well, have you ever seen a sixteen-year-old fall in love? The axe for the frozen sea becomes embedded in her. Or have you ever seen a woman get to be forty and never have any love in her life? What happens to her when she falls in love? The axe for the frozen sea" (*No Evil Star* 110).

Kafka's insight about books making one feel as if "on the verge of suicide" appealed to Sexton because she had made several suicide attempts and had been rescued each time, seemingly defying death. Writing many of her poems immediately before or after suicide attempts, she must have identified with Kafka's startling assertion. Poetry was, of the many therapies she encountered, the most powerful and least invasive form of the "talking cure." Poetry was an ax or, to change metaphors, a powerful jolt of electricity, mysteriously rousing her senses to health. These are only figures of speech; fortunately, none of her psychiatrists subjected her to the electroshock therapy that might have destroyed her creativity.

And yet there are disturbing ironies in Sexton's appropriation of Kafka's words, ironies that have only deepened with time. As long as she was the poet of survival, Sexton could speak about the necessity of writing books that make us feel as though we are on the verge of suicide. But when she came to believe, around 1968, that she would never permanently emerge from depression, Kafka's words assumed a more ominous meaning. The epigraph to *All My Pretty Ones* reminds us that if literature is the ax for the frozen sea within us, axes nevertheless remain dangerous instruments and must be wielded carefully. There are times when the frozen sea cannot be safely unlocked, times when even an icebreaker must proceed cautiously. Poetry can indeed move readers *to action*, but if a survival poet becomes a suicidal poet, readers may find themselves stranded on an ice floe.

These cautionary comments should not be interpreted as an endorsement of A. Alvarez's view that poets like Plath or Sexton were victimized by their "extremist" art. Writing about madness or suicide does not compel poets to dangle ever more precariously on the high wire of art, until they inevitably plunge to their deaths. Sexton viewed herself as an escape artist, and poetry gave her something for which to live. To cite Maxine Kumin's authoritative pronouncement in the foreword to Sexton's *Complete Poems*, "I am convinced that poetry kept Anne alive for the eighteen years of her creative endeavors" (xxiii–xxiv). Poetry therapy has its limitations, as do other therapies, but what needs to be affirmed is the degree to which poetry succeeded in strengthening her determination to live.

Live or Die

Nevertheless, the comparison of literature to an ax for the frozen sea within us has a very different meaning in light of Sexton's shifting attitude toward suicide. In early poems like "You, Doctor Martin" and "The Double Image," and in her correspondence and public interviews, Sexton refused to romanticize mental illness or suicide. She regarded herself as a survivor and recognized the role she could play in the recovery of others. But with the publication of her major suicide poems in *Live or Die*— "Sylvia's Death" (1963), "Wanting to Die" (1964), "Suicide Note" (1965), and "The Addict" (1966)—we see a darkening of her vision and an increasing attraction to suicide.

Sexton's title *Live or Die* alludes to a passage in the novel *Herzog* that Saul Bellow sent to her in response to her letters praising *Henderson the Rain King*. "I wrote Saul Bellow a fan letter about Henderson, saying that he was a monster of despair, that I understood his position because Henderson was the one who had ruined life, who had blown up the frogs, made a mess out of everything." Bellow responded with a letter containing a quote from *Herzog*, with the following words encircled: "With one long breath, caught and held in his chest, he fought his sadness over his solitary life. Don't cry, you idiot! Live or die, but don't poison everything." Bellow's words were so important to Sexton that she chose *Live or Die* as the title of her volume and used the entire passage as the epigraph to the volume. She interpreted the passage as a commentary on her life and vowed to heed its warning. "That I didn't want to poison the world, that I didn't want to be the killer; I wanted to be the one who gave birth, who encouraged things to grow and to flower, not the poisoner" (*No Evil Star* 95–96).

Sexton may not have realized, however, that the "Die" poems in this volume are more aesthetically convincing than the "Live" poems. One of Sexton's many paradoxes is that even as she spoke eloquently about the power of literature to save lives, she found the subject of suicide irresistible. She ends the volume with the moving poem "Live," but it is only with the greatest reluctance that she renounces death. Readers may also find themselves drawn to Sexton's darkening vision, unable to find the sources of hope that had been evident in the earlier poems. Sexton articulates in "Sylvia's Death," "Wanting to Die," "Suicide Note," and "The Addict" a poetics of suicide, one that requires us to approach her art with special caution.

"Sylvia's Death"

"Sylvia's Death" is the most prosuicide of the four poems. It opens with an invocation, "O Sylvia, Sylvia," and then makes passing reference to her two children, "two meteors / wandering loose in the tiny playroom" (*Complete Poems* 126). It is the only time the speaker indicates an awareness of suicide's shattering aftermath. The image of the two orphaned children recalls Adele Ratignolle's enigmatic statement to Edna in *The Awakening*—"Remember the children!"—a warning that Edna is unable to heed. Calling Plath a "Thief" because she crawled down alone "into the death I wanted so badly and for so long" (126), the speaker feels abandoned and betrayed. The reader infers that Plath and Sexton had made an antisuicide pact; now that the former has broken her promise, the latter feels cheated out of death. Sexton's speaker personifies death as a sleepy drummer whom the two poets simultaneously beckoned and resisted.

"Sylvia's Death" is problematic because rather than mourning Plath's loss or reflecting on the tragedy for those closest to her, the speaker dwells self-pityingly on her inability to accompany her friend in death. The lack of aesthetic distance between Sexton and the speaker suggests that the former has no awareness of the latter's envy and sentimentality. There is little indication of the devastation wrought by Plath's suicide on relatives and friends, the terrible sense of loss, the possibility that had the suicide attempt been thwarted, the poet might have resumed her life and dealt successfully with her problems. Nor does the poem give any reason why suicide should *not* be resisted. The news of Plath's death has created a "terrible taste for it, like salt" (*Complete Poems* 127).

Sexton never conceded that she romanticized Plath's suicide in "Sylvia's Death." She later wrote an essay called "The Bar Fly Ought to Sing" in which she elaborated on her relationship with Plath and reprinted the poem "Wanting to Die," composed on 3 February 1964 to mark the first anniversary of the poet's death. Sexton relates how she and Sylvia would talk at length "about our first suicides" (*No Evil Star* 7). Sexton ignores the pain and depression of their suicidal crises and dwells instead on their fascination with death: "We talked death with burned-up intensity, both of us drawn to it like moths to an electric light bulb. Sucking on it! She told the story of her first suicide in sweet and loving detail and her description in *The Bell Jar* is just the same story. It is a wonder that we didn't depress George [Starbuck] with our egocentricity" (*No Evil Star* 7). Sexton admits that "such fascination with death sounds strange (one does not argue that it isn't sick—one knows it *is*—there's no excuse), and that people cannot understand" (8). There is only one sentence in "The Bar Fly Ought to Sing" that indicates why an artist might resist the seduction of death—when Sexton remarks that "Suicide is, after all, the opposite of the poem" (7).

Plath's suicide had a permanent influence on Sexton, planting a seed, or at least fertilizing one that had already been planted, that would bear terrible fruit a decade later. Middlebrook quotes a statement Sexton made to Dr. Orne confirming her fascination with Plath's suicide. "Sylvia Plath's death disturbs me. . . . Makes me want it too. She took something that was mine, *that* death was mine! Of course it was hers too. But we both swore off it, the way you swear off smoking" (*Anne Sexton* 200).

Sexton viewed Plath's suicide as an outcome to which she was herself inevitably fated. Hemingway's suicide, of which she also approved, served as another literary model for her. "For Ernest Hemingway to shoot himself with a gun in his mouth is the greatest act of courage I can think of," she told Dr. Orne (Middlebrook, *Anne Sexton* 216), though she wanted to die unmutilated, like Sylvia Plath. Yet Sexton also recognized that a suicidal crisis is both temporary and treatable. She wrote to Lois Ames in 1965 about Plath: "After all she had the suicide inside her. As I do. As many of us do. But, if we're lucky, we don't get away with it and something or someone forces us to live" (*Self-Portrait* 261).

"Wanting to Die"

"Wanting to Die" is Sexton's most thoughtful meditation on suicide, exploring the desire for suicide without the emotionality and self-indulgence of "Sylvia's Death." The tone is mournful and subdued, unlike the exclamatory rhythms of the Plath elegy. "Wanting to Die" begins by involving the reader in the speaker's suicidal state of mind. "Since you ask, most days I cannot remember" (*Complete Poems* 142). Poet and speaker are not identical, and Sexton is able to analyze the yearning for death with detachment and objectivity. She observes, in what are probably her most famous lines:

But suicides have a special language.
Like carpenters they want to know *which tools*.
They never ask *why build*. (142)

"Wanting to Die" demonstrates, in its cool, reserved language, why death may seem preferable to life. Although the speaker notes that twice she has "possessed the enemy, eaten the enemy, / have taken on his craft, his magic" (*Complete Poems* 143), suicide seems less of an antagonist than an ally, a way to escape the pain of life. Sexton is a keen psychologist in the poem. She knows that suicide is an attempt to master terrifying fears of abandonment and loss, an effort to defeat the enemy at its own game. Suicide is the last refuge of a person who has exhausted hope.

"Wanting to Die" contains little of the active rage appearing in Plath's poems. Sexton admired Plath's courage in writing poems filled with intense anger and hate, though Sexton did not write about these emotions herself. "She had dared to do something quite different. She had dared to write hate poems, the one thing I had never dared to write. I'd always been afraid, even in my life, to express anger" (*No Evil Star* 93). The speakers in *The Bell Jar*, "Daddy," and "Lady Lazarus" are filled with murderous hostility and attempt suicide in large part to revenge themselves on those who have disappointed them. By contrast, revenge does not appear to be the speaker's motive in "Wanting to Die." There is only one moment when she conveys angry emotion: "suicides sometimes meet, / raging at the fruit" (*Complete Poems* 143).

Yet like Plath, Sexton suggests in "Wanting to Die" that suicide attempters have experienced pleasures that nonattempters can only imagine:

Still-born, they don't always die,
but dazzled, they can't forget a drug so sweet
that even children would look on and smile.

To thrust all that life under your tongue!—
that, all by itself, becomes a passion.
(*Complete Poems* 143)

It is at this point that "Wanting to Die" romanticizes suicide. The lust for death enlivens the otherwise dreary nature of quotidian life. The speaker cannot be dissuaded from her attraction to death despite the addressee's resistance: "Death's a sad bone; bruised, you'd say." The poem ends with the image of "the phone off the hook," an allusion to lines from Plath's "Daddy": "So daddy, I'm finally through. / The black telephone's off at the root, / The voices just can't worm through" (Plath, *Collected Poems* 224).

Sexton spoke about her intentions in "Wanting to Die" in a 1964 letter to Anne Clarke in which she offers her most extended statement on the meaning of suicide:

> My therapy is degenerating to SEX. Boy, there *are* some things that I do avoid, avoid, avoid! But we got to it by the back door, starting with the poem "Wanting to Die" . . . and the discussion of the sex of death. When (to me) death takes you and puts you thru the wringer, it's a man. But when you kill yourself it's a woman. And it goes on from there to his discovery that 1. I don't really think the dead are dead 2. that I certainly don't think I'll die even tho I'm dead 3. that suicides go to a special place . . . asleep for instance. 4. that suicide is a form of masturbation!!! (*Self-Portrait* 231)

Sexton is attracted to suicide because of the power it confers on her — the ability to cheat suffering by becoming the agent of her own destruction. She analyzes the reasons behind her yearning for oblivion and concludes, in an embarrassed voice, "Killing yourself is merely a way to avoid pain despite all my interesting ideas about it" (*Self-Portrait* 232).

"Suicide Note"

Written after Dr. Orne's departure, "Suicide Note" is addressed to a "Dear friend" to whom the speaker attempts to communicate her reasons for exiting life. She begins with a quote from Artaud — "You speak to me of narcissism but I reply that it is a matter of my life" (*Complete Poems* 156). The speaker gives the impression that she has carefully considered all the pros and cons of suicide and has reached a logical conclusion. She contrasts the vitality of her past self with the barrenness of her present self and observes, in a religious turn,

> Once upon a time
> my hunger was for Jesus.
> O my hunger. My hunger!
> Before he grew old
> he rode calmly into Jerusalem
> in search of death.
> (*Complete Poems* 157)

Sexton's speaker identifies with the Christian Messiah's martyrdom, an association that recalls Sylvia Plath's persona as "Lady Lazarus." The difference between "Suicide Note" and "Lady Lazarus" is that the former emphasizes crucifixion while the latter moves toward resurrection. "Suicide Note" is difficult to read because of its absence of hope: the poem awakens feelings of helplessness and frustration in the reader. The speaker refers twice to the addressee of the "Suicide Note" as "Dear friend." Readers of Sexton's poem may also regard themselves as her dear friend, caring deeply about the writer and therefore distressed by her impending death.

Indeed, we are so distressed that we may resist the speaker's argument:

> I could admit
> that I am only a coward
> crying *me me me*
> and not mention the little gnats, the moths,
> forced by circumstance
> to suck on the electric bulb.
> But surely you know that everyone has a death,
> his own death,
> waiting for him.
> (*Complete Poems* 158)

The fallacy in the speaker's argument is that unlike insects, which are unable to resist a deadly flame, a person chooses to commit suicide. Everyone must eventually die, but no one is forced to commit suicide. Sexton grants that she is not killing herself because of old age or disease, which might have made suicide a more rational decision; rather, she commits suicide "wildly but accurately, / knowing my best route"—a claim the reader does not have to accept.

It is a long distance from Sexton's poem "Suicide Note" to the audiotaped suicide note left by the Reverend Jim Jones, the messianic leader of the People's Temple in Guyana, who exhorted his nine hundred followers to commit mass suicide on 18 November 1978. Yet the constricted logic of Jones's rambling speech recalls Sexton's poem. "Well, some, everybody dies. Some place that hope runs out; because everybody dies. I haven't seen anybody yet didn't die. And I like to choose my own kind of death for a change. I'm tired of being tormented to hell, that's what I'm tired of. Tired of it [Applause from his followers]" (qtd. in Etkind 83).

Reading "Suicide Note" oppositionally does not imply reading it unempathically. I am moved by the speaker's anguish and can understand, to a degree, her efforts to spare those closest to her from being overwhelmed by her suffering. Sexton views the speaker's suicide as a gift to family and friends, enabling them to remember her with love and dignity. But she does not anticipate the devastation experienced by recipients of the gift.

Suicide survivors will resist the speaker's fatalistic argument to her dear friend. Surely a dear friend would reassure the speaker that she is not alone and that help is available. A dear friend would encourage the speaker to see a therapist or actually take her to an emergency room or walk-in clinic, as Sexton's family and friends did many times. To Sexton's lines, near the end of "Suicide Note," "I know that I have died before— / once in November, once in June. / How strange to choose June again, / so concrete with its green breasts and bellies" (159), a dear friend might respond: "You survived past crises; so can you survive this one."

"Suicide Note" also poses problems for Christian readers, who may sympathize with Sexton's religious impulse but who will be hard pressed to locate anything transcendent about her quest for death. They will have difficulty accepting the speaker's two premises in "Suicide Note": first, that Jesus was suicidal ("he rode calmly into Jerusalem / in search of death"); and second, that the speaker's suicide follows Jesus' preachings. While Judas has been vilified mainly for betraying Jesus, his more serious crime, as Friedrich Ohly has suggested, was suicide, since the hanging implied that Judas was beyond God's redemption, therefore beyond God's power. The church has been steadfastly opposed to suicide since the third or fourth century A.D., when so many Christians martyred themselves that it appeared the young religion might die out. The church's condemnation "was pronounced tardily, albeit clearly, by Augustine in his *De civitate Dei*, becoming official in 533, with the Second Council of Orleans. After 563 and the Council of Barga, anyone who committed suicide was denied Christian burial" (Carotenuto 143).

Sexton later realized the disturbing autobiographical implications of "Suicide Note" and attempted to distance herself from its theme. In one of her Crashaw Lectures at Colgate University, she jokingly observed about the poem, which had undergone several drafts: "If it were a real suicide note, there would have been one draft, I imagine. . . . One does not perfect at gunpoint" (Middlebrook, *Anne Sexton* 240). Her response may strike the reader as ingenuous. She insisted in her letters and interviews that poetry can save lives; if so, then it can endanger lives, particularly when it encourages us to ignore a cry for help. Additionally, as her creative talents declined due to drug and alcohol addiction, Sexton wrote suicidal poems that she did not revise, further blurring the difference between art and life.

The Therapeutics of Reading

Sexton's poetics of suicide requires a therapeutics of reading, a survival guide for reading suicidal literature. Based upon the principles of suicide prevention—knowledge of danger signals, the need to take suicide seriously, and the willingness to empathize and listen—a therapeutics of reading will help us respond to real and fictional suicidal characters. A reader's empathy for a suicidal character does not require acceptance of the fantasies associated with suicide: the belief that suicide leads to omnipotent control, rebirth, immortality, magical reunion with the dead, or reparation. Nor does empathy require acceptance of the dichotomous thinking and constricted logic associated with a suicidal crisis. Awareness of the countertransference feelings associated with suicide—including malice, aversion, and fear—enables a reader to avoid condemning or heroicizing self-death. Finally, the reader must guard against the temptation to blame a suicide on another character or agent, even when the text invites such a response.

"The Addict"

We can see many of the characteristics of suicidal thinking in "The Addict," in which Sexton, sounding like Plath, uses black humor to rationalize her obsession with death. Unlike earlier poems, "The Addict" portrays suicide as a ritualistic performance. The speaker in the poem refuses to explain why she has promised to die; instead, she describes the power of her addiction to pills, which are "a mother, but better" (*Complete Poems* 165). These multicolored "death pills," upon which Sexton herself was increasingly dependent during the last months of her life, have seized control of virtually all aspects of the speaker's life. The pills are a metaphor of a psychic battle in which she hurls "bombs" at herself—a civil war in which protagonist and antagonist coinhabit the same body.

Like Plath's suicide poems, "The Addict" dramatizes the vicissitudes of bearing witness. The poem challenges readers to observe a suicidal crisis without becoming horror-stricken or repelled. The poem distances readers in ways that make it difficult to remain compassionate to the speaker. We can become detached onlookers, watching the spectacle of the pill-popping performer with a mixture of voyeuristic fascination or jaded cynicism. We can retreat in horror, repelled by the situation of a woman intent "to kill myself in small amounts, / an innocuous occupation" (*Complete Poems* 166). We can distance ourselves from the suffering in the poem and limit our attention to its carefully wrought imagery, self-mocking irony, discordant end rhyme, and jarring conclusion: "Fee-fi-fo-fum- / Now I'm borrowed. / Now I'm numb" (166). Or we can adopt a therapeutics of reading and empathize with the speaker's pain without endorsing her despair.

Critical Reactions to Sexton's Poetry

Sexton's literary and extraliterary cries of help have bedeviled critics. One cannot recall another major poet who wrote about suicide with such frequency and intensity, and who, after making repeated suicide threats over a period of eighteen years, finally succeeded in taking her life. Although suicide always comes as a shock, many of her relatives and friends regarded Sexton's suicide as "inevitable"—and herein lies a major problem for her readers. Widely regarded as the first confessional poet, Sexton was fond of saying that the "difference between confession and poetry . . . is after all, art" (*Self-Portrait* 44). In Sexton's case, however, it is not always possible to locate a firm distinction between the two. She rightly insisted that the world she created in her poetry was not based solely upon autobiographical truth. She cited as an example "The Double Image," in which she deliberately failed to mention that she had not one daughter but two, and that she had been hospitalized not twice but five times. "[P]oetic truth," Sexton concluded, "is not necessarily autobiographical" (*No Evil Star* 103). Yet many of Sexton's most complex and moving poems *are* about her suicide attempts. Despite her remark to one of her students—"No, I do not want to be known as the mad suicide poet, the live Sylvia Plath" (qtd. in McCabe 225)—this is precisely the reputation she has acquired for many readers.

In the beginning of her career, many critics refused to accept the legitimacy of Sexton's poetic themes. The content of her poems appalled John Holmes, whose early poetry seminar was so important to her artistic development. "That isn't a fit subject for poetry," he advised her (*No Evil Star* 89), an opinion that proved representative of many male critics. Maxine Kumin's suggestion that Holmes's attitude was influenced by his wife's mental illness and suicide helps to explain his aversion to Sexton's poetry. Other critics disliked Sexton's candor. James Dickey wrote two influential reviews blasting Sexton's poetry for containing more pain than art. Dickey stated in his 1961 review of *To Bedlam and Part Way Back* that "Anne Sexton's poems so obviously come out of deep, painful sections of the author's life that one's literary opinions scarcely seem to matter; one feels tempted to drop them furtively into the nearest ashcan, rather than be caught with them in the presence of so much naked suffering" (Dickey 63).

Charles Gullans's 1970 review of *Live or Die* was even more dismissive:

> These are not poems at all and I feel that I have, without right or desire, been made a third party to her conversations with her psychiatrist. It is painful, embarrassing, and irritating. The immediacy and terror of her problem are painful; the personal character of the confessional detail is embarrassing; and the tone of hysterical melodrama which pervades most of the writing is finally irritating. Either this is the poetry of a monstrous self-indulgence, in which case it is despicable; or it is documentation of a neurosis, in which case to pretend to speak of it as literature at all is simply silly. (Gullans 148)

The balanced cadences of Gullans's prose belie his outrage over Sexton's poems; whatever the artistic merits of *Live or Die,* his reaction has less to do with her poetry than with his anxieties over mental illness. His resistance to *Live or Die* recalls the early critical response to Kate Chopin's *Awakening,* which was also regarded as pathological art.

Robert Boyers's glowing 1967 review of *Live or Die* is based upon the contrast he draws between Sexton and Plath: "Miss Sexton's propensities are similarly violent and suicidal, but she convinces herself, and her reader, that she has something to live for. We are grateful to Miss Sexton as we can be to few poets, for she has distinctly enlarged and enhanced the possibilities of endurance in that air of lost connections which so many of us inhabit" (Boyers 155–56). Boyers admired Sexton largely because, unlike Plath, she had not committed suicide. Sexton's endurance inspired many readers in the late 1960s and early 1970s, a period of "lost connections" and political turmoil. Boyers concludes his review with the observation that "Miss Sexton's decision to live, with her eyes open, and the responsibility for human values planted firmly on her competent shoulders, is a major statement of our poetry" (166). One can only imagine Boyers's grief when she committed suicide seven years later.

Adrienne Rich was one of the first critics to comment on Sexton's suicide, noting sadly in her 1974 essay "When We Dead Awaken": "We have had enough suicidal women poets, enough suicidal women, enough of self-destructiveness as the sole form of violence permitted to women" (rpt. in *On Lies, Secrets, and Silence* 122). Rich also worried about the impact of Plath's suicidal poems on readers. A prefatorial comment in *On Lies, Secrets, and Silence* suggests Rich's motive in writing her cautionary essay on Sexton. "Recalling the effect on so many young women poets of Sylvia Plath's suicide (an imaginative obsession with victimization and death, unfair to Plath herself and her own struggle for survival), I wanted to try to speak to the question of identification which a suicide always arouses" (121).

Kathleen Spivack and Denise Levertov explored in separate 1981 articles the relational implications of Sexton's suicide. They express deep sadness over Sexton's death, praise her exceptional talents, and worry about the effects of a celebrated female poet's suicide on other readers. Spivack argues that Sexton's death "confirms the importance of staying alive, not to cut off one's options and development prematurely, but to continue to grow" (Spivak 25). Spivack discusses the severity of Sexton's illness during the last two years of her life and her friends' despair over their inability to help her. She agrees with Sexton's own observation that she would have been a healthier person had the women's movement come along sooner. Spivack laments the loss of so many female poets of her acquaintance who glorified madness and eventually committed suicide.

Denise Levertov develops this theme in further detail, arguing that "while the creative impulse and the self-destructive impulse can, and often do, coexist, their relationship is distinctly acausal; self-destructiveness is a handicap to the life of art, not the reverse" (Levertov 56). She chides Alvarez for perpetuating the "myth that confounds a love-affair with death with a love-affair with art" (58), and widening her attack, criticizes "our exploitive society, which romanticizes its victims when they are of a certain kind (thus distracting us from the unromanticizable lives of the suffering multitude)" (59). I agree with these criticisms, though there is increasing evidence of a link between creativity and manic-depressive illness. The statement that most interests me occurs at the beginning of Levertov's essay: "Across the country, at different colleges, I have heard many stories of attempted—and sometimes successful—suicides by young students who loved the poetry of Plath and who supposed that somehow, in order to become poets themselves, they had to act out in their own lives the events of hers. I don't want to see a new epidemic of the same syndrome occurring as a response to Anne Sexton's death" (54).

The Werther Effect

Levertov does not provide any empirical evidence for this assertion, but there is good reason to heed her advice. On 5 April 1994, three weeks before the end of the Literary Suicide course, Kurt Cobain shot himself to death, and in the following weeks newspapers across the country reported a number of his bereaved followers taking their own lives. Although there was only one clear imitation suicide in the Seattle community, where Cobain lived—that of a twenty-eight-year-old man who, after attending a candlelight vigil memorializing the rock singer, went home and shot himself in the head with a shotgun, as his hero had done—there was a sharp increase in suicide crisis calls in the Seattle area. David Jobes and his colleagues theorize in a study appearing in *Suicide and Life-Threatening Behavior* that additional copycat suicides in the Seattle area were prevented by the media's refusal to glorify the suicide, Courtney Love's public expression of grief and anger over her husband's death, and the effectiveness of crisis centers and community outreach programs.

There were isolated instances of Cobain-inspired suicides throughout the world. The *New York Times* reported on 30 May 1997 in an article entitled "2 'Perfect Little Girls' Stir France in Suicide" about two teenagers who shot themselves to death in a small mining town 110 miles north of Paris. Described by their headmaster as "model girls and model students," they were part of a group of twenty who wore Cobain T-shirts and worshiped his grunge rock music. Beside the girls' bodies were several Cobain lyrics—the police would not say which ones for fear of their impact on other impressionable youths.

It is unlikely that Sexton's death was responsible for the jump in the suicide rate from 12.1 suicides per 100,000 in 1974 to 12.7 in 1975, one of the biggest leaps in the last twenty years (Leenaars and Lester 188). Far fewer people model their lives and deaths on poets than on rock stars or actresses. Nevertheless, writers' suicides, or those of their fictional characters, sometimes serve as the model for readers' copycat suicides or suicide attempts. Tolstoy's wife, Sophia, tried to throw herself beneath a train shortly after the publication of *Anna Karenina*, in obvious imitation of the novelist's doomed heroine. Psychologist Herbert Hendin reports the case of another woman who leaped in front of a train and lost both her legs. "She could recall the death scene in many novels, vividly recalling Anna Karenina's suicide in front of a train" ("Psychotherapy and Suicide" 438).

There is mounting evidence that the depiction of violence in films and television leads to heightened aggression in viewers. "Some researchers use the term 'priming' to refer to the agitated state that occurs when the mind receives and stores persuasive images, whether good or bad. For a short period after seeing images of violence, they say, viewers are more likely to interpret ambiguous behavior by others as aggressive, and to respond in kind" ("Does Life Imitate Violence on Film?" *New York Times*, 30 November 1995). Many films and television shows have provoked acts of copycat violence, including *The Deer Hunter*, *Taxi Driver*, *The Burning Bed*, *Boulevard Nights*, *Colors*, *New Jack City*, *The Program*, *Natural Born Killers*, and *Beavis and Butt-Head*. If we believe that literature, along with art, television, and music, can be a powerful humanizing force, then we must also admit that it can be a destructive force. It has been estimated that the typical American high school student views eight hundred suicides on film (Coleman). Researchers have concluded that the suicide rate rises following television broadcasts of fictional stories portraying suicide (Gould et al.) and that suicide stories "trigger deaths that would not have occurred otherwise" (Phillips and Carstensen 101).

Romanticizing Sexton's Suicide

In light of these observations, the tendency among critics to romanticize or rationalize Sexton's suicide should give us pause. A shift in attitude toward her suicide has occurred in the last ten years, mainly by critics proclaiming the maturity of her final vision. Their work appears in two major collections of essays on Sexton, one edited by Linda Wagner-Martin, the other by Francis Bixler.

William Shurr begins his essay on mysticism and suicide in Sexton's last poetry by noting the "chilling information" that she was actually reading the galley proofs of *The Awful Rowing toward God,* which she intended for posthumous publication, on the day she committed suicide. The "grim fact that the suicide is a consciously intended part of the book" makes *The Awful Rowing toward God* a more authentic work for Shurr (Shurr 193). He cites a passage from Emerson indicating that suicide has many causes: "It may be in one the effect of despair, in one of madness, in one of fear, in one of magnanimity, in one of ardent curiosity to know the wonders of the other world." Sexton's suicide, Shurr insists, was grounded in magnanimity and curiosity — "Sexton's way is not everyone's, but it has its own rationale and, as artistic vision, its own extraordinary beauty" (207–8).

To view Sexton's suicide as a deliberate attempt to authenticate her final book is to see her as literally dying for art. Suicide becomes for Shurr the logical and fitting conclusion to her long artistic obsession with death. He avoids discussing Sexton's prolonged psychiatric illness and the effects of the suicide on her family, friends, and readers. Shurr quotes Camus's statement in *The Myth of Sisyphus* — "There is only one philosophical problem which is truly serious; it is suicide. To judge whether life itself is or is not worth the trouble of being lived — that is the basic question of philosophy" — but then concludes, in opposition to Camus's existentialism, that suicide is justifiable. Nowhere does Shurr observe that had Sexton succeeded in committing suicide in the 1950s, she never would have written any poetry.

Other critics have praised Sexton's suicide as an escape from male oppression. Anne Marie Seward Barry compares Sexton's *Book of Folly* with Erasmus's *Praise of Folly* and claims that the former's suicide was the fate of the wise, according to Erasmus. "'Recall,' his narrator Folly tells us,

'What kind of people have committed suicide. . . . Have they not been the wise or near-wise?'" (Barry 47). Like Shurr, Barry attaches Christian symbolism to Sexton's death and sees her as a martyr, crucified by patriarchal and capitalist forces. "In the process of living, she observes that personal madness, as an inner psychical fragmentation caused by outer forces, is the inevitable result of domination of women by men, of countries by other countries, of art by business, of creativity by sterility" (64). Lynette McGrath argues that criticisms of Sexton's suicide reveal misunderstanding of her life and art. "A patriarchal view that expects in women weakness and loss of control will tend to interpret a woman's suicide not as a heroic act but as a sign of failure, seeing it as 'hysterically' interruptive of her more appropriate biological and nurturing functions" (McGrath 139). McGrath does not realize that one can lament suicide without being chauvinistic or controlling. Nor is Sexton's suicide the beginning of a "connection," as McGrath claims; experts agree that nothing leads to greater *dis*connection than does suicide. Similarly, it is hard to agree with Caroline King Barnard Hall's conclusion that for Sexton "escape and arrival are identical conclusions. Suicide is an act of female triumph, for it is the ultimate affirmation of self and of freedom from male domination" (173).

The "Inevitability" of Suicide

Diana Hume George, one of the most important Sexton scholars, has offered perhaps the most disturbing commentary on her suicide. I admire George's psychoanalytic study *Oedipus Anne* but disagree with her statement about undergraduates' reactions to "Wanting to Die":

> In my experience college students are rigorously normal in their response to suicide. In a discussion before we looked at this poem, the class in which I first taught it asserted positively that wanting to die because you are suffering physically is understandable; wanting to die without what they called "a real reason," by which they meant a physical one attached to disease, is sad — not merely sad but bad, reprehensible, morally irresponsible, and ethically debased. Depression, unlike cancer, said my students, must be reasoned with and always cured. One may never simply give over the struggle. My students almost uniformly denied the legitimacy — even the credibility — of an attitude that says from the beginning, "I would rather not live." (I think of Bartleby, who would always prefer not to, and who, by God, does not.) (131)

Unlike George, I have never attended a class in which students (or teachers) are "rigorously normal" in their response to anything, much less to a subject as fraught with ambivalence as suicide. As I have suggested throughout this study, not only do undergraduate and graduate students disagree widely over their feelings toward suicide, but this disagreement is reflected among literature professors and critics. There are important gender differences in reading suicidal literature, as we saw in our discussion of Hemingway. George also seems to cast her students in the role of Sir William Bradshaw in *Mrs. Dalloway*, who enjoins his patients to maintain a sense of "proportion." Few students are naive enough to believe that depression "must be reasoned with and always cured"— largely because many of them know from experience that mental illness is often more intractable than physical illness. Students are less judgmental toward suicide than George implies, less inclined to perceive it as morally evil. If some students maintain, as she suggests, that one "may never simply give over the struggle," then that attitude strikes me as less dangerous than the willingness to relinquish hope. For if we encourage our students to conclude that a real or fictional character's suicidal crisis is terminal, then we ignore a basic fact underlying most suicide attempts, namely, that people want to be rescued.

George invokes "Bartleby the Scrivener" to justify the legitimacy of suicide, but Melville's story can also be interpreted as a protest *against* suicide. Had the complacent narrator made a greater effort to understand and befriend Bartleby, whom he literally and symbolically walls up in the beginning of the story, and whom he later abandons, the forlorn young man might not have given up the will to live. Bartleby's increasingly desperate refrain, "I would prefer not to," is a reaction against a world that has preferred not to live with him. Like Bartleby, Sexton must have felt toward the end of her life that her situation was hopeless.

This judgment is shared by Diane Wood Middlebrook, who remains a central figure in Sexton scholarship. Her groundbreaking biography deepens our understanding of the relationship between the poet's life and art. Middlebrook used, with the permission and cooperation of the poet's family, the audiotapes of more than three hundred psychotherapy sessions with Dr. Orne. Middlebrook confronts the darker sides of her subject's life without reducing biography to pathography. She never romanticizes Sexton's death, but she does acknowledge in the 1994 conference "Wanting to Die: Suicide and American Literature," sponsored by the American Suicide Foundation, that she felt a conflicting set of beliefs when writing the biography. Middlebrook believed strongly, on the one hand, that suicides are preventable and should be prevented whenever possible. She believed equally strongly, on the other hand, that Sexton neither could have nor should have been prevented from suicide because of the devastating losses in her life: the departure of her husband, the growing up of her children, the abrupt departure of her psychiatrist, and the decline of her creativity.

Middlebrook's desire to write a biography of a heroine rather than a victim prompted her to agree with Sexton's decision to commit suicide. "The best thing I could do as a biographer was to honor her intention without flinching" (qtd. in *New York Times*, 14 November 1994). Middlebrook admits candidly in the 1994 conference that Dr. Orne was so disturbed by her belief in the inevitability of Sexton's suicide that he felt compelled to write a foreword in which he offered a contrary opinion. "Sadly, if in therapy Anne had been encouraged to hold on to the vital supports that had helped her build the innovative career that meant so much to her and others, it is my view that Anne Sexton would be alive today" (*Anne Sexton* xviii). No one can resolve the question of the inevitability of Sexton's suicide, but we can suggest, as Herbert Hendin did in his response to Middlebrook's 1994 talk, that had the poet received proper medical treatment, including appropriate psychotherapy and medication, she might have recovered. She was, after all, only forty-four when she died, and though her life seemed beyond repair, other artists have battled back to health from bleak situations. Were Sexton alive today, struggling with the same problems, her prognosis would be more positive.

Literature and Suicide Prevention

A teacher's failure to call into question the "inevitability" of Sexton's suicide may have unintended consequences. Hearing a teacher admit, as George does, that "[p]erhaps successful suicide attempts, figurative or otherwise, are strange things to celebrate" (*Oedipus Anne* 132), students may come to accept Sexton's vision of suicide. They may also come to believe that a suicidal depression is untreatable. George remarks that at the end of her class discussion of "Wanting to Die" her students came to an "uneasy, genuine understanding" of the poem. The statements she quotes by her students emphasize the utter hopelessness of the speaker's situation and the appropriateness of suicide. "'Wanting to Die' ends in the silence of suicide because, for me and for the students to whom I taught it, the poem is a successful attempt. As one of my students said, 'This poem self-destructs'" (132).

Are we putting our students at risk by teaching poems that celebrate suicide? If so, what special precautions should we take when reading suicidal literature with our students? I quoted lines from "Sylvia's Death" and asked my Literary Suicide students to respond to these questions. The following comments indicate the range of responses.

I don't believe that the misreading of anything, in itself, can be deadly. The idea that someone could read something that would make them decide to kill themselves is absurd. Too many factors enter into a suicide: mental health, psychosocial stressors, etc. I used to get really angry when a court case came up where parents were suing some singer or band, saying that a certain song caused their teenager to commit suicide. (Ozzy Osborne's "Suicide Solution" is the one I remember.) I think that these people are just so guilt-ridden and pained at the death of their child that they fail to see the big picture—they look for someone to blame.

Don't get me wrong: I think that it is a good idea to have a knowledge of suicide prevention if you are a teacher, regardless of what you teach. Those who teach suicidal literature should be even more aware because issues might come up in a suicide class that wouldn't in any other class. When you start to delve into really emotional stuff in a classroom, sometimes people are left feeling a little raw, with nowhere to turn in order to keep venting these feelings that come up.

Reading poems or listening to music does not make people kill themselves.

It's hard to disagree with your question. But I think much would depend on how much the suicide is emphasized, whether the teacher glorified it or not. In fact, I think high school teachers (and maybe college professors) should have some knowledge of what suicidal symptoms are and how to respond to them regardless of what they're teaching.

Yes, a misreading of this poem can be deadly, but no more deadly, I think, than most of what we've read this semester.

So much depends on the individual reader that it becomes impossible to give yes or no answers to these questions. I'm almost cynical enough to say that questions like this place too much power in words. You're lucky if you can get someone to read a book these days, let alone have it impel them to end their life.

One of the most interesting responses came from a student who had extensive teaching experience at another college and who had witnessed campus violence:

I have to respond in a practical, realistic way to this question because I have no other. If I teach adults, people over eighteen, perhaps, I must acknowledge their maturity, their self-containedness, at least to a large degree. So, I can assume that they are able to read and discuss anything. I must assume my adult students are sane people able to grapple with difficult ideas.

The problem is, however, that young adults are often not "sane," not fully able to separate themselves from the idea and the texts. I must, then, take care to consider how to present painful, troubling concepts such as suicide, violence, and murder.

Surely, I can't fear that my classroom, my syllabus, my lectures, and my discussion are so influential that they can cause suicide. Still, I have experienced a student's rampage; I do know that, while he was a very, very disturbed young man, he was also influenced in part by his classes, the readings, and his teachers' responses to his papers.

Sometimes, then, classwork can be very powerful, and as teachers, especially of young adults, we must take some precaution.

Others echoed the need to take special precautions when teaching suicidal literature. "People everywhere imitate suicides of famous people all the time," wrote one student; "[l]ast week I heard of at least two Kurt Cobain–inspired suicides. Why not, then, Anne Sexton?" A second suggested that all teachers should have knowledge of suicide prevention regardless of the courses they teach. "I realize teachers are not always the people a student turns to, but especially in literature, teachers often grow to know their students through their work." A third recalled an acquaintance who had become suicidal after reading *The Bell Jar* in high school. A fourth argued that "it is not uncommon for a student to choose a teacher as a figure of transference, and obviously it could be a teacher in any field. Just as schools now insist on teachers being able to recognize child abuse, they should be able to recognize the signs of suicidal behavior." And a fifth wrote:

I think a teacher should have some knowledge of suicide prevention, because I believe that for certain personality types, reading and discussing and writing about suicidal literature is hazardous. Just as there are types who always want to find out how fast a car can go, how much they can cheat on their income tax, or on their husband or wife, or how much they can drink, there are those who have an attraction toward dangerous or darker impulses.

If I left a group of children alone with matches and kerosene, I'd want to know something about extinguishing a fire. I think a misreading could be deadly, because having the text in print somehow legitimizes the idea—and may lead, suggest, or influence others to believe that this is a craving they should pursue, like pushing the pedal to the floor, seducing the neighbor's wife, drinking the bottle of vodka. Yes, I would want to know about suicide prevention were I the teacher.

Nietzsche, not known for optimism, observed that "[w]e possess art lest we perish of the truth" (435). Perhaps he should have added a corollary: we possess truth lest we perish of art. If art can be life-affirming, it can also be life-denying, as we can see in suicidal literature. Sexton confronts in her greatest poems the pain of existence and offers us, without false hope, the courage to endure. Poetry prolonged her life, and if we take seriously her Kafkaesque belief that literature should serve as the ax for the frozen sea within us, then we honor her memory best by celebrating her not as a poet of suicide but as a poet of survival.

CHAPTER 7

William Styron and the
Landscape of Depression

Darkness Visible *[was] the first book by William Styron that I read, and it remains for me the most impressive, even after reading several of his works of fiction. I think that any reader would find his portrayal of his struggle with depression and suicide moving; Styron writes with honesty and clarity. For me, however, this account has a special meaning. I have been grappling with my own depressive illness for more than five years now, and Styron has eloquently put into words many of the feelings that I have been unable to grasp in my mind or on paper. Reading Styron has helped me to organize my own thoughts and feelings about this sickness that I have been experiencing mostly alone.*

This semester has, I believe, been cathartic for me in many ways. It has made me come face to face with my illness at least on a daily basis, and has encouraged me to relate my own experiences to the writers we have examined in class. Literary Suicide has given me a feeling of camaraderie. I feel a connection to many of the writers we have studied, and also to many of the class members, including yourself, who have shared their own experiences with the class through their diaries. Aloneness is one of the worst parts of depression, and in this class the truth that I am not alone has been reinforced. This is still a very difficult subject for me to write about; it cuts very close to the bone. However, my own story is a long time coming, and now is as good a time as any. I write now more for myself than for the class (forgive me).

Because one of the most irritating symptoms of depression is a muddled thought process, I have made only a few haphazard attempts to write about my experience with mental illness. Styron calls this confusion and lack of

210

*focus some of depression's "most famous and sinister hallmarks." He re-
counts to the reader his inability even to compose a suicide note at his most
desperate moment. Many times for this class I have found myself sitting at
the computer, with thousands of ideas running through my mind, only to
be frustrated at my inability to set them down in any sort of order. For now
I will just write, in hopes of organizing my thoughts after they have all
been spilled onto the page.*

LAURA

Darkness Visible (1990), William Styron's extraordinary account of his
descent into mental illness, chronicles the development of his depression from its origins in October 1985 to its near-fatal conclusion two
months later, when the novelist narrowly rejected suicide, hospitalized
himself, and initiated the healing process. Styron tells us in the author's
note that the book originated as a lecture given at a 1989 symposium on
affective disorders sponsored by the Department of Psychiatry of the Johns
Hopkins University School of Medicine. Like A. Alvarez's *Savage God,
Darkness Visible* situates the writer's suicide attempt in the larger context
of the many nineteenth- and twentieth-century artists who have taken
their own lives. Styron explores the personal, psychological, and literary
implications of depression, a mysterious disease that has "yielded its secrets to science far more reluctantly than many of the other major ills
besetting us" (11).

Darkness Visible was the last book we read in Literary Suicide, and it
had by far the most powerful impact upon the students. Reading it proved
to be a profound experience not only for Julie, who found it indispensable to her own recovery, but also for Laura, who had been grappling
with depression for several years. I knew that many students would find
Darkness Visible an uplifting work—hence, my decision to end the course
with an author who overcame suicidal depression—yet I was nevertheless surprised by the number of people who regarded it as a transformative work.

Darkness Visible is Styron's most accessible book, and it has elicited an
outpouring of responses from his readers. There are many reasons for its
astonishing popularity, but if I had to identify one, it would be the unsentimental hope *Darkness Visible* offers to anyone suffering from mental
illness. To appreciate the book's affirmative ending, one must recognize

that Styron, an ironist in the tradition of James Joyce and William Faulkner, has been wary of "inspirational" literature throughout his forty-five-year artistic career. He has long been skeptical of professional healers, and his fictional psychiatrists and ministers inspire little hope for those searching for psychological relief or redemption. Yet it is precisely Styron's irony and skepticism, his refusal to accept anything on faith alone, that make the ending of *Darkness Visible* so convincing.

"I'm sick . . . un Problème Psychiatrique"

The difficulty of writing about depression, Styron notes at the beginning of *Darkness Visible*, is that it remains "nearly incomprehensible to those who have not experienced it in its extreme mode" (7). He returns to this theme at the end of the book, observing that "the horror of depression is so overwhelming as to be quite beyond expression, hence the frustrated sense of inadequacy found in the work of even the greatest artists" (83). Styron's literary brilliance enables him to describe the indescribable feelings of madness to which he almost succumbed in late 1985: the gloom slowly closing in on him, the growing dread and alienation, the indefinable anxiety that seized hold of him. He singles out, among the most debilitating symptoms of depression, "confusion, failure of mental focus and lapse of memory" (14). His mind was dominated at a later stage of the illness by "anarchic disconnections." There was also a bifurcation of mood: "lucidity of sorts in the early hours of the day, gathering murk in the afternoon and evening" (14–15). He likens the pain to drowning and suffocation, metaphors also used by Sylvia Plath in *The Bell Jar* to describe her suicidal depression.

Like Plath and others who have written autobiographically about depression, Styron identifies a "sense of self-hatred—or, put less categorically, a failure of self-esteem" as one of the worst manifestations of the illness (*Darkness Visible* 5). The self-loathing became so virulent that he lost the ability to write. He concluded that he was not worthy of receiving the prestigious French award Prix Mondial Cino del Duca, given annually to an outstanding humanistic scientist or artist, which had been bestowed upon him when the paralyzing illness struck. Styron recounts his bizarre behavior in Paris upon receiving the award, and only when he hears himself blurt out the words—"I'm sick . . . *un problème psychiatrique"* — does he overcome the "smug belief in the impregnability of my psychic health" (15).

Styron records the other symptoms of depression eroding his will to live: a growing hypochondria, including "twitches and pains, sometimes intermittent, often seemingly constant, that seemed to presage all sorts of dire infirmities" (*Darkness Visible* 43–44); exhaustion combined with sleeplessness, producing a "rare torture" (48); the loss of libido and an indifference to food; and a growing obsession with suicide, to the point that he felt compelled to revise his will and pen a farewell note — a task the novelist was unable to execute. "It turned out that putting together a suicide note, which I felt obsessed with a necessity to compose, was the most difficult task of writing that I had ever tackled" (65). He finally had to abandon the effort because he was unable to reconcile the intention to maintain the "sheer dirgelike solemnity" of the suicide letter with the melodramatic words he heard himself contrive. He also describes a phenomenon experienced by other people suffering from severe depression, the "sense of being accompanied by a second self — a wraithlike observer who, not sharing the dementia of his double, is able to watch with dispassionate curiosity as his companion struggles against the oncoming disaster, or decides to embrace it" (64).

Styron's depression was not of the manic type, associated with euphoric highs, but of the unipolar form, leading straight down into an abyss. The two physical factors that contributed most to the onset of the illness were fits of anxiety resulting from his body's sudden intolerance to alcohol, a substance that had been abusing his body for forty years, and a dangerous dependency upon Halcion, a tranquilizer prescribed to him for insomnia by a physician who was unaware that it could precipitate a major depression, especially in the heavy doses he recommended.

Styron has few good words for the psychiatrists who treated him before and during his six-week stay at Yale–New Haven hospital. The physician he sardonically calls "Dr. Gold" spoke with the dry platitudes of the *Diagnostic and Statistical Manual of Mental Disorders*, the psychiatric reference work that Styron himself read, during the early stages of the illness, in an unsuccessful effort to cure himself. Dr. Gold prescribed antidepressants that did nothing to lessen Styron's pain. When the illness progressed to the point that the novelist feared committing suicide, the psychiatrist remained reluctant to hospitalize him because of the "stigma" involved—an attitude Styron finds appalling. He encountered in the hospital an "odiously smug young shrink, with a spade-shaped dark beard *(der junge Freud?)*" (*Darkness Visible* 73), who used group therapy to belittle and bully his patients. None of this speaks well for psychiatrists who, in Styron's view, as in Virginia Woolf's, rarely empathize with a mentally ill person. Styron concedes that although pharmacology and psychotherapy can help many patients, neither was able to arrest his descent into hell. The real healers for him, as for Virginia Woolf, were the hospital environment—with its enforced safety, solitude, and stability—and time. After his release from the hospital, the love and support he received from his family, particularly his wife, Rose, were also invaluable.

Styron insists that despite the effort to understand the origins of depression, the illness remains beyond comprehension. "I shall never learn what 'caused' my depression, as no one will ever learn about their own" (*Darkness Visible* 38). Acknowledging that there were probably multiple causes, he singles out one psychological factor that may inhere in all cases of depression, namely, loss, particularly if it is followed by incomplete mourning. As we have seen, childhood loss and incomplete mourning played a decisive role in the life and art of Virginia Woolf, Ernest Hemingway, Sylvia Plath, and Anne Sexton. In Styron's case, childhood loss led to a more massive loss of self in later life, resulting in dependency, infantile dread, and fear of abandonment. He mentions tersely two crucial childhood losses in his own life: the early hospitalization of his father, who battled the gorgon of depression for much of his life, and the death of his mother when he was thirteen, an event with which he had never come to terms.

"The Landscape of Depression"

An "autodidact in medicine" for much of his life, Styron was surprised to learn upon falling ill that he was "close to a total ignoramus about depression" despite the later realization that he was probably always an "incipient depressive" (*Darkness Visible* 9). "Until the onslaught of my own illness and its denouement, I never gave much thought to my work in terms of its connection with the subconscious—an area of investigation belonging to literary detectives" (78). Styron was astonished to discover after recovering from his illness that his novels had long foreshadowed his suicidal obsession:

> Suicide has been a persistent theme in my books—three of my major characters killed themselves. In rereading, for the first time in years, sequences from my novels—passages where my heroines have lurched down pathways toward doom—I was stunned to perceive how accurately I had created the landscape of depression in the minds of these young women, describing with what could only be instinct, out of a subconscious already roiled by disturbances of mood, the psychic imbalance that led them to destruction. (78–79)

The landscape of depression dominates Styron's earliest novel, *Lie Down in Darkness* (1951), and constitutes the psychic setting of his later novels, including *Set This House on Fire* (1960), *The Confessions of Nat Turner* (1967), and *Sophie's Choice* (1979). Styron mentions that three of his major characters commit suicide; others, including Cass Kinsolving, the tormented hero of *Set This House on Fire*, remain obsessed with self-destruction. Like Woolf, Hemingway, Plath, and Sexton, Styron has remained preoccupied with suicide from the beginning of his writing career, and no less than theirs, his artistic interest in the subject arises from his own inner conflicts. To observe this is not to imply that Styron will share the fates of these writers. As he points out in *Darkness Visible*, "one need not sound the false or inspirational note to stress the truth that depression is not the soul's annihilation; men and women who have recovered from the disease—and they are countless—bear witness to what is probably its only saving grace: it is conquerable" (84).

Lie Down in Darkness

Reading *Lie Down in Darkness* in the light of *Darkness Visible,* one is struck by the extent to which Styron's fictional characters anticipate the symptoms of clinical depression that he himself writes about nearly four decades later in his memoir of madness: gloom, dread, alienation, confusion, panic, memory loss, drug and alcohol addiction, hypochondria. Characters are driven in despair to physicians and analysts who, like Drs. Holmes and Bradshaw in *Mrs. Dalloway,* offer maddening platitudes and glib diagnoses rather than insight and compassion. Before the novel's heroine jumps to her death from the twelfth story of a Harlem building, she is oppressed by the same feelings of self-loathing, dependency, and abandonment that Styron writes about in *Darkness Visible*. Moreover, she dwells morbidly upon all the losses in her life; describes the torment of mental illness in ways that are most closely connected to drowning and suffocation; and, perhaps most striking of all, experiences in the final hours of her life the same wraithlike observer that her creator personally experienced thirty-five years later. The landscape of depression in *Lie Down in Darkness* does not prefigure the psychic scenery of *Darkness Visible* in every detail, but the similarities are uncanny.

Lie Down in Darkness chronicles an American family's inexorable drift toward madness and self-destruction. Milton Loftis is a Virginia attorney in his fifties who is devastated by the suicide of his beloved daughter Peyton. His wife, Helen, is a nervous, straitlaced woman whose frail health collapses as a result of the earlier death of her older daughter Maudie, born with severe physical and mental disabilities. Maudie's death deepens Helen's bitterness toward life, producing a black depression from which she never recovers. Nor does Loftis psychically recover from Peyton's death. While neither Loftis, Helen, nor Peyton bears a precise resemblance to the portrait of clinical depression Styron presents in *Darkness Visible*, they experience collectively nearly all the symptoms of their creator's mind-numbing descent into mental illness.

Lie Down in Darkness begins in August 1945, immediately after the atomic bombing of Japan, but for Milton Loftis a more catastrophic event has occurred. The novel opens with a train carrying Peyton's coffin home to Port Warwick, Virginia, where her parents await its arrival. Juxtaposing past and present, Styron uses flashbacks, interior monologues, and in Peyton's final fifty-page section, first-person stream of consciousness prose to illuminate the family tragedy. Loftis cannot defend himself against the "bewildering sorrow" of Peyton's loss. "Yesterday he had been happy, but this sorrow—descending upon him as it had the night before—seemed to have confounded him beyond all hope, since, for the first time in his life, he was unable to cut his trouble adrift, to shed it like some startling and unwelcome chrysalis, and finally to explain it away as 'one of those things'" (10). Styron emphasizes the numbing, paralyzing, bewildering nature of sorrow: it is not a passive but an active adversary, a force that seizes control of body and spirit and overpowers the will to live.

Loftis does not seem to be constitutionally predisposed to mental illness, as Helen is, but he finds himself confronting depression whenever he dwells upon the losses in his life. Even before Peyton's death, Loftis dwells morbidly upon loss. He recalls the "fog of hostility" hanging over the entire family during Christmas dinner the year Peyton was eighteen, and this memory evokes earlier holiday celebrations that were similarly grim. "A terrible melancholy seized him; his mind trembled upon loss, upon the sounds of ancient forgotten Christmases" (*Lie Down in Darkness* 159). The novel never clarifies these memories, which remain as mysterious and unsettling to us as they do to Loftis. In Styron's world, memory serves mainly as a brooding reminder of loss, and there is danger when his characters meditate on the past. Later, on Peyton's wedding day, Loftis feels "unbelievably depressed and neurotic" (257), yet he cannot explain why he feels this way. He knows only that the "unbearable depression" is destroying his life.

Helen Loftis's struggle against depression begins long before the deaths of her two children—her adored Maudie, whom she has always favored and fiercely protected, and Peyton, with whom she has fought bitterly her entire life. Even when the family is intact, Helen is a "hurt" and "neurotic" woman. Loftis finds "something still imposingly youthful about her in spite of everything—the complaints, the headaches, the moments of eerie and popeyed hysteria" (*Lie Down in Darkness* 88). Helen's psychological conflicts take the form of physical complaints, and she becomes as dependent upon sleeping pills as her husband is on alcohol. In her bitterness toward those whom she views as betraying her, she becomes, in the words of one character, a "*nest* of little hatreds" (105). Not that Helen lacks reasons to be disappointed with life. Her husband's womanizing and alcoholism distress her, as does his capacity for self-indulgence and rationalization; Maudie's disabilities fill Helen with sorrow and guilt; and Peyton's intimacy with her father fuels Helen's jealousy and anger.

Helen's only passion in life is Maudie, who remains childlike and passive until her death at the age of twenty from tuberculosis. By favoring Maudie over Peyton, Helen reveals her preference for dependence over independence, compliance over rebellion, control over freedom. In contrast to the saintly Maudie, who resembles the severely retarded Benjy in William Faulkner's *The Sound and the Fury*, Peyton is self-centered, willful, solipsistic. Peyton is not, however, the "little devil!" that her mother viciously calls her (58). Helen's criticisms of Peyton are unrelenting. She cannot forgive Peyton for dropping Maudie as a child, even though Maudie herself does not hold her sister responsible, and despite the absence of clear evidence that Peyton intended the accident. Peyton remains throughout the novel the target for her mother's pent-up anger.

"There's Something Wrong with You Beyond Curing"

"God help me please, I'm going crazy" (*Lie Down in Darkness* 124), the panic-stricken Helen thinks to herself after Maudie's injury, acknowledging for the first time her fear of madness. She momentarily considers swallowing ten or fifteen nembutal pills but rejects the idea as hateful. "[T]he whole idea of insanity was forgotten as too difficult and too gross a thing to contemplate for more than an instant" (124). Helen's mental health continues to deteriorate, producing a cancerous religiosity that sees sin and damnation everywhere. Maudie's death shatters Helen's life, resulting in loss of religious faith and deepening hatred toward Peyton. Helen's inability to create a meaningful life, given the bright future that her privileged background presaged, also contributes to her depression. She sinks into suicidal despair and swallows an overdose of pills; her last thought before drifting into unconsciousness is a mysterious, whispered apology to her father, a West Point officer who died years ago.

Loftis saves Helen from death but cannot rescue her from the wild paranoia engulfing her life. Her dreams become "crowded with enemies, dreams bizarre and frantic, villainous beyond men's wildest imaginings" (*Lie Down in Darkness* 283). The most striking symptom of Helen's paranoia is the split between her idealization of Maudie and her virulent devaluation of Peyton; she elevates the former into an angel and casts off the latter as a devil. The tension between idealization and devaluation suggests Helen's inability to integrate love and hate, her failure to acknowledge the massive ambivalence she feels toward her family. Her condemnation of Peyton exceeds anything her daughter deserves, and the accusation that Peyton has "half-killed her own sister through negligence — did kill her in fact, she let Maudie fall!" reveals the irrationality of Helen's thoughts (286). Peyton expresses to her mother during their last exchange what is surely the authorial point of view: "You know, I suspect you've always hated me for one thing or another, but lately I've become a symbol to you you couldn't stand," adding, "the terrible thing is that you hate yourself so much that you just don't hate men or Daddy but you hate everything, animal, vegetable and mineral" (297–98).

Carey Carr, the Episcopal minister to whom Helen unburdens herself, recognizes that she is consumed by hatred and guilt. He tells her, significantly, that she suffers from low self-esteem and that she must love herself before she can love other people. He also suspects that Helen's obsession with evil is the result of infantile emotions rigidly repressed. Priding himself on his intuitive understanding of psychology and his advocacy of free inquiry, he scorns less liberal American religious movements because of their tendency to invoke the devil as a scapegoat for disowned sexual and aggressive drives. He welcomes the opportunity to counsel Helen, flattered by her willingness to allow him to be her minister and analyst. Like a therapist, he encourages Helen to share her feelings with him, repeats her statements back to her, and reassures her that everyone has shameful thoughts.

As Helen's visits increase, however, Carey becomes annoyed by her growing dependency upon him. His tangled erotic feelings toward her prevent him from maintaining the healthy professional distance necessary for a minister or therapist. The projection of his unconscious feelings onto others makes him an ineffective counselor. His hostility toward psychiatry also emerges. "He thought that he was enlightened, and he wanted to be, but this business of psychology and such matters was to him maddening and strange: that so potentially strong an ally should still possess no real Godhead and be so indecently inquisitive and expensive, and have no respect for the tender and infinite mutations of the heart" (*Lie Down in Darkness* 135). His depression over Peyton's suicide momentarily shatters his faith, almost resulting in apostasy. Two years earlier, during Peyton's wedding, Carey is so unnerved by Helen's paranoid actions that he loses patience and verbally attacks her: "I think you're a very sick woman. I don't know whether it's proper to call a spade a spade in such a case, but you asked me. There's something wrong with you beyond curing, beyond anything I can do, anyway" (281). He thus implicitly acknowledges his failure as Helen's minister and analyst.

Carey Carr is one of Styron's many ineffectual ministers, physicians, and therapists. Styron's "healers" are naive, insincere, glib, and pietistic. They are driven to cure others in an effort to cure themselves, a motive that Styron satirizes in *Lie Down in Darkness*. As a youth, Carey Carr was overly sensitive and unsure of his masculinity, and he exhausted himself by writing hundreds of sonnets that he knew were miserably bad. Writing brought no relief to Carr, as it does to Stingo in *Sophie's Choice*, and his mother hurried him to a sanitarium following his nervous breakdown. He later entered a seminary upon her prompting and emerged a changed man: "He had put on thirty pounds and through a violent struggle had learned how to swim and play softball, and had in general cast out his womanish failings" (100).

The minister's passion to save Helen from religious despair derives as much from his own incomplete relationship to God, along with unanalyzed egotism and eroticism, as from the need to offer a helping hand. He is disappointed that Helen's temporary recovery after Maudie's death is due to Loftis's decision to abstain from drinking rather than to his own powers of religious salvation. Unable finally to understand or empathize with Helen, Carey Carr is the first of many members of the helping professions whom Styron depicts in his writings. Because Loftis, too, fails in his efforts to "cure" Helen, to "make her well" (97), Styron suggests that recovery can come only from within.

Like her mother, Peyton Loftis proves to be beyond cure or redemption. The two-page suicide letter she writes to her father on her twenty-second birthday gives us a few clues into her state of mind. Beginning the letter "Dearest Bunny," a name, we later find out, that her great-grandmother used to call him, Peyton tells her father how much she misses him now that she is living in New York City and is estranged from her husband, Harry Miller. "After you've lived with someone for a time it leaves a huge gap in your life when they're gone" (*Lie Down in Darkness* 34). She recounts to Loftis her growing sleeplessness and morbid thoughts: "They've just started lately it seems. I've had these moments before, but never for so long—and they're absolutely terrible. The trouble is that they don't—these thoughts—seem to have any distinctness or real point of reference. It's more like some sort of black, terrible mistiness like the beginning of a disease, the way you know you feel when you're catching the flu" (35).

Peyton compares her illness to a physical disease, yet her language, both here and in the convoluted stream of consciousness interior monologue at the end of the novel, evokes a symptomatology startlingly similar to Styron's description of clinical depression in *Darkness Visible*: sleeplessness, loss of mental clarity, panic, and most striking of all, a sense of drowning. The rebirth imagery associated with Edna's movement toward the sea in *The Awakening* is absent from Peyton's feeling of drowning. "I feel adrift, as if I were drowning out in dark space somewhere without anything to pull me back to earth again. You'd think that feeling would be nice — drowning like that — but it isn't. It's terrible" (*Lie Down in Darkness* 35). She refers in the same letter to the "absolute panic" upon seeing her husband and the feeling that "something terrible is happening to me" (36). The letter reveals Peyton's other preoccupations that become more evident later in the novel: an enigmatic reference to an alarm clock she has bought recently, a symbol of her desperate need for order, unity, and perfection; the belief that she has been unkind to the people in her life, whom she fears have now abandoned her; and her growing obsession with death. "I think of Maudie. Why did she have to die? Why do we have to die?" (36). Loftis cannot finish the letter because "it all became so crazy and confused" (36).

Until Peyton's final monologue, we see only isolated glimpses of her, often from her father's point of view as he agonizes over her death. One of Loftis's earliest recollections is hearing a small voice announce passionately, on a dewy spring morning, "Daddy, Daddy, I'm beautiful!" He stares at his nine-year-old daughter who is standing in the grass, gazing into a little mirror and exclaiming: "I'm beautiful, Daddy!" He picks up the budding Narcissus and, "with a sudden, almost savage upwelling of love," presses her against him and murmurs, in a voice choked with desire: "'*Yes*, my baby's beautiful,' with wonder and vague embarrassment paying homage to this beautiful part of him, in which life would continue limitlessly" (*Lie Down in Darkness* 42). Loftis recalls another incident, one Christmas morning nine years later, when he tiptoes into the room where Peyton is sleeping, rouses her with a kiss, spanks her across the bottom, and asks: "Who do you love?" — to which she replies, "Me" (155).

"A Freudian Attachment"

Styron's suggestion in *Darkness Visible* that depression usually originates from childhood loss leads us to Peyton's own childhood, where we encounter severe Oedipal and pre-Oedipal conflicts. *Lie Down in Darkness* contains one of the most striking Oedipal father-daughter relationships in twentieth-century American fiction. Loftis loves Peyton more than anyone else in his life, and he is always kissing, fondling, or gazing at her as if she were a lover instead of a daughter. Judging from the way he embraces Peyton on her wedding day, one might conclude that he is the aroused groom: "He shoved the book away and swept her up toward him, laughing, kissing her helplessly. She lay tender and unresisting against his shoulder; he breathed the perfume in her hair, and was stricken by beauty at the sight of a gardenia pinned there, nestling just beneath his left eye. 'Bunny,' she said finally, pushing away from him, 'you are such a demonstrative old bum. Come on, quit it now. I've got lipstick on your neck'" (249).

Peyton's response to her father's overwhelming desire for her is contradictory. At times, she is embarrassed by her father's advances and pushes him away. It is harder for her to separate herself from him when he is drinking, when his lust for her becomes almost uncontrollable. After the wedding is over and Peyton prepares to leave with her husband for New York City, Loftis, driven by mad desire and sodden despair, makes one last effort to cling to her. "He bent down to kiss her. She didn't move when he kissed her cheek, her ear, her hair. He kissed her on the mouth. 'Don't—' she whispered, pushing him away" (*Lie Down in Darkness* 299). At other times, Peyton encourages her father's erotic advances in order to manipulate him into giving in to her wishes, as when she succeeds in getting him to buy her a car on her sixteenth birthday. "'Come on, honey, buy me a car.' She pressed a big smear of lipstick on his neck" (90). He himself believes that it was "unfair of Peyton to seduce him" (252) into giving her on her wedding day a half-pint of whisky he had secretly stored in a cough syrup bottle sometime after Maudie's death eight months before, when he decided to give up drinking. Unable to resist Peyton's request for whisky, he begins drinking again at the wedding—with disastrous results, since his body has grown intolerant to alcohol.

Loftis cannot take his eyes off his daughter's body during the wedding ceremony. "Peyton's dress was drawn tightly against her hips; he could see them, the two crescent shadows that a tight girdle makes when you look at a woman's behind, joining above like a curved Dutch roof: it was too obvious, or something; she should have dressed more demurely" (*Lie Down in Darkness* 257). The more the father pursues her, the more the daughter recoils. "Please don't smother me," she tells him crossly, "just don't *smother* me, Bunny!" adding: "You'd love me half to death if you could" (254–55). Helen overhears Peyton's rebuke of Loftis and, in a fit of insane jealousy and rage, accuses her of being a "shameless little seducer" (286).

Threatened by Peyton's beauty, youth, and intimacy with her father, Helen has long seen her daughter as a seductress. Peyton is indeed manipulative at times, but Helen is blind to her husband's aggressive pursuit of her. The father's incestuous attraction to his daughter is hinted at earlier in the story when Loftis, in response to Peyton being "pinned" to Dick Cartwright, gives her his University of Virginia ring, as if he were the betrothed. "Look at Daddy, I love him so," Peyton later tells her ex-boyfriend. "'But he lost me and he doesn't even know it.' She took the ring out of her pocket and looked down at it. 'The dear. I think we've got a Freudian attachment'" (*Lie Down in Darkness* 224). Loftis has invoked the same psychoanalytic theory to explain the intense family dynamics; earlier in the novel, his mistress Dolly Bonner ruminates over the family tragedy and recalls something he once told her: *"It's somehow Freudian, he says"* (71).

It is impossible to know precisely whether Loftis and Peyton have actually committed incest together and, if so, the circumstances. There are moments in the novel when both characters brood darkly over a distant memory involving the other, the language intimating each time an erotic encounter. Loftis recalls walking one summer day with his young daughter to a church, where they climb the creaking stairs and stand at the belfry door. Suddenly the church bells begin to chime, deafening them, and the frightened Peyton bursts into tears and clings to her father. The intensity of his desire for her would hardly be reassuring to a young girl:

> He smooths dust from her skirt, saying, "Peyton, don't be scared," and then kisses her. The weeping stops. Beneath his cheek he can feel cool, tiny beads of sweat on her brow.
>
> He doesn't know why his heart pounds so nor, when he kisses her again, in an agony of love, why she should push him so violently away with her warm small hands. (*Lie Down in Darkness* 277)

In an even murkier passage describing Peyton's wedding, Loftis gazes at his daughter's body, closes his eyes, and recalls an ancient memory so horrifying in its animality that he is forced to break off the thought and return to a safer object of his lust, his mistress Dolly:

> He let his eyes close, began to perspire, and thought of the blessed release whisky might give. Yet it was not only this; his eyelids slid open, he saw Peyton, those solid curved hips trembling ever so faintly; he thought desperately, hopelessly, of something he could not admit to himself, but did: of now being above—most animal and horrid, but loving—someone young and dear that

he had loved ever since he was child enough to love the face of woman and the flesh, too. Yes, dear God, he thought (and he thought *dear God, what am I thinking?*) the flesh, too, the wet hot flesh, straining like a beautiful, bloody savage. He thought vaguely of Dolly, wondering why she was not here. (258)

Whatever the meaning of this passage, Loftis is consumed by dark desire for his daughter, and she too is tormented by an ancient memory involving her father. She recalls toward the end of her monologue a fierce battle with her husband over her repeated sexual infidelities with men whom she meets on the street. As she tries to tell Harry that she has derived no joy from the sordid affairs that bring only pain and humiliation, her mind travels back beyond "dreaming or memory" to dwell upon a terrifying memory in which she hears herself pulling away from her father and crying out the word "no":

> [C]ouldn't he see, couldn't I convince him of, instead of joy, my agony when I lay down with all the other hostile men, the gin and the guilt, the feathers that rustled in the darkness, my drowning? Then I would say: oh, my Harry, my lost sweet Harry, I have not fornicated in the darkness because I wanted to but because I was punishing myself for punishing you: yet something far past dreaming or memory, and darker than either, impels me, and you do not know, for once I awoke, half-sleeping, and pulled away. "No, Bunny," I said. That fright. (*Lie Down in Darkness* 359)

New evidence that Milton Loftis and Peyton may have attempted or committed incest appears in the publication of *Inheritance of Night*, the unfinished predecessor of *Lie Down in Darkness*. Peyton's childhood classmate Marcus Bonner is "filled with an enormous contempt" toward Milton as a result of something Peyton had told Bonner "one night in New York in a fury of grief and drunkenness." Peyton confessed "things he refused to believe until later when, carefully retrieving in his memory all those curious and unnamed gestures of the past, he came to know that the things she told him were true indeed" (*Inheritance of Night* 41). James L. W. West III, the editor of *Inheritance of Night*, concludes from these statements that Peyton "had told Marcus of some kind of incestuous relationship between herself and her father—whether sexually consummated or not, one cannot tell from the surviving drafts" (xiv). West suggests additionally that this incestuous element may have been omitted from Peyton's final monologue in *Lie Down in Darkness* at the insistence of Styron's publisher, Bobbs-Merrill.

Fright motivates Peyton to visit Newark psychiatrist Dr. Irving Strassman. She has expressed interest in psychoanalysis, confiding to Harry that "[m]aybe I need to be analyzed" (*Lie Down in Darkness* 315), yet she is immediately hostile to Strassman. "I don't think I like you," she tells him, "I think I'm more intelligent than you." Strassman is no less insulting: "Perhaps so, but certainly less stable" (330). The therapy never progresses beyond this impasse: Peyton is a recalcitrant patient; Strassman, an antagonistic analyst. Like Dr. Gold in *Darkness Visible*, Dr. Strassman reflects Styron's belief that psychiatrists are ineffectual and unimaginative. "Be calm. Be calm" (329), Strassman blandly tells his patient and then labels her "dangerously abstracted" (330), a term she mockingly repeats to herself. When Peyton offers a promising clue to her illness — "all hope lies beyond memory, back in the slick dark womb" — Dr. Strassman responds dismissively: "That's what I mean, your abstraction" (355). Peyton concludes that he cannot help her and breaks off therapy.

Peyton's suicide seems motivated primarily by the wish for self-punishment. She comes to accept Helen's accusations that she has tried to harm Maudie — Peyton's sororal guilt is excruciating. Helen brings up this incident several times in the story, always with the intention to hurt her daughter. Peyton repeats her mother's accusation to Strassman, who inexplicably refuses to pursue it. Peyton's suicide is symbolic murder of the (m)other and accomplishes several goals: it confirms Helen's judgment that her daughter is unfit to live, symbolically destroys the mother who has rejected her, and represents the ultimate self-punishment for harboring matricidal feelings.

Had Dr. Strassman read Freud's "Mourning and Melancholia" (1917), he would also have recognized the relationship between Peyton's depression and object loss. "The distinguishing mental features of melancholia," Freud writes, "are a profoundly painful dejection, cessation of interest in the outside world, loss of the capacity to love, inhibition of all activity, and a lowering of the self-regarding feelings to a degree that finds utterance in self-reproaches and self-revilings, and culminates in a delusional expectation of punishment" (244). These symptoms unerringly characterize Peyton's illness. Her need for self-punishment is so intense that near the end of her monologue she imagines her head on an executioner's block.

Peyton's suicide is also a response to her tangled feelings toward her father. If, as seems likely, father and daughter committed incest in the distant past, we can understand Peyton's sexual acting out and frigidity, her need to punish herself masochistically by entering into affairs with men who reinforce her feelings of self-loathing. Childhood incest casts light on other shadowy aspects of Peyton's life: her fixation on a past memory she can neither remember nor forget; the repeated flashbacks involving her father, ending in her anxious "no!"; the emotional instability, panic attacks, promiscuity, and self-hatred accompanying her relationship with men; the fear that she is pursued by angry, stinging bees, a recurrent image that may be a displacement of her relentlessly pursuing phallic father; and the ever-present pains in her womb, a physical and psychic reminder of the fear and revulsion engendered by a shameful act.

There may also be a connection between the clock Peyton carries around with her everywhere during her last days and the pains in her womb, reflecting sexual revulsion. Freud argues in the *Introductory Lectures on Psycho-Analysis* that clocks and watches often symbolize in dreams menstruation and other periodic biological processes (266). Guilt arising from incest is a primary source of Peyton's physical and psychological suffering. Smashing the clock moments prior to her suicide may symbolize the wish to escape from the biological and temporal rhythms of existence. The clock is also, as James Nashold has observed, a "place of refuge from Peyton's world of pain, existing beyond time, place, and space, and represents a place of psychical refuge and sanctuary" (personal communication, 9 December 1997).

Additionally, although the term was not in existence when Styron was writing *Lie Down in Darkness*, many of Peyton's symptoms are similar to those of post-traumatic stress disorder, which is defined as a psychologically distressing event, outside the range of ordinary human experience, that produces recurrent and intrusive recollections of a traumatic incident, along with intense fear, terror, and helplessness. Peyton's flashbacks, horrified recollections of the past, sexual numbness, feelings of estrangement from others, and sense of a foreshortened future are all characteristic of this disorder.

Climbing the staircase of the Harlem building from which she leaps to her death, Peyton experiences an inner observer watching her every action. "I stood erect: Did I have a companion? I felt that someone was watching me, myself perhaps; at least I knew I was not alone" (*Lie Down in Darkness* 367). This wraithlike observer may be viewed, psychologically, as a form of splitting. John Maltsberger and Dan Buie theorize in their essay "The Devices of Suicide" that many self-inflicted deaths arise from a "hostile introject" or killer self that orders a person to die. This destructive introject is internalized within one part of the self and succeeds in persecuting the other part of the self. The hostile observer is experienced in less pathological states not as a killer self but as a chronically nagging conscience that makes relentlessly perfectionistic or omnipotent demands upon the self—a state of mind that Styron's major characters know all too well.

The description of Peyton's wraithlike observer unerringly foreshadows Styron's account of his own inner observer almost forty years later in *Darkness Visible*. Not that the author and his fictional character experience the identical depression: there is a manic quality to Peyton's interior monologue in *Lie Down in Darkness* that is absent from the gray landscape of depression in *Darkness Visible*. Peyton's monologue contains some of the most poetic descriptions of a suicidal consciousness found anywhere in literature. Her flight to oblivion recalls, in its lyricism and haunting birdlike imagery, Septimus Warren Smith's fatal plunge in *Mrs. Dalloway*. But whereas Septimus's death is motivated by the fear of being institutionalized by his medical-jailers Holmes and Sir William Bradshaw, Peyton's suicide seems to be caused by the desire to end her self-punishing guilt and to discover a more positive father surrogate of whom she has long been in pursuit. Peyton tells Harry that she has sinned "only in order to lie down in darkness and find, somewhere in the net of dreams, a new father, a new home" (*Lie Down in Darkness* 362).

Peyton is also in quest of a mother figure, a pre-Oedipal theme that has remained largely ignored by critics. Peyton has never had a loving, attentive mother; psychologically speaking, she was abandoned by Helen at birth. Maternal loss figures prominently in Peyton's depression along with Oedipal fixation. Ironically, Peyton is her mother's daughter: both women are incapable of loving others or themselves, are in precarious mental health, accuse their husbands of neglecting them, regard sex as a torture, and are governed by sinister moods they can neither understand nor control. "You're a Helen with her obsessions directed in a different way" (337), Harry tells her. Like her mother, Peyton has been searching for a rescuer.

"You left me just like you always do," she reproaches her husband. "When I needed you. *Why* didn't you come and rescue me?" (304).

We know from the beginning of *Lie Down in Darkness* that Peyton has committed suicide, and thus we are thrust into the position of helpless observers. The novel's suspense lies in discovering the reasons for her death and its impact on her family and friends. We see throughout the novel the devastating interpersonal consequences of suicide: Peyton's father remains deranged with grief, her mother embittered and withdrawn, her husband sick with sorrow. Walking along the mass graves at Potter's Field, Harry tells a grave-digger, "I could have stopped her"; moments later, his stomach churning, he thinks: *"I just don't know whose fault it is"* (318).

The history of the published criticism on *Lie Down in Darkness* reveals a growing tendency to heroicize Peyton's suicide. Richard Pearce suggests in his 1971 monograph that "Peyton's suicide ends with a note of resurrection" (17) but acknowledges that this is not in character for the unreligious young woman. Samuel Coale argues in his 1991 *William Styron Revisited* that while all the figures in the novel are cocooned, "Peyton's suicide seems a triumph, in that she ejects herself from this cocoon" (43). David Hadaller's 1996 book *Gynicide* offers the most affirmative reading of Peyton's suicide. Citing an observation by the feminist critic Dale Marie Bauer that "self-violence is a subversive strategy against a culture which has internalized violence," Hadaller claims that Peyton commits suicide "as a way of finalizing her desire to remain *unenclosed* by the language of the patriarchy" (76). The problem with these readings is that they ignore not only the jumbled thought processes contributing to Peyton's suicide but also her anguished cries for help. If we take Peyton's character seriously, we must acknowledge her terrifying psychotic depression. We may cite in this context Styron's observation in *Darkness Visible*: "To most of those who have experienced it, the horror of depression is so overwhelming as to be quite beyond expression, hence the frustrated sense of inadequacy found in the work of even the greatest artists" (83). To romanticize or rationalize an act that is the culmination of psychotic depression is as misguided as to judge or condemn it.

As *Lie Down in Darkness* closes, we are left with the image of a dead and dying family. Maudie and Peyton are in the earth, and Loftis and Helen are beyond recovery. Loftis becomes so enraged by Helen's refusal to take him back that he tries to choke her after Peyton's funeral; years later, Carey Carr cannot forget the sudden eruption of violence. The last few pages of the novel describe a black evangelical speaker named "Daddy Faith," a smiling, avuncular man who holds out the promise of everlasting peace to the mesmerized masses gathered for baptism. "Who loves you, my people?" he asks, to which they respond, "You, Daddy! Daddy Faith! You loves us! You, Daddy!" (378). As Marc Ratner has noted, Daddy Faith is a "showman, not a healer of souls" (52), and it is difficult to find convincing affirmation in the final pages of the novel.

A Mirror of Styron's Family Life

Styron stated in a 1982 interview in the *New York Times Book Review* that *Lie Down in Darkness* is a "mirror" of his early family life. Helen Loftis was modeled on his stepmother, "as close to the wicked stepmother image as one can possibly imagine," while Milton Loftis was modeled on his father: "The basic torment between Peyton and her family was really a projection of my own sense of alienation from my own tiny family — that is, my father, whom I really loved and this strange woman who had just come on the scene and who — I think I'm speaking as objectively as I can — was really trying to make my life a hell" (Styron, "Interview with William Styron" 26). Styron's other father figures, while more sympathetically portrayed than Milton Loftis, are cut from the same cloth as Styron's own father. Yet it is important to recognize, as John Kenny Crane does, that in each of Styron's major novels we see an admired father figure who, unlike Milton, "does not drink, does not do battle with a shrewish wife, does not flounder in self-pity and inertia" (117).

The shadowy figure in Styron's life whom future biographers will need to discuss is the absent mother, whose death was one of the crucial determinants of his later depression. Judith Ruderman notes that soon after the future novelist was born, Styron's mother developed cancer, underwent a series of operations, and remained bedridden for the rest of her life. Styron's portrait of Pauline Styron appears in "A Tidewater Morning," first published in *Esquire* in August 1987 and then republished along with two other semiautobiographical stories as a book of the same title in 1993. The story, which might be called more aptly "A Tidewater Mourning," describes a thirteen-year-old boy's grief as he watches his mother die, riddled with cancer. Her unbearable suffering visibly affects the father, but the son is also overwhelmed. One can imagine the physical and psychical toll on both father and son as they witnessed Pauline Styron slowly and painfully succumb to cancer. It seems probable that her illness produced in the boy a desire to rescue his mother from death; when the rescue fantasy ultimately failed, feelings of guilt and helplessness emerged. This may be one of the sources of the pervasive rescue fantasies of Styron's characters, who similarly fail to save loved ones from illness and death.

Set This House on Fire

"I've Got a Lust to Be Gone from This Place"

The landscape of depression haunts Styron's 1960 novel, *Set This House on Fire*. The main character in the story, set mostly in Italy, is Cass Kinsolving, a struggling alcoholic American painter who falls under the evil spell of the wealthy American playwright Mason Flagg. The story is narrated by an American lawyer named Peter Leverett. The plot centers on Flagg's rape of the thirteen-year-old Italian peasant girl Francesca and her brutal death. The sadistic Flagg controls Cass for most of the novel, but when the latter assumes that the former has slain the virginal Francesca, the outraged Cass bashes his skull and hurls his hated enemy off a steep precipice. It is not Flagg, however, but another man, a "village idiot," who has committed the murder. Upon discovering that he has executed the wrong person, Cass is prepared either to kill himself or to spend the rest of his life in prison, but he is befriended by an Italian policeman, Luigi Migliore, who convinces the authorities that Flagg's death is a suicide. The novel ends with Cass's repudiation of his lifelong death wish and his renewed commitment to life.

Set This House on Fire is a sprawling and sometimes melodramatic novel, but in light of Styron's comments in *Darkness Visible* about his lifelong tendency toward depression, it takes on new significance. Cass tells Leverett that one of the turning points in his life occurred when he was discharged from a California psychiatric hospital after World War II:

> There was this chief noodle specialist there—one hell of a guy. He was a Navy captain, name of Slotkin. I'd told him about my schoolboy interest in painting, and he got me in one of these therapy painting classes, and I reckon I was a painter from then on out. That's how I ended up after the war in New

York instead of back in Carolina, I guess. Anyway, we couldn't come to any agreement whatsoever about my melancholia or whatever it was, with its manic-depressive overtones, but I had a lot of long talks with him, and there was some patient gentle quality the guy had that almost swung me out of my blues, and just before I left the place—uncured—he gave me a two-volume edition of Greek drama. (129)

It is never precisely clear why Cass is so filled with self-loathing. Styron describes rather than analyzes this poisonous psychic phenomenon. Thus Cass records in his journal: "At least I understand the quality & the quantity of what I do possess which is a mysterious self-hatred so prideless & engulfing it would turn a Hitler or a Himmler purple with envy and which I at least understand enough to keep it (roughly speaking) within the bounds of reason" (293). Cass is tortured by dreams and fantasies of murdering his sleeping wife and family and then killing himself; when one of his children falls ill with scarlet fever and almost dies, he views it as God's punishment for his infanticidal thoughts. Styron does not glorify Cass's suicidal longings, but readers may grow weary of his drunken excesses and self-pity. Some of Cass's speeches seem bombastic, as when he exclaims to Leverett:

> "Yes, I'll tell you how you can help old Cass," he said somberly. "Now I'll tell you, my bleeding dark angel. Fetch him the machine, fetch him the wherewithal—a dagger, see, a dirk, well honed around the edges—and bring it here, and place it on his breastbone, and then with all your muscle drive it to the core." He paused, swaying lightly from side to side, never removing his gaze from my face. "No bullshit, Pete. I've got a lust to be gone from this place. Make me up a nice potion, see? Make it up out of all these bitter-tasting, deadly things and pour it down my gullet." (*Set This House on Fire* 238)

Apart from the plot's contrived double murder, Cass Kinsolving is an artist figure who closely resembles the novelist in several ways. Like Styron, Cass is born in the South in 1925 and serves in the U.S. Marines during World War II. He is blessed with prodigious creative talent and cursed with periodic artist's block. "Hell, I knew I could paint rings around anyone—at least of my own age and experience. Anyone! Yet in front of a sketch pad or a canvas I was like a man who had suddenly had both hands chopped off at the wrist. Completely paralyzed, I was" (*Set This House on Fire* 250). Additionally, both Cass and Styron share an almost spiritual devotion to classical music; an abiding love for serious literature, philosophy, and psychology; an ambivalence toward Freud; and the same ironic sensibility. Cass reports that while in Europe about half his nightmares involve Negroes waiting to be executed — a foreshadowing, perhaps, of Styron's next novel, *The Confessions of Nat Turner*. The anxiety and panic attacks Cass experiences prefigure those that Styron writes about in *Darkness Visible*. Styron's reading of the *Diagnostic and Statistical Manual of Mental Disorders* in an attempt to diagnose and heal himself has its counterpart in Cass's reading of the *Merck Manual of Diagnosis and Therapy* in an attempt to cure Francesca's dying father. Perhaps most intriguing of all, Styron's wraithlike observer appears in *Set This House on Fire*, as Cass admits in his journal: "What saves me in the last analysis I have no way of telling. Sometimes the sensation I have that I am 2 persons & by that I mean the man of my dreams & the man who walks in daylight is so strong and frightening that at times I am actually scared to look into a mirror for fear of seeing some face there that I have never seen before" (361).

The movement toward self-destruction in *Set This House on Fire* is opposed by a stronger movement toward self-preservation. Luigi, who is responsible not only for Cass's freedom from prison at the end of the novel but also for his redemption, observes authorially:

> I'm not a religious man . . . and this you well know. However, I studied among the humanist philosophers — the Frenchman Montaigne, Croce, the Greek Plato, not to speak, of course, of Gabriele D'Annunzio — and if there's one thing of the highest value I've discovered, it is simply this: that the primary moral sin is self-destruction — the wish for death which you so painfully and obviously manifest. I exclude madness, of course. The single good is respect for the force of life. (195)

Styron does not regard suicide as a moral sin, as Luigi does, but he endorses his policeman's words. (Luigi's fascist political views do not undercut his role as Cass's consultant in humanist philosophy and guardian angel.) Cass discovers, through Slotkin's wise counsel and Luigi's timely intervention, that acute self-loathing need not be terminal. Cass's murder of Mason Flagg is a crime for which he must repent the rest of his days, recognizing, as he does, that "to kill a man, even in hatred, even in revenge, is like an amputation. Though this man may have done you the foulest injustice in the world, when you have killed him you have removed a part of yourself, forever" (446).

Cass's destruction of Flagg, who in a Dostoevskian sense symbolizes his darker self, seems to release him from the virulent self-hatred poisoning his life. Some readers have been troubled by Cass's escape from punishment for his crime, but he has been ennobled through suffering and is prepared at the end to start life anew, purged of his toxic self-destructiveness. Cass's Kierkegaardian choice of being over nothingness underscores the novel's existentialist ending. Speaking from painful experience, Cass voices Styron's rejection of suicide: "'Suicide?' Cass put in. He removed the cigar from his teeth and squinted at me, making a thin smile. 'It does not take anything whatsoever, my friend. Maybe desperation. Guts is the last thing it takes.' He gazed at me, not without humor, shrewd, tugging gently at his line. 'It doesn't take courage, guts, or anything else. You're talking to a man that knows'" (49).

The Confessions of Nat Turner

Suicide does not appear explicitly in Styron's next novel, the Pulitzer Prize–winning *Confessions of Nat Turner* (1967). "I had never known of a Negro who had killed himself," Nat acknowledges in response to a slaveowner's statement, "and in trying to explain this fact I tended to believe (especially the more I examined the Bible and the teachings of the great Prophets) that in the face of such adversity it must be a Negro's Christian faith, his understanding of a kind of righteousness at the heart of suffering, and the will toward patience and forbearance in the knowledge of life everlasting, which swerved him away from the idea of self-destruction" (27). Yet Nat Turner may be viewed as a chronic suicide: one who engages in repetitive, risky behavior that ultimately results in his or her own death. "While Nat Turner did not commit suicide," Jim Nashold notes, "he was so deluded by his beliefs that he completely misread the social climate of slavery and was shocked when other slaves did not rise up with him to kill the white owners. Thus, despite overwhelming evidence against the chances of success with a slave revolt, Nat acted in such a way that not only caused his own death but the deaths of over two hundred other slaves killed in revenge after the failed revolt" (personal communication, 9 December 1997).

Sophie's Choice

Peyton, Sophie, and Maria Hunt

Suicide figures prominently in Styron's masterpiece, *Sophie's Choice*. The novel remained on the *New York Times* best-seller list for more than forty weeks and received in 1980 the first American Book Award for fiction.

Sophie's Choice is Styron's darkest and most autobiographical novel. The narrator Stingo is a portrait of the artist as a young man. Apart from having names that are near anagrams, both Styron and Stingo are born in Tidewater, Virginia, in 1925, lose their mothers at the age of thirteen, enlist in the U.S. Marines during World War II, after which they complete their education at Duke, work briefly for the publisher McGraw-Hill, write similar first novels based on their infatuation with a woman who commits suicide and a later novel about Nat Turner that provokes sharp controversy, and meet a Polish survivor of Auschwitz whose story they later immortalize. We see two Stingos, the callow youth who is self-centered and inexperienced in the 1940s, when the story takes place, and the older Stingo who narrates *Sophie's Choice* in the 1970s. The older Stingo regards his younger self with a mixture of affection and scorn. Styron constantly plays off the older narrator against his younger counterpart, as novelists often do in a bildungsroman. Styron forces his readers to revise their understanding of Sophie's and Stingo's complex and often confusing stories.

The inspiration behind Stingo's first novel *Inheritance of Night* (the early draft of *Lie Down in Darkness*) was a letter he received from his father in 1947 informing him of the recent death of a beautiful twenty-two-year-old woman, Maria Hunt, with whom Stingo had been hopelessly in love during his early adolescence. Styron describes this woman in his nonfictional *This Quiet Dust* (1982) as the "source of my earliest and most aching infatuation" (290). Maria Hunt killed herself, Stingo discovers, by leaping from the window of a Manhattan building. She came from a tragic household: her father was a "near-alcoholic and always at loose ends," and her mother was "pretty unremitting and cruel in her moral demands upon people," particularly upon her daughter (*Sophie's Choice* 44).

James West's new biography of Styron casts more light on the shadowy woman who served as the model for Maria Hunt. West notes that when Styron was fifteen years old, he became infatuated with a beautiful and popular teenager whose parents fought bitterly and finally divorced. Anna, as she is referred to in the biography, was psychologically unstable, as was her mother, who was institutionalized frequently for mental problems. Anna married a young naval officer, gave birth to a child, and then began suffering from postpartum depression. Her mental health soon deteriorated, and after attempting to drown her baby in a bathtub, she was committed to a Williamsburg state sanitarium, where her mother had been confined earlier. Of the several women who served as models for Peyton Loftis in *Lie Down in Darkness*, Anna was the "tragic source." Styron completed the novel before she was released, but then, in an eerie example of life imitating art, she committed suicide in late July 1951 by driving her automobile off a dock in Newport News. Styron's father, unaware that she served as the source for Peyton, sent his son a newspaper clipping of the bizarre suicide, which proved terribly upsetting to the novelist. "She had been alive during the time he was writing *Lie Down in Darkness*," West observes, "which concluded with the suicide of the fictional character based on her. Now she had killed herself. Had he predicted, in writing the novel, that Anna would take her own life? Or worse, had he somehow caused her to kill herself" (*William Styron* 201-02). Though Styron knew that he was not responsible for Anna's fate, her suicide became a troubling postscript to the publication of *Lie Down in Darkness*.

Maria Hunt's death gave birth not only to Peyton Loftis but to her other avatar, Sophie Zawistowska, who commits suicide with her psychotic lover Nathan Landau at the close of *Sophie's Choice*. Although Sophie was based on a Polish survivor of Auschwitz whom Styron knew briefly while living in New York City immediately after World War II, she also seemed to be an incarnation of Maria Hunt. "And what is still ineffaceable about my first glimpse" of Sophie, Stingo observes, "is not simply the lovely simulacrum she seemed to me of the dead girl but the despair on her face worn as Maria surely must have worn it, along with the premonitory, grieving shadows of someone hurtling headlong toward death" (46).

"Malignant Depression"

Sophie's life is a case study of what Stingo calls "malignant depression" (94). The word "guilt" dominates her vocabulary, guilt so pervasive that it recalls Little Father Time in Thomas Hardy's *Jude the Obscure*, the morbid boy who hangs himself and his younger half-brother and half-sister because of the conviction that the world would be better without them. *"Done because we are too menny"* (405), he scrawls in his suicide note. But whereas Father Time remains a two-dimensional character, illustrative of Hardy's Schopenhauerian belief in an impending universal death wish, the three-dimensional Sophie experiences a depression that arises from the most horrendous event in history.

Sophie is the daughter of a prominent anti-Semitic Polish professor, yet despite her family's position she and her two children are shipped to Auschwitz in 1943. Fiercely protective of her children, she encounters a sadistic doctor who forces her to make a horrifying choice: she must decide which child will live and which will perish in the gas chambers. It is, of course, an impossible choice, but one she must nevertheless make lest she lose both children. She chooses to save her son though he, too, later perishes. Sophie's guilt is so overwhelming that she cannot live with herself after surviving Auschwitz. She is sent to a Swedish displacement camp in 1945 where she tries to kill herself by cutting her wrist with a piece of glass. She chooses a church for the suicide in order to rage against God, who she believes has abandoned her. A more serious suicide attempt occurs when she tries to drown herself at Jones Beach shortly after Nathan forsakes her. Stingo rescues her, and after he drags her onto the beach she cries out, regurgitating half a gallon of seawater onto the sand, "Oh God . . . why didn't you let me die? Why didn't you let me drown? I've been so *bad*—I've been so awful bad! Why didn't you let me drown?" (364).

Sophie's feelings of "drowning" establish her kinship with Peyton Loftis. Their need for self-punishment arises from the fear that they have killed or injured a beloved daughter or sister. Each sees herself as abandoned by a lover or husband. Stingo has little sympathy for psychoanalysis, yet his interpretation of Sophie's unhealthy relationship with Nathan evokes contemporary attachment theory: "Her love for Nathan was so totally consuming, yet at the same time was defined by such childlike dependence in a hundred ways, that the terror that surrounded her in his unexplained absence was utterly demoralizing, like being caught in that strangling fear—the fear that she might be abandoned by her parents—which she had often felt as a little girl" (*Sophie's Choice* 318).

Sophie's farewell letter to Stingo conveys poignantly in broken English the depth of her self-loathing, her rage against God, and her wish to remain united with Nathan in life or in death:

> My dearest Stingo, your such a beautiful Lover I hate to leave and forgive me for not saying Good-Bye but I must go back to Nathan. Believe me you will find some wunderful Mademoiselle to make you happy on the Farm. I am so fond of you—you must not think bei this I am being cruel. But when I woke I was feeling so terrible and in Despair about Nathan, bei that I mean so filled with Gilt and thoughts of Death it was like Eis Ice flowing in my Blut. So I must be with Nathan again for whatever that mean. I may not see you again but do believe me how much knowing you have meaned to me. Your a great Lover Stingo. I feel so bad, I must go now. Forgive my poor englisch. I love Nathan but now feel this Hate of Life and God. FUCK God and all his Hande Werk. And Life too. And even what remain of Love. (*Sophie's Choice* 499–500)

Earlier in *Sophie's Choice* Nathan tells Stingo that the novel he admires above all others is *Madame Bovary*, not only because of its formal perfection but also because of its resolution of the suicide theme: "Emma's death by self-poisoning seeming to be so beautifully inevitable as to become one of the supreme emblems, in Western literature, of the human condition" (185). The same can be said about Styron's portrayal of suicide in *Sophie's Choice*. Without romanticizing the double suicide, Styron depicts the chain of events that leads inexorably to a horrifying conclusion. Sophie has symbolically died in Auschwitz's gas chambers years earlier, and the sodium cyanide she and Nathan swallow in their Brooklyn rooming house is the culmination of her obsession with death. Stingo has hinted repeatedly that Sophie's story will end tragically, and we are saddened but not shocked at her fate.

Does Sophie freely choose suicide, or is it thrust upon her by a deranged lover? The reader infers from her farewell letter to Stingo that she is prepared to accept whatever course of action Nathan decides. Sophie's rage toward God is evident in her letter, as is her belief that life no longer holds any meaning or value to her. Sophie presumably chooses suicide, for she knows that by returning to Nathan, her savior and destroyer, she may be required to carry out the suicide pact to which she has agreed in the past. Sophie makes two terrible choices, the first in Auschwitz, the second in Brooklyn, and in both cases she is swayed by the thinking of a man who is not in his right mind.

Unlike Sophie, whose violence is directed only against herself, Nathan's fury always threatens to destroy anyone in its path. Stingo remains oblivious to this violence in the beginning of the novel but soon recognizes Nathan's mad instability. Several times Nathan inexplicably turns against Stingo and verbally abuses him. Nathan's paranoid schizophrenia may have a biochemical component, but he also contains a characterological darkness that has moral as well as psychological dimensions. His monstrous hatred of non-Jews connects him to the Nazis he despises. Although Sophie agrees to the suicide pact, Nathan would have felt no hesitation in murdering her before killing himself. His sadistic violence is apparent when he beats her and urinates in her face during their weekend in Connecticut the previous autumn. Nathan's suicide pact with Sophie, enacted by swallowing the same form of cyanide poison used by officers like Hermann Göring to escape the Nuremberg Trials, identifies him with the final solution that the Nazis intended to impose upon the world.

Stingo's Rescue Fantasies

Stingo cannot prevent Sophie's suicide, just as earlier he is unable to avert Maria Hunt's suicide. "I pondered whether I might not have been able to save her, to prevent her from taking such a terrible course, had I only known of her existence in the city, and her whereabouts" (44). And yet Stingo can rescue them in another way, through the immortality of art. He resolves to write about Sophie's life, just as earlier he decides to write about Maria Hunt's, and while it takes him thirty years to complete the former's story, the result is Styron's magnificent *Sophie's Choice*. Stingo seems to be well suited for writing about Sophie, acknowledging that in his career as a writer he has "always been attracted to morbid themes — suicide, rape, murder, military life, marriage, slavery" (110). Apart from the wry inclusion of marriage in this list of violent subjects, Stingo is particularly drawn to characters whose crimes are ultimately beyond expiation.

Sophie's Choice is finally about Stingo's choice — his decision to devote more than a decade of his life to writing a single novel. He reveals a great deal about himself and his creator, including the extent to which early loss shapes the content of their art. The childhood incident that has the greatest formative impact on Stingo involves an unforgivable crime he committed against his mother when he was twelve, a year before her death. Stingo's mother suffers from terminal bone cancer and is confined to a bed or a chair, from which she passes the day reading. She is the same dying figure whom Styron later writes about in "A Tidewater Morning." Stingo's responsibility during the chilly winter months is to hurry home after school so that he can stoke the fireplace. He "abandons" her one particularly frigid afternoon by accepting a schoolmate's invitation to ride in his new Packard-Clipper. Stingo arrives home hours later, long after the fire died out, to find his father massaging his wife's numbed hands, both parents silently reproaching him. The father later marches his wayward son to the woodshed, where he receives his just deserts by shivering for the rest of the evening. Stingo recalls how he would have willingly frozen to death in order to expiate his heinous crime, one that was "ultimately beyond expiation, for in my mind it would inescapably and always be entangled in the sordid animal fact of my mother's death" (*Sophie's Choice* 297).

Daniel Ross's perceptive psychoanalytic interpretation of Stingo's dreams reveals that Styron's narrator is oppressed by guilt over the failure to rescue the three most important women in his life — his mother, Maria Hunt, and Sophie. The guilt is heightened by the fact that Stingo waits so long before he finally writes about the story that Sophie entrusted to him years earlier. "It is certainly a curious fact," Ross writes, "that a storyteller as gifted as he would withhold so dramatic a tale for a quarter of a century, especially when, as I have suggested, Sophie seems to have bequeathed the story to him as a special gift, the surviving offspring of their relationship." Stingo's narration evokes the "compulsive obsessiveness of the Ancient Mariner, insisting repeatedly on the necessity of speaking the unspeakable" (Ross 144–45).

"A Study in the Conquest of Grief"

Stingo's attitude toward suicide changes in the course of the novel. In the beginning, he recalls his brief career as a junior editor at McGraw-Hill and his dismay over the sentimental or juvenile manuscripts that he had to evaluate for publication. He cites a letter from a desperate author whose manuscript has been rejected by several publishers. To the author's veiled threat of suicide should her manuscript be rejected again, Stingo writes in his reader's report: "I should hate to be responsible for anyone's death but it is absolutely imperative that this book never be published. *Decline!*

(Why do I have to keep reading such shit?)" (Sophie's Choice 7). Stingo's supercilious response slowly gives way to empathy when he reflects upon Maria Hunt's life. He asks himself: "Would I be able to summon the passion, the insight to portray this young suicide? Could I make it all seem *real?"* (449). Stingo never seriously doubts his ability to capture Maria Hunt's and Sophie's stories. His task as a novelist is complicated by the fact that he is both an observer of and participant in Sophie's history.

Sophie's Choice is a more compassionate novel than *Lie Down in Darkness.* Styron's narrator is older, wiser, and more vulnerable. Suffering has expanded his vision. Not since the death of his mother has he allowed himself to cry, but on the last pages of *Sophie's Choice* Stingo breaks down and weeps, an act that allows him to purge his rage and sorrow. The final entries, which he describes as "A Study in the Conquest of Grief" (508), represent both his cathartic outpouring of emotion and his decision to re-create the story of all the doomed characters in his life. Stingo mourns not only Sophie's and Nathan's deaths but also Maria Hunt's and Nat Turner's. These characters will live forever in the novelist's imagination—and in his reader's as well.

"My Writing Had Kept Serious Emotional Distress Safely at Bay"

Writing serves multiple purposes for Stingo, enabling him to memorialize lost friends and to cast light on two subjects about which it is nearly impossible to write: the Holocaust, with its unspeakable crimes against humanity, and depression, which Styron calls in *Darkness Visible* a "simulacrum of all the evil of our world" (83). Writing also allows Stingo to ward off his own demons. "[M]y writing had kept serious emotional distress safely at bay, in the sense that the novel I was working on served as a cathartic instrument through which I was able to discharge on paper many of my more vexing tensions and miseries" (*Sophie's Choice* 438).

For a writer who has long mistrusted psychoanalysis, and who has satirized the spirit of Freudianism in *Lie Down in Darkness* and *Sophie's Choice,* Styron surprisingly believes in the writing cure. "When I'm writing," he declares in his 1958 *Paris Review* interview, "I find it's the only time that I feel completely self-possessed, even when the writing itself is not going too well. It's fine therapy for people who are perpetually scared of nameless threats as I am most of the time—for jittery people. Besides, I've discovered that when I'm not writing I'm prone to developing certain nervous tics, and hypochondria. Writing alleviates those quite a bit" (Cowley, *Writers at Work* 272). Styron adds in the same interview that while much of the morbidity and depression of modern life arises from the explosive increase of scientific knowledge of the self associated with Freudianism, the "good writing of any age has always been the product of *someone's* neurosis, and we'd have a mighty dull literature if all the writers that came along were a bunch of happy chuckleheads" (282).

Reading is also cathartic for Stingo. He remarks early in *Sophie's Choice* that when he was in his early twenties, "reading was still a passion and thus, save for a happy marriage, the best state possible in which to keep absolute loneliness at bay" (11–12). Nothing in the later pages of the novel undercuts or qualifies this affirmation. Stingo's observation about André Gide's diaries affirms the power of literature to change the writer's and reader's lives: "the more catastrophic the humiliation or the disappointment, I noted, the more cleansing and luminous became Gide's account in his *Journals*—a catharsis in which the reader, too, could participate" (173).

Styron's Heart of Darkness

Nowhere is the cathartic power of literature more evident than in *Darkness Visible*, where Styron does more than perhaps any other literary writer to educate readers about the reality of suicidal depression. *Darkness Visible* is an essential text for anyone seeking bibliotherapy. It is not a how-to book: there is none of the unrestrained theorizing or psychobabble that characterizes the vast popular literature on survival. Nor does the story offer false hope to the millions of people who suffer from mental illness. Styron's openness, insight, and wry humor in *Darkness Visible* enable readers to participate in his frightening descent into black depression— in Conradian terms, a journey to the heart of darkness—and to emerge slowly into the world of radiant light. In the process, we see the landscape of depression dissolving into a scene of renewal and rebirth.

The authenticity of *Darkness Visible* derives from Styron's ability to evoke through vivid details the commonalities of suicidal depression. He writes with the clinical detachment of a psychologist about his unbearable psychic pain, self-loathing, mental constriction, dichotomous thinking, isolation, helplessness, and longing for death. *Darkness Visible* abounds in Styron's self-deprecating humor, which allows us to see the tragicomic elements of the story. He describes his "better-than-average amateur's knowledge about medical matters" but then adds, parenthetically, that it is a knowledge "to which many of my friends, surely unwisely, have often deferred" (9). He observes that although Madame del Duca graciously accepted his psychiatric explanation of his bizarre behavior after the presentation ceremony, she probably still regarded him as a "weird number" (16). He uses the word "zombielike" to characterize his state of mind during the celebration dinner, when he lost the twenty-five-thousand-dollar del Duca prize check. The psychiatrist's warning that the antidepressant he is about to prescribe might result in impotence provokes this mordant sentence: "Putting myself in Dr. Gold's shoes, I wondered if he seriously thought that this juiceless and ravaged semi-invalid with the shuffle and the ancient wheeze woke up each morning from his Halcion sleep eager for carnal fun" (60).

Darkness Visible is about depression but never becomes depressing. Styron reminds his readers that just as he was able to survive a potentially fatal illness, so might others. There is nothing breezily optimistic about *Darkness Visible*; the hope Styron offers is hard earned. He is careful not to overgeneralize from his experience. He acknowledges that his suicidal depression was atypical; neither medication nor psychotherapy helped him, but he does not rule out their efficacy to others. He does not conceal his indignation toward "Dr. Gold" but refuses to condemn psychiatrists in general. At no time in *Darkness Visible* does Styron intimate, as both Kate Chopin and Virginia Woolf do, that suicide is an act of heroic defiance or transcendence. Nor does he stigmatize suicide, as Hemingway does. Styron would sympathize with the yearning for suicide in Sylvia Plath's and Anne Sexton's poetry but would also suggest that such desire should be resisted fiercely.

Styron is aware of the high suicide rate among artists and cites several who took their own lives, including Hart Crane, Randall Jarrell, Vincent van Gogh, Virginia Woolf, Arshile Gorky, Cesare Pavese, Romain Gary, Vachel Lindsay, Sylvia Plath, Henry de Montherlant, Mark Rothko, John Berryman, Jack London, Ernest Hemingway, William Inge, Diane Arbus, Tadeusz Borowski, Paul Celan, Anne Sexton, Sergei Esenin, and Vladimir Mayakovsky. He also mentions Abbie Hoffman and Primo Levi. Styron views these people as fallen comrades who deserve sympathy for the private horrors they were unable to endure.

"The Fundamental Question"

The artist about whom Styron writes at greatest length in *Darkness Visible* is not on the above list—Albert Camus. Styron's indebtedness to the French existentialist is well known. Styron stated in a 1963 letter to Pierre Brodin that "[o]f the moderns of any nationality, including the United States, Camus has had the largest effect upon my thinking, and I have valued the quality of his moral intensity more than anything I have found in any other contemporary" (qtd. in Ratner 136). Camus was a "great cleanser of my intellect," he declares in *Darkness Visible* (21). In Styron's judgment, Camus's *Myth of Sisyphus* contains the century's most famous pronouncement on suicide: "There is but one truly serious philosophical problem, and that is suicide. Judging whether life is or is not worth considering amounts to answering the fundamental question of philosophy" (qtd. in *Darkness Visible* 23).

Camus's death in a car accident in 1960, at the age of forty-six, horrified Styron. "I have almost never felt so intensely the loss of someone I didn't know" (*Darkness Visible* 22). Styron reflected on the death endlessly and began to suspect that although Camus had not been driving the death car, he must have known the driver was a "speed demon." Styron sensed "there was an element of recklessness in the accident that bore overtones of the near-suicidal, at least of a death flirtation" (*Darkness Visible* 22). The death reinforced Styron's earlier suspicion that Camus's rejection of suicide in *The Myth of Sisyphus* does not ring true. Roman Gary, who had tried to arrange a meeting between the two writers in 1960, later told Styron that Camus had hinted about being suicidal. Gary visited Styron in 1978, and the two men continued to discuss Camus's death. Gary was himself becoming depressed around this time. "He said that he was able to perceive a flicker of the desperate state of mind which had been described to him by Camus" (25). Gary's ex-wife, Jean Seberg, was also severely depressed. Styron reports that not long afterward she took a fatal overdose of pills and that in 1980 Gary shot himself in the head.

Styron's discussion of Camus and Gary is important because it suggests that their deaths seemed to heighten his risk of self-destruction. Styron does not explicitly invoke the contagion theory of suicide, but it may be inferred from *Darkness Visible*. Nor is this the first time that Styron has expressed interest in the contagion theory. His 1971 short story "Marriott, the Marine" contains an unexpected discussion of a little-known copycat suicide. Lt. Col. Paul Marriott of the U.S. Marine Corps speaks with the authority of a literary historian when he informs the narrator, himself a Flaubert votary, of the disturbing case of Eleanor Marx Aveling, the English translator of *Madame Bovary* and daughter of Karl Marx: "Yes, and another strange thing about her—she was rather badly unbalanced mentally and finally became totally obsessed by the life of Bovary, by the career of this woman she'd rendered into English. Finally she killed herself and in the identical manner of Emma Bovary—by taking poison. It's one of the most curious tales in the history of literature" ("Marriott, the Marine" 200).

It would be false to say that *Darkness Visible* reveals Styron's similar obsession with Camus's and Gary's deaths. Nevertheless, the subtext of his remarks suggests that Styron's deteriorating mental health in 1985 may have been further undermined by his identification with two admired writers whom he associated with suicide. Styron does not imply that Camus's premature death invalidates his rejection of suicide in *The Myth of Sisyphus*—Olivier Todd's new biography of Camus reveals nothing to indicate that he was depressed or suicidal near the end of his life—but Styron does intimate, as he describes his feelings leaving Paris in 1985, that his own fate seemed inextricably linked to Camus's. Paraphrasing his deceased mentor, Styron began to fear that "I would be forced to judge that life was not worth living and thereby answer, for myself at least, the fundamental question of philosophy" (*Darkness Visible* 28).

Styron's instincts as a writer prompted him to draft a suicide note, yet his failure to find the right words may have saved his life. The suicide note was the most difficult writing task of his life; there was something "almost comically offensive in the pomposity" of the sentence he intended to use as his final farewell: "For some time now I have sensed in my work a growing psychosis that is doubtless a reflection of the psychotic strain tainting my life" (*Darkness Visible* 65). Unaware that the sentence's lucidity disproved he was psychotic, the perfectionistic Styron tore up the suicide note and vowed to leave in silence. Fortunately, art came to his aid when he most needed it. As he prepared for his death, he happened to watch the tape of a film in which could be heard a soaring passage from Brahms's *Alto Rhapsody*. A lover of classic music his entire life, Styron had been numb to its pleasures for months, but when he heard the joyful sounds, which he recalls hearing his mother sing in his childhood, he realized he could not forsake art and life. The next day he hospitalized himself and began the healing process.

Styron pays tribute in *Darkness Visible* to a close friend, a "celebrated newspaper columnist," who was hospitalized for severe manic depression in the summer of 1985 and whose recovery, largely due to lithium and psychotherapy, inspired his own. "It was he who kept admonishing me that suicide was 'unacceptable' (he had been intensely suicidal), and it was also he who made the prospect of going to the hospital less fearsomely intimidating." Each writer became part of the other's support system. "The help he gave me, he later said, had been a continuing therapy for him, thus demonstrating that, if nothing else, the disease engenders lasting fellowship" (*Darkness Visible* 76–77).

Coming Out of the Closet

Styron's decision to write about his near-fatal psychiatric illness was both courageous and risky, involving not only the loss of his cherished privacy but also the stigma of being branded a "mad" writer. *Darkness Visible* was a difficult work for him to write, and he tried for years to write the story in third person, each time failing. He decided to switch to first person and completed the book in a few months (personal communication, 5 October 1993). He does not tell us the whole story of his illness and recovery. Some of the observations Styron made to Philip Caputo in an interview begun shortly before the breakdown and resumed a few months afterward indicate he was still seriously contemplating suicide in the hospital and had actually telephoned a friend to bring him a lethal dose of barbiturates (Caputo 157). Styron's friend advised him to wait a few days, at which point the suicidal depression had begun to lift.

The tremendous attention generated by *Darkness Visible* testifies to Styron's literary power as well as to the wide interest in the subject. He told a newspaper reporter that in some ways *Darkness Visible* is his most important work. "I think my book has allowed other people to write frankly and openly about their own experience with mental illness. . . . I like to think it sort of opened up a closet in which millions of Americans afflicted by this disease have suffered silently" (*Albany Times-Union* 3 October 1993).

With the publication of *Darkness Visible*, Styron has come full circle from his initial depiction of suicidal depression in *Lie Down in Darkness* almost forty years earlier. He has matured as an author and writes about madness with the authenticity of one who has survived it. Styron is one of those artists in the tradition of writing as rescue, and it is clear now that a central driving force behind his creativity is the need to master psychic conflict and heal himself. *Darkness Visible* contains an almost evangelical fervor that Styron might have treated satirically in *Lie Down in Darkness*. "It may require on the part of friends, lovers, family, admirers, an almost religious devotion to persuade the sufferers of life's worth, which is so often in conflict with a sense of their own worthlessness, but such devotion has prevented countless suicides" (*Darkness Visible* 76). This message would have been ironically undercut in the words of the Reverend Carey Carr, Dr. Strassman, or Daddy Faith, but in *Darkness Visible* it is expressed with humility and urgency. *Darkness Visible* is the work of a man who has plunged into the murky depths of depression and emerged stronger and wiser. Styron's life affirms the possibility of surviving the landscape of depression and transmuting it into profoundly moving literature.

CHAPTER 8

Conclusion
RETURNING FROM THE DEAD

When I mention to people that I am in this course, I usually receive responses from them which everyone else in this course has no doubt heard too. "Sounds cheery," people say. Or, "Sounds like a lot of fun." Then silence.

Sometimes when you tell people that you are in this class, you become afraid that they will think that you are suicidal. I guess if you are suicidal, you should not be afraid to admit it, but there is such a stigma attached to suicide that you wouldn't want to admit it. And if you are not suicidal, you still don't want to be suspected of it. After you mention that you are taking this course, an invisible barrier seems to go up between you and the person you are speaking to.

A similar barrier seems to appear when we have gotten half an hour or an hour into one of our classes. I begin to have this feeling, and I cannot stop having this feeling, that we in this classroom are the only people on the planet at this moment discussing the subject of suicide. There is one person in one pocket of the country and another person in another pocket privately considering committing suicide, but we in this class are the only ones engaged in discussing it aloud. That's the feeling I begin to have, and when we leave the classroom at the end of class, it seems like we have returned from the dead. Everything seems quiet in the hallways and in the outdoors, and no one seems to notice us. While I recognize the risk of comparing our experiences to the terrible struggle of someone considering suicide, I can't avoid thinking how similar our worlds are. We both feel to some extent cut off from the world.

By the same token, the people who are not in this course seem themselves to have something in common with suicidal people. People want to cut us out of their lives, as it were, when they find out we are taking this course. I have heard some people say about this course, "I don't think I could take the feeling of being in that course." Similarly, you hear about suicides who can't "take it" anymore.

I guess this diary is trying to show me that all people like to cut themselves off from others. While we are intuitively aware of this fact, this course is making it more vivid.

JONATHAN

"Oh, my God," exclaimed my mother when she heard the title of the present book, "Why can't you stop writing about that subject?" Her reaction was only slightly less guarded than those of others who, as Jonathan records in his diary, find the topic of suicide depressing if not morbid. While I had no difficulty convincing my department chair to allow me to teach a course on literary suicide, I certainly did receive unusual stares from my colleagues and friends. I suspect that more than a few of them wondered about my motivation and the course's impact upon the students.

Many scholars who write about a particular subject do so for personal reasons, usually to work through a conflict. As a child I remember thinking, after my grandmother, grandfather, and uncle all succumbed to cancer after prolonged suffering, that I would become a cancer researcher and find the cure that would prevent the rest of my relatives from dying of this dreaded disease. A string of C's in college biology and chemistry courses convinced me that oncology was not a realistic career choice. Yet even as I struggled with my premed courses, I was gravitating toward literature. The suicide of the professor who awakened my passion for literature and psychoanalysis left me wondering why anyone would renounce life—and as the years passed, I found my childhood fantasy of finding a cure for cancer replaced by the wish to find a cure for suicide, or at least a way in which literature might help us to understand and alleviate suffering.

Teaching a course on literary suicide was not depressing or morbid for me. Quite the opposite. I had the feeling, in both the 1992 and 1994 courses, that we were not only reading some of the century's most compelling literature but also discussing life-and-death issues that affected writers and readers alike. The course's interdisciplinary focus, combining literature, psychoanalysis, and biography, enabled us to explore suicide from a variety of perspectives. The addition of a diary-writing and reader-response component in the 1994 course encouraged students to write openly and candidly about their experiences with suicide and depression, experiences that were more extensive than most people would have predicted.

As I observe in chapter 1, more than one-quarter of all American high school students think seriously about committing suicide every year. "The 1996 Index of Social Health," published by Fordham University, indicates that the nation's social well-being has fallen to its lowest level in nearly twenty-five years. "Of the six problems concerning Americans younger than eighteen, four of them—child abuse, teen-age suicide, drug abuse and the high school dropout rate—worsened in 1994, the most recent year covered by the index" (*New York Times*, 14 October 1996). One of the authors of the study noted that "the teen suicide rate is 95 percent higher than it was in 1970." Since the suicide rate increases with age, it's likely that more than one-quarter of American undergraduate and graduate students have been suicidal at some point in their lives. And so it should not be entirely surprising that if students have the opportunity to write about their experiences, in a safe and supportive classroom environment, they will comment on issues reflecting the decline of the nation's social health, such as depression and suicide.

I was gratified that so many students gave me permission to use their diaries, and after the course ended in May 1994, I invited two of them to collaborate with me on their experiences. They agreed and decided to use their own names for publication. The diaries record their week-by-week responses to the course and their efforts to apply insights from class readings and discussions to their own lives. "Suicide Diaries and the Therapeutics of Anonymous Self-Disclosure" (Berman and Luna) investigates the ways in which the course enabled one person to write about a frightening experience and distance herself from a past that kept mingling with the present. "Writing about Suicide" (Berman and Schiff) examines the ways in which the course enabled another person to probe the vagaries of memory and unlock a family secret, the mystery of his father's death, which was not, as it was thought to be, a suicide. Students also used their formal essays to discuss the extent to which suicide has played a role in their critical and creative writings prior to taking my course. I have included Alyssa Colton's essay "Elegy for a Suicide: Writing and a Suicide Survivor" in the appendix.

"What Is the Most Important Insight You Have Acquired in the Course?"

I asked the students to describe briefly (and anonymously) the most important insight they acquired in the course, the insight that might have the most far-reaching impact upon their lives. The most striking aspect of the course, for one student, was discovering the shocking reality of suicide, a reality seldom captured in literature:

It's very weird, but I'd never thought about exact suicide scenes before I started this class. But after reading some biographies and some scenes of the writers' suicides, for the first time I realized that actually there were people who found them dead, touched the bodies. For some reason, somewhere in my mind I believed that suicides don't have corpses. I believed that their bodies vanish upon committing suicide. This is strange, because suicide issues have always been my interest. I believe that anyone, including me, has the possibility of committing suicide. For example, during the very tense period when my boyfriend and I were talking about breaking up, I realized that it is not hard to commit suicide. It could happen, say, in a minute. But still now, I can't believe that the dead bodies are left behind after the suicides.

Many students were startled by the extent to which suicide is a recurrent biographical and artistic theme in the writers studied in the course. Since biographical criticism has been largely ignored in contemporary literary studies, the students were intrigued by the close interrelationship between life and art. Knowledge of a writer's suicide invariably affects the reader's responses. "I have definitely come to a new understanding about how biographical information affects our reading of texts, particularly when that knowledge is about an author's suicide. A slightly less literary insight—or surprise, I suppose—is how many people seem to suffer emotionally and mentally (as well as physically). These two insights are related, I think." Another student found the relationship between biography and art problematic and tried, with difficulty, to separate the two:

I think that more than anything, this course has taught me to separate the writer from the suicide, if, in fact, that is at all possible. Maybe that's not what I mean. I've learned that a writer is not her suicide, if that makes any sense. When I used to consider Sylvia Plath, for example, all I saw was her suicide. The suicide doesn't make the artist; the artist is a victim of suicide. This, for me, is important. I will no longer shy away from authors who I fear may be too depressing. I'll read them first and then make up my mind.

The students affirmed the courage of the writers who had endured a lifelong struggle with mental illness and praised the compassionate support of relatives and friends: "I now understand how frail, mentally frail, writers are who have committed suicide. I applaud their friends for trying to shelter them and encourage them to carry on. I am sure that there were times when those nurturing people must have found [their task most] difficult. I am particularly amazed at Anne Sexton's friends, especially Maxine Kumin, her psychiatrist Dr. Orne, and others. Also Virginia Woolf's husband and family."

One student who had met William Styron the year before observed:

The course, or rather my participation in the course (specifically the diaries and the reader-response paragraphs), did change my ability and willingness to talk about suicides, both real life and literary. Experiencing the insights of others and how they were presented, I became more able to express my own. I suppose if I were to meet William Styron now, as opposed to last semester when I stood before him like an open-mouthed idiot, I would have the "courage," in a sense, to ask him about his experiences with suicide and depression. I was curious then, but I couldn't bring myself to ask him: I felt as though I might have been intruding on his personal life.

I wondered before the course began whether the students would find themselves identifying or counteridentifying with suicidal writers. It became clear at the end of the semester that they experienced the writers not as distant authors but as fellow human beings struggling with universal problems.

I used to wonder about my desire to write, to make up stories, since I was about ten years old. "How come I like to do this?" I would ask myself. "This would be more convenient or more enjoyable if I was happy." But I wasn't really happy as a kid, and yet I found many things to write about that made me feel better.

Now, in this course, I've learned that this is so with many writers. And many of the class diaries have indicated this too. Why? It is fascinating. I feel like I'm in a club. Don't always know who the other members are, but it's a club just the same.

We've discussed some really interesting things in this class. For me, learning about a person's work in light of their life is very rewarding. And for many reasons, very comforting.

Significantly, the diary component had the greatest impact upon the students. Hearing about their classmates' experiences was often a revelation, and they felt a heightened sensitivity to those who struggle with suicidal feelings, be they famous authors or classmates.

For me, the biggest surprise was the effect that writing and hearing the diaries had on me. Specifically, it made me aware of how many people have such a difficult time dealing with life and have had such strong, hard things happen to them. This has made me feel less alone in my own difficulties, my own struggles. I think this same experience has also helped me to respond more empathically to suicidal literature. Though I have always responded in this way to "actual people" (that is, people I know) who have killed themselves or tried to do so, authors and their characters have, until now, seemed more remote. Now, at times I can imagine Sylvia Plath or Virginia Woolf sitting among us and feel as if, when we read their works, we are reading their suicide diaries.

Many students indicated that their most important insight was discovering the prevalence of suicidal thinking in the writers discussed in the course as well as in society in general. Even those who knew a great deal about depression and suicide in the beginning of the semester were astonished by the ubiquity of mood disorders. The following are representative comments:

The prevalence of suicide, suicidal depression, and suicidal ideation in the world at large and the world of literature [has surprised me]. I came into this course feeling like a person who was well educated in both the worlds of literature and psychology. But how little I knew about suicide! And it seems to be staring me in the face now every time I turn around. I guess that for me, a person who perceives herself to be an intuitive, sensitive person, this has been an eye opener (boy, am I full of clichés tonight!). I hope I can be aware of the psychology of students when I am a teacher.

There have been lots of insights I have acquired, but the most important one is a very basic one. I realized how much I overlook the problem of suicide in our society and in literature. I have always considered myself a compassionate person, and I have always felt that I am attentive to problems that society tends to sweep under the rug. This may be so, but I see now how much more compassionate I could be. In short, while I have learned many facts about suicide, more importantly, I learned about myself.

I am amazed at how much people suffer! Listening to the diaries read in class, reading the literature, and learning biographical details about the artists, I am constantly surprised at people's stories of pain. I don't think I am particularly naive, and I have always been aware of misery around me. But this class just brings home how many ways there are to be unhappy. I could say something ennobling here about how strong people are in overcoming this pain, but that would be dishonest. The theme of this class is the failure to overcome pain, except by that ultimate *triumph. Maybe I'm just overtired from working on the final paper, but there it is.*

And yet paradoxically, the prevalence of suicidal thinking was reassuring to those who have struggled with this problem. For at least two students, the main value of the course was that it helped them identify personal issues that required immediate attention. They spoke about the course as a journey of self-discovery and self-healing.

The most important, actually crucial, insight is how suicide affected my life, both familially and personally. It was the first class that began my journey into the depths of my own rage and its impact on my own struggle with suicide. Suicidal moments had come briefly in my life, and I had always triumphed over them, but looking down the tube of suicidal literature and the science and theories of suicide put it uppermost in my mind.

It was then that I had to reckon and fight with my own death wish bearing its weight against the strength and determination of a life wish. I won the battle against suicide and began to blossom into light fully and more intrinsically than I ever had before.

I must honestly say that I began this course feeling, logically, I suppose as I did about my past experiences with psychotherapy (i.e., I thought it was sort of touchy-feely bullshit). It is not that I am averse to touchy-feely (and I have been known to lay on the B.S. in the past pretty thick, though I am not in this passage). On the contrary. But anything like this always has rung false for me, very contrived. The diaries made me feel as if I were obligated to disclose personal things (regardless of the fact that I was told I was not obligated to write them). But something has changed. (Boy, does this sound touchy-feely: music swells.) This class has made me aware that I still (after having stopped therapy) have problems. When I overreact, when I have my daily crying jags, I think about symptoms we have talked about in this class. I think how they relate to me. I am wondering about how to help myself, something I had ceased to do before this class. Has this class put me at risk? In an immediate visceral sense, yes. In a long-term sense, I think, I hope, it has made me see how very at risk I have been for a very long time.

"Not Everyone Around You Is Suicidal"

Did the course place students at risk? This was the question that remained uppermost on my mind before, during, and after the semester. The question is complicated by the fact that, as the above student observes, some people discovered they have been at risk for a long time. No one indicated in the brief "insights acquired" paragraphs that he or she was becoming seriously depressed or suicidal as a result of the class readings, writings, or discussions. I suspect that most of the students would identify with the following comment: "What has surprised me the most, although this may not count as an insight, is that this course has been less upsetting and/or depressing to me than I thought. Not that it hasn't been a bit upsetting and depressing, just not as much as I had thought." Students often remarked upon the course's intensity, but there were also moments of welcome comic relief, as can be seen in the following diary:

In an effort to inject some humor into the diary readings, I'll relate an incident that happened last week. It began as I got on an afternoon bus heading from Albany to New York City. Blessed with luck as I am, I wound up having to take the last remaining seat which was, you guessed it, the sliver of seat on that three-seater "lounge seat" in the back, the one right next to the bathroom.

The ride started off on an ominous note. After only a few minutes on the Thruway, the driver pulled to the side of the road and announced he felt light-headed and that he was going to stand outside the bus for a while. I couldn't hear most of what he said, but it had something to do with a lack of air circulation. However, that soon became the least of my worries. About an hour into the ride, the man sitting diagonally across from me turned and said, "Is this bus headed to New York?"

"Yes."

He nodded and a moment later stood up and, holding a large brown paper bag, went into the bathroom. My mind immediately gnawed away on the questions why he waited an hour to ask where the bus was going and what the contents of the bag were. When he didn't emerge for a few minutes I wondered if the bag contained drugs. But that speculation didn't last long, and soon enough I had somehow resolved he was preparing to commit suicide and that the bag contained a bomb. He was about to blow himself up and take us all with him.

No, I thought, this doesn't make any sense. Then I heard bang bang bang from the bathroom. What was that? What was he doing? Assembling something? Then tap tap tap tap tap — maybe he was funneling gunpowder into a pipe bomb and tapping in the last of it.

Stop it, stop it, I thought. It's just the class, the Literary Suicide class, making you think everyone is suicidal. Who cares what the banging is. Just read your book.

Bang bang bang — Ignore it. Why would he wait till now to build the thing? (Maybe he's having trouble setting it off.) Why would someone kill himself in a Greyhound bus toilet? (Maybe he's a former Greyhound driver who lost his job in the strike and didn't get it back when the strike ended.)

Tap tap tap bang bang rattle. Rationality slipped from me. I grew convinced I was about to die. I wondered if everyone who dies in a bomb explosion has the same urgent presentiment but never does anything about it because it seems so ludicrous.

I sat staring at the doors and walls surrounding the toilet and wondered how thick the metal was and if it would be able to contain the force of the blast. I found myself closing my book and, making as if stretching my arms, held the book at the side of my head, hoping it might absorb the brunt of the blast.

This was it. I visualized the bus from the viewpoint of the car behind us, watching the back abruptly erupt into a fireball. I wondered if I would feel anything at all.

It's just the class, I kept repeating. Not everyone around you is suicidal. Look, he has a bag under his seat. Why would someone planning suicide carry luggage with them? (Maybe he took the bag to fool his housemates or loved ones.) And, after all, no one suspected Edna in The Awakening— *"Oh, I'm just going down to the beach."*

I imagined him in there—tapping, rattling, banging away, ready to light the fuse, but also thinking, like Septimus Warren Smith in Mrs. Dalloway: *I do not want to die. Life is good. Spring is coming.*

Finally, perhaps sensing my consternation, the woman next to me said something starting with "Vou." She was from Montreal. Then she laughed and said, "His face. Shave."

I sighed in relief. He was shaving his face! But doubts assailed me. How did she know? How could she know? What on earth made it so obvious? Had she been a man once, who traveled a lot and had to shave on buses?

Well, he emerged ultimately, clean-shaven. I shrugged, closed my eyes, and thought about what I would eat for dinner.

I read the above diary to the class, and everyone appreciated its nervous humor. Indeed, when I asked the students to indicate the most memorable diaries that were read aloud, this was the one that was most often selected. The seriousness of suicide made humor a necessity, and I was especially pleased with the following observation at the end of the course: "The biggest surprise is how much I enjoyed the class and how much laughter occurred, not the strained kind that came from trying to mask a depressing situation, but genuine laughter. And though the diaries often saddened me, they didn't depress me; instead they made me think how strong some of the people in the class are, how courageous it was to put down what they had written."

Evaluating the Diaries

The students' "insights acquired" paragraphs were consistent with their responses to an anonymous questionnaire I distributed on the last class of the semester. All found the diary component of the course valuable, twelve rating it an "A" and five a "B" (one person was absent). To the question: "Did you find diary writing therapeutic? That is, did writing about conflicts encourage you to understand those conflicts better and find constructive ways to deal with them?"—fourteen indicated "yes" and two were "not sure" (one did not answer the question). No one believed that writing about suicide increased his or her vulnerability to suicide; one was "not sure." Four believed that writing about suicide decreased their vulnerability to suicide. Hearing the diaries proved to be as valuable as diary writing. There was nearly unanimous agreement that the diary component heightened their understanding of literature, their classmates, and themselves. In addition, the diaries made them feel more connected to everyone in the classroom. Nearly all believed the course would have been very different without the diary component. All seventeen recommended that I continue to ask future students to write a weekly diary.

My own experience of the diaries was similarly positive. I enjoy all my courses, including those in which students do not submit diaries, but I feel more connected to my "diary students," more aware of their weekly progress, more attuned to their questions and concerns. Quite apart from the literary and personal issues discussed in the diaries, the students offered me nearly instant feedback on the successes and failures of each week's class. The diaries gave a voice, albeit an anonymous one, to the students, many of whom felt uncomfortable speaking in class. I have found that learning takes on a new dimension in every course with a diary component, a dimension that integrates the intellectual (and theoretical) with the personal. As one student observed,

The course has been absolutely great!! There is so much I have learned that it's hard to reduce to just one insight. We have listened to classmates' concerns and fears about death, but we have also gone deeper into the analysis of different motives in the writers' suicide attempts. We read poems and short stories from a new perspective: the one which allows us to see the writer, his inner conflicts, and his environment. Since our reading went beyond the literal meaning of a sentence or any piece of discourse, we learned to understand a little more about suicide, yet we learned a lot about life.

"Reading His Work Proved Not Purgative But Pernicious"

I would be remiss if I did not acknowledge the potential risks of a course like Literary Suicide, risks that came to light, unexpectedly, in two students, one toward the end of the semester, the other, not long afterward.

Sadly, I fear the one thing you'd taken precautions against all semester and which I'd dismissed as a possibility has happened. Shortly after reading Darkness Visible *I found myself slipping into a depression the likes of which I have not experienced in years. Styron's descriptions of what his depression felt like disturbingly matched my own experiences with depression. In fact, his accuracy was uncanny.*

Oddly, and for reasons I can't determine or explain, reading his work proved not purgative but pernicious. It seemed to literally "stir up" feelings that hadn't plagued me in at least two years. The effects were swift and encompassing, and while there were other factors that could have served as proximate causes (a deteriorating relationship), there's something so familiar to this depression that I know it's not just due to outside influences.

To allay your concerns, the intensity of these feelings has decreased over the past few days and will hopefully subside. I'm hoping that the letter Julie will read in class will help as well.

So, no, I'm not in danger of suicide or anything, but Darkness Visible *had a pronounced and immediate effect upon me, one I had no way of foreseeing, and it's something you may want to consider in future classes. I really hate ending on a note like this, because I felt the diary writing was an incredibly beneficial experience for me, and truly appreciated your consistently insightful and empathic comments. Thanks and take care.*

I had a conference with the student (who signed his diaries "Ultra") in which we discussed the issues raised in his entry. His reaction to *Darkness Visible* mystified me, for of all the texts we read in the course, Styron's was the most uplifting, providing hope and reassurance for those afflicted with mood disorders. Julie had cited *Darkness Visible* as instrumental to her recovery, and it was partly for this reason that I invited her to read her

"Letter to William Styron" to the 1994 Literary Suicide course on the last day of the semester. Why was Ultra's response to *Darkness Visible* so different from Julie's? Would its countertherapeutic impact on him, if that's what it was, be long-lasting? I asked Ultra to stay in touch with me, and he sent me the following letter a month after the semester ended:

Dear Jeff,

Having put aside my final diary for a few weeks following our discussion, I've just finished rereading it and have some comments to offer.

In the weeks that have passed, the depression I had feared approaching has faded away. My last diary now strikes me as hyperbolic, if not hysterical. I can, however, remember how I felt at the time clearly enough to know these emotions were genuine when written.

When we met, we discussed other possible causes for my reaction to Darkness Visible; *the end of the semester, for example. I'm still certain that what I felt was distinct from the stress brought on by papers coming due or something similar, but again, it's gone. Hearing Julie read her letter to Styron helped a great deal, as did speaking with you about what I had experienced.*

In a sense I now consider reading Darkness Visible *as a kind of inoculation against depression. You know the way inoculations work: you get infected with a little bit of a virus and your body develops a resistance to it that protects you from it in the future. (Right?) In doing so, however, you may come down with some symptoms of the disease you're being immunized against. So I suppose in this analogy, my evanescent depression was simply a side effect of the inoculation. (Or something like that.)*

That's about all I have to say on the subject for now. Thanks for this chance to elaborate on my last diary. Moreover, thank you for the concern you showed. It was very much appreciated.

Ultra's analogy of reading *Darkness Visible* as an inoculation against depression anticipates many of the questions Roger Shattuck discusses in *Forbidden Knowledge*. One can never know whether literature will have an infectious or cathartic influence on readers, and even when a text seeks to empower readers, its impact remains unpredictable. Shattuck quotes a statement by Edgar Wind suggesting that "[a]rt has the power to intensify (not just to purge) emotions," an intensification that may have unexpected consequences (291–92). Ultra's analogy recalls the mythic story of King Mithradates, who upon being warned that he was being murdered by slow poison laced in his food, took an antidote to counteract the poison, thus ensuring his survival.

"It Was a Bad Time to Be Taking a Course Like That"

I doubt, however, that a mithradatic interpretation accounts for the letter I received from Mary less than two months after the semester ended. The breakup of a relationship triggered a depression culminating in a drug overdose, and while she did not attribute the suicide attempt to the course itself, she could not rule out the possibility that reading suicidal literature might have placed her at risk. She noted that even as she swallowed a small number of sleeping pills, a line from one of Edwin Shneidman's articles ran through her mind: *"Suicide is characterized by ambivalence."* Mary knew she was ambivalent about suicide; she did not wish to die but to find a solution to her pain, guilt, and anxiety. She phoned her therapist immediately after taking the pills and rushed to an emergency room where she had her stomach pumped. She ended her letter by observing that Julie's presentation had a powerful effect on her: Julie had recovered, and she hoped she would too. She also said that writing brought her relief by allowing her to escape, momentarily, from her pain.

Mary wrote in a subsequent letter that amid her depression she felt like Dorothy Parker, on whom she had written one of her essays for my course. Like Parker, she felt she was in a kind of limbo, estranged from family and friends and enveloped in a black depression. She said that antidepressants had helped her and that when she found herself becoming anxious again, writing a letter to a friend or teacher also made her feel better.

I have often thought about Mary in the four years since the course ended, and though she gave me permission to quote her letters, I have chosen to paraphrase them because they contain too much raw pain and confusion. Mary subsequently recovered and completed her graduate studies; I would like to think that my course was more helpful than harmful to her, but I cannot be sure. Did the course plant a "seed" of suicide that had not existed before? Was her suicide attempt an imitation of Dorothy Parker's drug overdose? As we have seen, both real and fictional characters sometimes find themselves at risk as a result of reading accounts of suicide. Was Mary one of these people? Do certain students experience at the end of a semester feelings of disconnection or abandonment that some patients feel at the end of therapy? I cannot answer these troubling questions. Nor could I have predicted Ultra's or Mary's responses. Those who argue that courses like Literary Suicide are inherently dangerous, unleashing powerful forces that may prove explosive, will find confirmation in Mary's suicide attempt. Those who counter that these courses are valuable precisely because they allow students to recognize when they are at risk and take appropriate actions will point out that Mary had the presence of mind to seek immediate help.

"The Roar Which Lies on the Other Side of Silence"

I have suggested throughout this study that teachers must be sensitive to the special risks posed by suicidal literature. Yet there are also special rewards, including a recognition of the fragility of life and an appreciation of the courage of those writers who have provided us with an unwavering account of their struggle to survive. Two of my favorite literary passages affirm literature's ability to sensitize us to suffering.

> If we had a keen vision and feeling of all ordinary human life, it would be like hearing the grass grow and the squirrel's heart beat, and we should die of that roar which lies on the other side of silence. As it is, the quickest of us walks about well wadded with stupidity. (Eliot 189)

> Behind the door of every contented, happy man there ought to be someone standing with a little hammer and continually reminding him with a knock that there are unhappy people, that however happy he may be, life will sooner or later show him its claws, and trouble will come to him—illness, poverty, losses, and then no one will see or hear him, just as now he neither sees nor hears others. (Chekhov 381)

Literature has a unique ability to remove some of the wadding from our ears and remind us, with a jarring knock—or, in the words of the student riding on the Greyhound bus, with a tapping in the lavatory—of the extent of human unhappiness. Recall Kafka's 1904 letter to Oskar Pollack, a part of which Anne Sexton used for her epigraph to *All My Pretty Ones*: "the books we need are the kind that act upon us like a misfortune, that make us suffer like the death of someone we love more than ourselves, that make us feel as though we were on the verge of suicide, or lost in a forest remote from all human habitation—a book should serve as the ax for the frozen sea within us" (Kafka 16). Literature has a transformative power, for good and for ill, and nowhere is this better seen than in suicidal literature, which records the roar that lies on the other side of silence. For this reason, it is probably unwise to remove all of the self-preservative wadding from our ears. One must approach artistic hammers and axes with special care.

Appendix

"ELEGY FOR A SUICIDE: WRITING AND A SUICIDE SURVIVOR"

Alyssa Colton

Students in our graduate program have the opportunity to fulfill written requirements for course work in a number of ways, including through creative and personal writing. Many students welcome the challenge to investigate the relationship between course content and their own lives, in the process discovering important insights about literature and themselves. They also become more critically self-aware, able to see how one's psyche shapes scholarly and artistic writings.

Alyssa Colton was one of these students, and I conclude with her introspective essay "Elegy for a Suicide: Writing and a Suicide Survivor." Alyssa's first essay was a thoughtful discussion of the link between mental illness and creativity in Anne Sexton's life and art. I readily agreed to her request to write her second essay on a more personal topic. "Elegy for a Suicide" is noteworthy for many reasons. Alyssa investigates with unflinching honesty the ways in which suicide haunts her writings. Suicide is a dark specter emerging in the least likely of places and over which the writer has only partial control. She seeks to exorcise this apparition through rigorous self-analysis. Alyssa writes about suicide from the perspective of an insider and outsider and refuses the temptation to romanticize death.

Alyssa's essay also affirms the value of writing and reading about suicide. She describes the various genres in which she has written about suicide—in essays, diaries, short stories, poems, and a novel-in-progress. Suicide awakens intense resistance within her, as it does within most people, but we can see how the process of writing enables her to arrive at new interpretations of her art and life, thus making her a more sophisticated writer and reader.

Alyssa does not speculate on the reasons behind her literary preoccupation with suicide, but Freud's repetition-compulsion principle may help to explain one of the driving forces behind her critical and creative writings: the need to relive painful experiences for self-mastery. Additionally, we can see a reparative impulse—the wish to eulogize a friend who committed suicide. In honoring his memory, she hopes to avert future losses.

In the first section of her essay, Alyssa writes about the impact of suicide on her life, and in the second, she analyzes her writings about suicide, both before and after her friend's death. She also reveals her own suicide attempt when she was a high school freshman. In the epilogue, she discusses a friend's experience with a recent suicide, an event that seems a repetition of a past loss. I close with Alyssa's letter to me, written in response to my request to use her essay for this book.

On the morning of April 11, 1987, my friend committed suicide. I was sixteen, a junior in high school. I'd just returned to school from a doctor's appointment. It was the middle of a class period so the halls were quiet. I walked slowly, looking outside at the gray mist and rain, wondering when spring would come. I climbed the stairs to the second floor. As I turned the corner, I saw somebody sitting outside of the social studies teacher's classroom. I realized right away it was my sister. She was crying uncontrollably. I rushed to her, took her in my arms, and asked her what was wrong. Through sobs she told me, "Carlos is dead." I heard the words with incomprehension. Carlos was my friend, our friend: how could he be dead? "He killed himself. I just found out." I began to cry, too.

Carlos and I first met when I was nine. He was a year older but in the same grade. We got in trouble for throwing spitballs at each other during class and had to stay after school to write "I will not throw spitballs" one hundred times. It was one of the first times I was punished in school, and I resented Carlos for getting me in trouble.

My next memory of him is from middle school. He lived a few blocks away, and he would come over after school after we got off the bus together.

In early November, just before Election Day, I took a job delivering a candidate's pamphlets door to door in the neighborhood. Carlos came with me one day. We held gloved hands in the cold November wind. He asked me to be his girlfriend. Delighted that someone actually wanted me, I agreed. He was my first boyfriend.

Our relationship was innocent. I was thirteen, and he was fourteen. I think he kissed me once. We mostly just hung out together after school, watching TV or playing games. We rarely went to his house. I'm not sure why. He gave the impression that his mother and stepfather were very strict. I don't really remember "breaking up." I guess we must have, or the relationship just faded away. I think he went away for the summer. But the next year, when we started high school, we were friends. My best friend had gone away to London for a year with her family, so I needed the friendship more than ever. We tried out for the play together, stumbling over our lines and feeling foolish. When I joined the volleyball team, he came and watched the games.

During my freshman year, I met Jason, a senior, my next boyfriend. One day Carlos asked me out again. I told him I had feelings for Jason. He acted nonchalant about it; I knew he was more hurt than he let on.

Carlos was well-liked in high school. He was able to move in and out of different social sets without losing his popularity. He was also very talented. In high school he developed his talents in the arts, particularly painting. He became one of those people who lurked in that wing of the school where the art rooms were. Yet despite his "artsiness" he wasn't given to sitting around, dressed in black, and being depressed like so many creative students were in my school. Though I knew at times he did get sad and depressed, he never showed it; he was very outgoing and always exhibited an upbeat personality. One reason for his depressions was a lisp he had had since he was young. He was very self-conscious about it, even in high school when people had long since stopped teasing him for it.

After Jason and I broke up, Carlos and I renewed our friendship. I began to expand my circle of friends and acquaintances. I started going to parties with him. At one party Carlos and I tried smoking cigarettes together. He also became friends with my sister, who was already part of that "party" crowd. I don't remember him having any girlfriends; though we talked occasionally, we weren't always very close. I would get phone calls from him at times when he was depressed. Usually he would complain about his family. He had older stepbrothers and sisters, but I don't think they lived at home. Though I can't say exactly what the situation was, I knew he felt that he was always being treated unfairly by his parents. I certainly got a sense of his feeling unloved; whether or not it was true, his feelings were definitely genuine. I didn't think there was anything really abnormal about it, but I did think some of the things his parents did were unfair.

There is one incident around this time that pains me particularly to re-

member. Carlos and I went on a ski trip with the school's ski club. Carlos roomed with a longtime friend of his, Thomas. I was at the time not seeing anyone and was attracted to Thomas. That night I went to Thomas's room and we made out in the room. Carlos was asleep in the bed a few feet away. I am appalled at myself whenever I think of this. Even if Carlos were still alive, I would feel still ashamed, for it was a very unfeeling and tacky thing to do. Especially since I knew he still had feelings for me.

I don't know for sure if he heard us, but the chances are pretty good that he did. The next day we skied together, being about the same level of ability. We had a great time trying to get down a difficult trail together. In the middle of it we gave up and had to stomp over to another trail. We were laughing so hysterically we couldn't even move. I remember wondering if he knew about the night before. If it hadn't been for that night, the day would be a happy memory.

In the spring of the following year the police found Carlos dead in his car from carbon monoxide poisoning. There were notes to his friends and family beside him on the seat. A few weeks before then, Carlos told me he was giving away some of his pictures. He asked me to come over. At his house, he gave me a picture he had done: it was two eyes, crying. The picture hung in my dorm room for a few years after that, haunting me whenever I looked at it.

The day we found out about Carlos's death was chaotic. All of Carlos's friends clustered together in a room where the counselors were. I remember seeing Thomas and hugging him, not saying a word. At some point we found out Carlos had left some notes. We were told there was a note for my sister and me, but we weren't able to see them until a week later, and then we were given Xeroxes. The note said something to the effect that he appreciated the friends we had been to him, to be happy, and he would miss us. You could tell when the gas started taking effect by the shakiness of his writing.

It was around the same time that a group of teenagers in New Jersey had killed themselves by the same method. It had been in all the newspapers. A friend remarked how true to Carlos's character it was that he followed the "trend," even in his death. In recalling this, I think there were probably also some practical reasons—I doubt Carlos had access to a gun, and he wasn't a violent person. Drugs are too risky. Carbon monoxide poisoning is one of the more efficient and least painful methods of suicide. In the stories of those reports, Carlos had found a method; but because he started giving his artwork away much before then, he had already made up his mind what he was going to do. Anne Sexton, a poet who battled with depression for half her life and eventually succeeded (after numerous attempts) in committing suicide by the same method Carlos used, expressed it best in her poem "Wanting to Die":

> But suicides have a special language.
> Like carpenters they want to know *which tools.*
> They never ask *why build. (Selected Poems* 98)

At the time of Carlos's death, my friend Anne had recently become a born-again Christian. I was still friends with her, but it was difficult at times to put up with her preachings. At the same time, I think I was struck by her faith. She had already been through a lot in life, coming from a very troubled family, and her ability to find happiness amazed me. Anne told me that unless Carlos had accepted Jesus before he died, he wasn't in Heaven. Naturally, I was angry. I could only think of Carlos at peace, finally. I loved to walk in cemeteries and felt a sublime peace whenever I did. But after awhile, after the initial shock had worn off, I began to ask some questions. My parents couldn't give me any answers: they only told me some people believe in God, some don't.

That summer Anne invited me to come to her church. I went. Sitting in the church, I felt loved. The sun was streaming in the windows, and the pastor was telling me to give myself over to God. I did. I told Anne, and of course she was ecstatic. That summer we spent a lot of time together, going to church and Bible study. I became part of a warm community of people who cared about me. It was a relief to give myself over to a higher power.

Within a few months I rejected this faith. I realized that the love and support I was looking for was in myself, in my friends, and in my family. I couldn't accept some of the things the church taught. It was also very exhausting to commit myself to something I could never fully believe in. And I had never been able to accept that Carlos wasn't somewhere at peace. I still believe this.

I often wonder what it would be like to still have him around. Perhaps we wouldn't even be in touch, since I'm not in touch with too many people from high school. But somehow it seems like he's still around. Perhaps we would have kept renewing our friendship through our interests in art and dance. *Maybe we would have gone to the same college, or seen each other on weekends home. It saddens me so much to think the world has lost such marvelous talent as he had. He would have gone on to study art, I think. His art teacher was very encouraging. Why wasn't it enough to keep him going? I should be angry at him, but I got over being angry. Once in awhile I think perhaps he's better off, life is just so much pain. Then a part of me strikes back; there's also so much beauty, and the beauty makes you ache and you want to live forever to keep soaking it in. It's so ironic he died in April. If he had only waited a few more weeks, he would have seen the flowers coming up, the greening of the trees, the promise of summer and renewal.*

Writing about Suicide

I first wrote about suicide before Carlos's death. When I was a freshman in high school I had a teacher who encouraged a lot of creative writing. Our assignment was to take an "issue" and write about it in an essay, a story, and a play. My topic was suicide. I can't remember the essay: I think it was just your basic research paper on the facts and figures of suicide. I do remember the story and play quite clearly.

The story was loosely based on personal experience. I don't really remember when this happened, but I think it was shortly before writing the story. I was feeling very low about myself, and I downed half a package of cold medicine (cold medicine made me sleepy, so I logically concluded it would put me to sleep forever). Fortunately, the result was only a very bad stomachache: I threw up the pills. I felt stupid shortly after I took them. It did allow me to stay home from school the next day, and that was probably more beneficial than anything. I wrote about the experience in my diary, which I've been keeping since I was eight years old. A while later I was in my sister's room looking for something. I came across her diary and read an entry. In it she wrote that she had read my diary and found out about the suicide attempt. She was quite upset about it. I was enraged, but it also made me feel guilty for reading her diary. Yet somehow it helped to know she really cared.

The story I wrote was about two sisters. Their personalities mirrored those of my sister and me. One sister comes home to find the other dead from slashing her wrists. In thinking about this story, for the first time I made a conscious connection between my attempt and the story. As horrible as the act of reading my sister's diary was, it enabled me to envision her view. It helped me cross the boundary of myself to understand how those who loved me might feel if I had succeeded. It also echoed the irony that help and love are always close by.

The play was quite a different story. In it an elderly man who perceives himself to be a burden on his family kills himself, a kind of euthanasia. The scene consists of the man's grandson innocently giving him the scissors with which he kills himself. I have a harder time drawing connections with the play to my life, but I do think that this may be about the time my grandfather was diagnosed with emphysema. Perhaps I was attempting to imagine what his life might have felt like for him. Perhaps I saw his life-long cigarette habit (which he promptly quit when he was diagnosed) as a form of suicide.

Sometime after Carlos's death, I tried to write a story about it. I wrote down every detail I could remember. I described the rain streaking down the huge plastic windows in the stairwell of the school. I described the shock of hearing my sister tell me the news. I described the anger and the pain that I felt as I stood around at his funeral. The story I wrote clearly fits into the second stage of recovery described by Judith Lewis Herman in Trauma and Recovery: "In the second stage of recovery, the survivor tells the story of the trauma. She tells it completely, in depth and in detail. This work of reconstruction actually transforms the traumatic memory, so that it can be integrated into the survivor's story" (175).

I soon grew frustrated with the story and discarded it. The characters were flat. I didn't know what point I was trying to make. It seemed unreal when it was in fact too real. It seemed contrived, clichéd. Herman again provides some support for the judgment of my work: "The survivor's initial account of the event may be repetitious, stereotyped, and emotionless. . . . It does not develop or progress in time, and it does not reveal the storyteller's feelings or interpretation of events. Another therapist describes traumatic memory as a series of still snapshots or a silent movie; the role of therapy is to provide the music and words" (175).

When I first read these words, before I even began planning the contents of this essay, I immediately remembered finding out about Carlos's death. The memory is like still snapshots in my mind: I see myself walking up the stairs; I see the rain outside; I see my sister huddled outside the door, cry-

ing. They are so clear to me I feel I could take these pictures out and look at them physically. It is reminiscent of accident victims who remember clearly what they were doing immediately before the accident: "then everything becomes a blur."

I didn't attempt to write consciously about my friend's death again until a year ago, but it has crept into my work before then. One story that stands out is one I wrote for a creative writing workshop when I was a senior in college. In the story, four friends drive into a cemetery at night, bored with the nightlife of the small town where they live. Their car gets stuck, and two of the characters take a walk and wind up breaking into a mausoleum, where they see the bones of a dead woman. When they see her, they suddenly feel vulnerable and mortal and quickly leave.

However, there is an undeveloped subplot in the story, which the professor seized on and questioned. The woman in the story, Emma, is aware of a friend who is buried in the same cemetery. As they drive past his grave she thinks: "Just over there. That's where Lucas is buried." The story continues: "But they wouldn't go that way. Emma had never seen his grave at night. Once she and Joel tried to find it, but they couldn't, and so they sat in the grass and talked by moonlight." A few minutes later, another character in the story, Connie, asks: "'Isn't this near where Lucas is buried?' This caught Emma off guard, and for a split second she wondered if she had inadvertently voiced her thoughts. 'Actually, it's over in the other direction.'"

A few paragraphs later, Emma's thoughts return to Lucas: "Then a strange, cold feeling crept up on her. Lucas was all of a sudden there, standing in the middle of her thoughts. For so long she couldn't conjure up his whole image, and now he was all there: his curly black hair, his ever-unhappy brown eyes, his slightly sour smile. Why didn't Lucas do anything like this? And her next thought was, Lucas, I'm sorry . . ."

Here Emma's thoughts are interrupted by the car hitting a rock. The next thought of Lucas comes when Emma is alone inside the tomb: "Then, vividly, the image of Lucas again appeared in her mind. Lucas, protect me. She had never thought of him that way before, as if he were some kind of guardian angel."

The last mention of Lucas is three paragraphs to the end: "When they passed the road that led to Lucas's grave, Emma's chest tightened. A new guilt crept in and attached herself to the old guilt. She closed her eyes and breathed in deeply, searching for the other, comforting image of Lucas.

But all she saw was the picture of the woman's body in the coffin."

The criticism that the professor made was that Lucas's death is never really integrated into the story. "Why new guilt?" he wrote, "What is the old guilt? What is the nature of the guilt? Guilt about what?" Of course, the guilt is the guilt Emma feels that she is somehow responsible for Lucas's death. Semi-consciously I was describing my own feelings of guilt about Carlos's suicide. Because Connie asks her where he's buried, it's obvious she had a relationship with him, but I never explain the nature of the relationship or the circumstances around his death. And of course, since I never say it, the reader can never know how Lucas died (and he could have died in another way that makes the guilt understandable — an accident, perhaps) or why Emma feels guilty. I didn't plan on including Lucas in the story, but he popped up: the cemetery where I imagined the story taking place is the cemetery where Carlos is buried. One of the landmarks of that cemetery in my mind is his grave. Similar to the way Lucas "was all of a sudden standing in the middle of her thoughts," Carlos all of a sudden appeared in my story. The story about Emma wasn't the only expression of my guilt, as the following poem attests:

In my heart is a bitter stone
it sinks deeply;
burrows in like a worm
through dirt,
Churning the organs of my guilt
pushing and pulling
against my heart.

For a long time I felt guilty about Carlos's death. I felt guilty that I rejected him, that I wasn't always there for him, that I somehow let him down and made him think life wasn't worth living. Even now I need to remind myself sometimes that there were other factors at work. Even if my actions were a part of it, they couldn't have caused Carlos to decide to kill himself. People get rejected all the time and don't take their lives. As I think back on what I know of his life, many plausible explanations come to mind. He had a troubled family life. He was often depressed, and also a very sensitive artist. Perhaps it was something biological. Much recent research indicates that some cases of depression are caused by neurochemical factors.

In my senior year when our high school established an award to black *artists in honor of his memory, one of Carlos's friends declined to attend the ceremony and implied that others were responsible for his suicide. I was enraged. In the time that had intervened, I had realized that the factors leading to his death couldn't have been the fault of one person or situation. I had just gotten over my own sense of guilt; I resented Carlos's friend for lashing out at others.*

A year ago I came up with an idea for a novel, or a series of short stories. Each story would focus on one character. Each of these characters would be linked by a mutual friend's suicide. I wanted to explore how a suicide might affect different people differently, how they might be dealing with it, how the memory affects their lives. Instead of focusing on the suicide itself, I would be focusing on the aftermath, in a long-term perspective. The novel is unfinished; I've worked on it in stops and starts. I'm still not sure I will go through with it.

One story I've been working on is the story of Corinne. She goes away to a Caribbean island to study indigenous art. The island calls up memories in her mind of her friend Octavio, who committed suicide. Octavio's family was from the Caribbean. Again, Octavio is a subplot as the story is now written. He doesn't appear until page 14:

It was during the first storm that Octavio's face began to haunt her, though frankly she was surprised she hadn't thought of him before then. She woke up to the wind bellowing through the open window in her room. She jumped up just in time to close the window before the rain began to sleet inside. She glanced out to the trees waving wildly in the wind, and that's where she saw his face, wild-eyed in the storm. His mouth was moving. He was crying out to her. She could see his lips forming her name.

Later, Corinne confides in Tara, a friend she had met on the island, after an evening at a bar:

The night was stunning, and they got sober just from staring out at the white foam like specks in the darkness of the ocean. They chatted for a while, then fell silent, sobered by the spectacle in front of them.

"Octavio," Corinne whispered.

"Who is Octavio?" Tara asked. She already knew all about Ansel, and secretly wondered why Corinne had been with him for so long.

Corinne glanced at Tara, but she was barely a shadow in the dark night, so she looked back out to the sea.

"Octavio was my friend when I was nine. We'd walk home from school together. We played on the playground. He was an alien and I was a moonwalker. He was an FBI agent, and I was the bad guy. In high school, Octavio got jealous when I was around other boys. We were a couple for awhile, but I needed to be with other people, to find out what they were like. When we went away to college, we called each other almost every night to fight the loneliness, we missed each other so much. Sometimes I thought maybe I loved him. It was harder for him . . . in the middle of his sophomore year he had to stop. He was a brilliant painter, an artist. I always thought he'd be around." Her voice trailed off.

"What then?" Tara's voice was soft, prodding.

"That summer he bought a gun and killed himself."

"Whoa." Tara sucked in her breath and turned back to the sea.

I think the main problem I have in writing about suicide is creating enough distance from it to be able to make it a full-fledged plot. I know I can't create the details of Carlos's death, because it still comes off as sounding flat and unreal; this always happens whenever I try to write about real events. I need to fictionalize it to make it into good fiction. If I'm going to write about Carlos, I also have to write honestly about myself: about my past actions, about my guilty feelings, about my own bouts with depression and attempt at suicide.

In the year following Carlos's death, I made a promise to myself to never commit suicide. I had bouts of depression and had tried to do it before, so I knew I needed to make this promise. At times I think this is the only thing that has kept me alive during some really hard times. It's hard enough to have someone you know commit suicide; it's even more difficult when you yourself have had suicidal thoughts. You think at times maybe they had the answer. In my novel I wrote: "Somewhere in that storm, Octavio had seen a way out." It's tantalizing in a way. As shocking as it may be that Anne Sexton was jealous of Sylvia Plath's suicide, it makes sense to me. One person has given in, why not me? Suicide becomes a temptation always to be resisted, the "unnameable lust" Sexton writes of in "Wanting to Die":

Still-born, they don't always die,
but dazzled, they can't forget a drug so sweet
that even children would look on and smile. (98)

The more I think and talk and write about suicide, the more I feel how pointless suicide is. One night I was watching the TV program ER *where a*

*girl who attempted suicide was being rescued. She was resisting their ef-
forts. Inside I cried out for her, a character on a TV show—"No! It's not
that bad! Live!" I also saw the doctors working away on her, trying to save
her, and how extreme and selfish the act of suicide seemed to be. I do not
condemn those who think of suicide, for I would condemn myself; but taking on the perspective of an outsider always keeps me in check, reminds me
of the world around me, and that I'm not alone.*

*I believe that this concept can extend similarly to readers of suicide lit-
erature. After Carlos's death there was some discussion in my school about
the amount of morbid literature we read in English classes. I would argue
such literature helps readers to learn and grow from others' experience,
provided the proper contexts are given. Too often this literature is taught
with only an emphasis on characterization, setting, plotting, and themes.
When discussing something as sensitive as suicide, the author's treatment
of suicide should be discussed. Also, if there is less emphasis given to the
"greatness" of a work and more on the problems of one, it might help students to understand that authors are human.*

*It has always been my feeling that biography is important to under-
standing an author's work. Authors draw upon their own life experiences,
and in order to understand a work better, it often helps to know some details about their life. In my own research on the poet Anne Sexton, I read
not only her poems, but her letters and biographies. Reading Sexton's letters to mental health patients was particularly illuminating. Sexton
struggled nearly her whole adult life with wanting to kill herself. She tried
on many occasions, but usually at times and in ways that would allow her
to be saved. Though she finally did succeed, the end of her life doesn't
appear glamorous. Instead of romanticizing her death, her death becomes
symbolic of the many sufferers of mental illness. Her illness becomes linked
with physical illnesses such as cancer and AIDS that are often romanticized in books, TV, and movies, yet we don't find ourselves wanting these
diseases. By coming to an understanding of Sexton's struggles with her depressions, and realizing that she mainly wrote when she was not depressed,
suicide loses much of its glamour and becomes real and terrible.*

*In addition, my research helped confirm that my own experiences of de-
pression were legitimate and cause for concern. By analyzing her poetry, I
can better understand and analyze my own feelings and thoughts on the
subject as they relate to both myself and to Carlos's suicide. Conversely, it
also helps to find that even in the works of artists who have committed*

suicide, they have expressed a hope that endures for future generations. Even in the work of a poet such as Dylan Thomas, who in essence killed himself slowly with alcohol, we find an expression of hope in his famous poem that endures for future generations:

> Do not go gentle into that good night,
> Old age should burn and rave at close of day;
> Rage, rage against the dying of the light.

Epilogue

Recently one morning I got a call from the office where I used to work. I'm still doing some freelance work for them, so I am occasionally in touch with them. During this particular call, a former coworker told me that another coworker there, Susan, had a friend who had committed suicide the week before. After I finished my business with the person on the phone, I asked to speak to Susan.

"I heard about Kevin. I'm so sorry. Are you OK?"

"Oh, I'm so mad at him! I'm done crying—I cried my eyes out this weekend. I just can't believe he did it. He had so many people that cared about him. He was on some drugs, Prozac or something. We thought he was better. He'd been happier. He just got out of bed in the morning and did it. I was the one who found him. Bastard!"

I imagined Susan going downstairs in her apartment building and knocking on her friend Kevin's door, then getting in and finding his body. The image sickened me.

"The police say they see this all the time: people who think they're alone, then when they die they have so many friends. Damn it! Alyssa, don't you ever do this. I was depressed before I came here, and I'd thought about it, but I'd never do it."

I told her I understood, that I had a friend who did the same thing, and that for the same reason I would never commit suicide.

"It's hard to believe how many people have friends who have done this. It's like everyone's coming out of the closet when they find out about this." She wasn't complaining; she was in shock, as I was, that together we could know so many people who have killed themselves.

"His brother killed himself . . . and his uncle. They never talked about it in his family. It was always like this joke to Kevin. They never talked about it . . . What? Hold on. Just a minute, Alyssa." I heard her ruffling papers. I

heard my former boss's voice in the background. I wished I could give Susan a hug.

Susan came back. "Aargh, sorry. I'm glad I'm not on vacation anymore— I was on vacation last week. I need to work. It helps."

"Yeah, I guess it keeps your mind off things. Listen, Susan, I don't want to keep you. You sound busy. I just wanted to let you know I'm here for you."

"Thanks. I have a strong network of support . . . it helps a lot." Her voice was shaky but somehow strong.

"Are you coming to visit soon?"

"I think when the semester's over, in a few weeks. We'll get together, OK?"

"OK. I'll talk to you later."

We said goodbye and hung up.

I felt helpless like people often do when trying to comfort a grieving person, but I felt a little less helpless, because for once when I said "I understand," I could really mean it. There's nothing worse than hearing someone say they understand when they've never been through what you've been through. Susan is around supportive, empathic people: the people I worked with, her family, her boyfriend. She's a strong person, full of humor, and I know she'll be OK. It just takes time. I know.

.   .   .

Dear Jeff,

Enclosed is the copy of my paper, which you requested I mail to you. I was reading it over and thought of so many things I wish I had included, though I am happy with the final product. There was one thing I thought might interest you. As a brainstorming technique for the paper, I sat at my computer and wrote out every thought and memory I could think of connected to Carlos. It was only when I allowed myself total openness and freedom to write anything that I remembered Thomas in the motel room. I hadn't forgotten about it completely, but I hadn't thought of it in a long time. And as soon as I remembered that, I hit upon where all that guilt over [Carlos's] death was really coming from. Proof that free-writing really works, not only for writing but, perhaps, for therapy?

With best wishes,
Alyssa

Works Cited

Abel, Elizabeth. *Virginia Woolf and the Fictions of Psychoanalysis*. Chicago: University of Chicago Press, 1989.

Alexander, Paul. *Rough Magic: A Biography of Sylvia Plath*. New York: Viking, 1991.

Alexander, Peter. *Leonard and Virginia Woolf: A Literary Partnership*. New York: St. Martin's Press, 1992.

Allen, Thomas. "Suicidal Impulse in Depression and Paranoia." In *Essential Papers on Suicide*, ed. John Maltsberger and Mark Goldblatt, 173–84. New York: New York University Press, 1996.

Alvarez, A. *The Savage God*. New York: Random House, 1972; Bantam, 1973.

Anderson, Olive. *Suicide in Victorian and Edwardian England*. Oxford: Clarendon Press, 1987.

Annas, Pamela. *A Disturbance in Mirrors*. New York: Greenwood Press, 1988.

Apter, T. E. *Virginia Woolf: A Study of Her Novels*. London: Macmillan, 1979.

Arnold, Lloyd. *High on the Wild with Hemingway*. Caldwell, Idaho: Caxton, 1969.

Axelrod, Steven Gould. *Sylvia Plath: The Wound and the Cure of Words*. Baltimore: Johns Hopkins University Press, 1990.

Baker, Carlos. *Ernest Hemingway: A Life Story*. New York: Bantam, 1970.

Barry, Ann Marie Seward. "In Praise of Anne Sexton's *The Book of Folly*: A Study of the Woman/Victim/Poet." In *Original Essays on the Poetry of Anne Sexton*, ed. Francis Bixler, 46–65. N.p.: University of Central Arkansas Press, 1988.

Bell, Quentin. *Virginia Woolf: A Biography*. New York: Harcourt Brace Jovanovich, 1972.

Berman, Jeffrey. *Diaries to an English Professor: Pain and Growth in the Classroom*. Amherst: University of Massachusetts Press, 1994.

———. *Narcissism and the Novel*. New York: New York University Press, 1990.

———. *The Talking Cure: Literary Representations of Psychoanalysis*. New York: New York University Press, 1985.

Berman, Jeffrey, and Alina M. Luna. "Suicide Diaries and the Therapeutics of Anonymous Self-Disclosure." *JPCS: Journal for the Psychoanalysis of Culture and Society* 1 (1996): 63–75.

Berman, Jeffrey, and Jonathan Schiff. "Writing about Suicide." In *Writing and Healing: Toward an Informed Practice*, ed. Charles Anderson and Marian MacCurdy. New York: NCTE, forthcoming.

Berryman, John. *The Dream Songs*. New York: Farrar, Straus, and Giroux, 1977.

Bixler, Francis, ed. *Original Essays on the Poetry of Anne Sexton.* N.p.: University of Central Arkansas Press, 1988.

Blake, William. *Complete Writings.* Ed. Geoffrey Keynes. London: Oxford University Press, 1966.

Boker, Pamela. *The Grief Taboo in American Literature.* New York: New York University Press, 1995.

Bond, Alma Halbert. *Who Killed Virginia Woolf?* New York: Human Sciences Press, 1989.

Boyers, Robert. *"Live or Die:* The Achievement of Anne Sexton." In *Anne Sexton: Telling the Tale,* ed. Steven E. Colburn, 155–66. Ann Arbor: University of Michigan Press, 1988.

Brian, Denis. *The True Gen.* New York: Grove Press, 1988.

Broe, Mary Lynn. *Protean Poetic: The Poetry of Sylvia Plath.* Columbia: University of Missouri Press, 1980.

Bruccoli, Matthew, ed. *Conversations with Ernest Hemingway.* Jackson: University Press of Mississippi, 1986.

Buie, Dan, and John Maltsberger. "The Psychological Vulnerability to Suicide." In *Suicide: Understanding and Responding,* ed. Douglas Jacobs and Herbert Brown, 59–71. Madison, Conn.: International Universities Press, 1989.

Butscher, Edward. *Sylvia Plath: Method and Madness.* New York: Seabury Press, 1976.

Caputo, Philip. "Styron's Choices." *Esquire,* December 1986.

Caramagno, Thomas C. *The Flight of the Mind: Virginia Woolf's Art and Manic-Depressive Illness.* Berkeley: University of California Press, 1992.

Carotenuto, Aldo. *To Love to Betray.* Trans. Joan Tambureno. Wilmette, Ill.: Chiron Publications, 1996.

Chekhov, Anton. "Gooseberries." In *The Portable Chekhov,* ed. Avraham Yarmolinsky. New York: Viking, 1968.

Chopin, Kate. *The Awakening.* Ed. Margo Culley. 2d ed. New York: Norton Critical Edition, 1994.

———. *The Awakening.* Ed. Nancy Walker. New York: St. Martin's Press, 1993.

Coale, Samuel. *William Styron Revisited.* Boston: Twayne, 1991.

Colburn, Steven E., ed. *Anne Sexton: Telling the Tale.* Ann Arbor: University of Michigan Press, 1988.

Coleman, L. *Suicide Clusters.* Boston: Faber and Faber, 1987.

Cowley, Malcolm, ed. *Writers at Work: The Paris Review Interviews.* New York: Viking, 1958; 1973.

Crane, John Kenny. *The Root of All Evil.* Columbia: University of South Carolina Press, 1984.

Culley, Margo, ed. *The Awakening,* by Kate Chopin. 2d ed. New York: Norton Critical Edition, 1994.

DeSalvo, Louise A. *Virginia Woolf: The Impact of Childhood Sexual Abuse on Her Life and Work.* Boston: Beacon Press, 1989.

Dickey, James. Rev. of *To Bedlam and Part Way Back.* In *Anne Sexton: Telling the Tale,* ed. Steven E. Colburn, 63–64. Ann Arbor: University of Michigan Press, 1988.

Diekstra, Rene, and Keith Hawton, eds. *Suicide in Adolescence.* Dordrecht, Netherlands: Martinus Nijhoff, 1987.

Dix, Dorothea. "Women and Suicide." In *The Awakening,* by Kate Chopin, 150–51. Ed. Margo Culley. 2d ed. New York: Norton Critical Edition, 1994.

Donaldson, Scott. *By Force of Will.* New York: Viking, 1977.

Dunne, Edward J., and Karen Dunne-Maxim. Preface to *Suicide and Its Aftermath.* Ed. Edward J. Dunne, John L. McIntosh, and Karen Dunne-Maxim. New York: Norton, 1986.

Dyer, Joyce. "Symbolism and Imagery in *The Awakening.*" In *Approaches to Teaching Chopin's* The Awakening, ed. Bernard Koloski, 126–31. New York: MLA, 1988.

Eliot, George. *Middlemarch.* London: Zodiac Press, 1967.

Etkind, Marc. . . . *Or Not to Be: A Collection of Suicide Notes.* New York: Riverhead Books, 1997.

Flaubert, Gustave. *Madame Bovary.* Trans. Francis Steegmuller. New York: Modern Library, 1957.

Freud, Sigmund. *Introductory Lectures on Psycho-Analysis.* Vol. 16 of *The Standard Edition of the Complete Psychological Works of Sigmund Freud.* Trans. and ed. James Strachey. London: Hogarth Press, 1963.

———. "Mourning and Melancholia." In vol. 14 of *The Standard Edition of the Complete Psychological Works of Sigmund Freud.* Trans. and ed. James Strachey. London: Hogarth Press, 1974.

George, Diana Hume. *Oedipus Anne: The Poetry of Anne Sexton.* Urbana: University of Illinois Press, 1987.

Gilbert, Sandra. "The Second Coming of Aphrodite." In *Kate Chopin,* ed. Harold Bloom, 89–114. New York: Chelsea House, 1987.

Gilbert, Sandra, and Susan Gubar. *Letters from the Front.* Vol. 3 of *No Man's Land: The Place of the Woman Writer in the Twentieth Century.* New Haven: Yale University Press, 1994.

Gilman, Charlotte Perkins. *The Yellow Wallpaper.* New York: Feminist Press, 1973.

Goldstein, Jan Ellen. "The Woolfs' Response to Freud: Water Spiders, Singing Canaries, and the Second Apple." In *Literature and Psychoanalysis,* ed. Edith Kurzweil and William Phillips, 232–55. New York: Columbia University Press, 1983.

Gordon, Lyndall. *Virginia Woolf: A Writer's Life.* New York: Norton, 1984.

Gould, Madelyn, David Shaffer, and Marjorie Kleinman, "The Impact of Suicide in Television Movies: Replication and Commentary." *Suicide and Life-Threatening Behavior* 18 (1988): 90–99.

Griffin, Peter. *Along with Youth: Hemingway, the Early Years.* New York: Oxford University Press, 1985.

Gullans, Charles. Rev. of *Love or Die.* In *Anne Sexton: Telling the Tale,* ed. Steven E. Colburn, 148–49. Ann Arbor: University of Michigan Press, 1988.

Hadaller, David. *Gynicide: Women in the Novels of William Styron.* Madison, N.J.: Fairleigh Dickinson University Press, 1996.

Hall, Caroline King Barnard. *Anne Sexton.* Boston: Twayne, 1989.

Hardy, Thomas. *Jude the Obscure.* London: Macmillan, 1971.

Hayman, Ronald. *The Death and Life of Sylvia Plath.* London: Heinemann, 1991.

Hemingway, Ernest. *Complete Poems.* Ed. Nicholas Gerogiannis. Lincoln: University of Nebraska Press, 1979.

———. *Death in the Afternoon.* New York: Scribner's, 1932.

————. *For Whom the Bell Tolls.* New York: Scribner's, 1940.

————. *Green Hills of Africa.* New York: Scribner's, 1935.

————. *In Our Time.* New York: Scribner's, 1925.

————. *Islands in the Stream.* New York: Scribner's, 1970.

————. *Selected Letters.* Ed. Carlos Baker. New York: Scribner's, 1981.

————. *The Short Stories of Ernest Hemingway.* New York: Scribner's, 1966.

————. *To Have and Have Not.* New York: Scribner's, 1937.

Hemingway, Gregory. *Papa: A Personal Memoir.* Boston: Houghton Mifflin, 1976.

Hemingway, Leicester. *My Brother, Ernest Hemingway.* Cleveland: World, 1962.

Hendin, Herbert. "On Anne Sexton." Paper presented at "Wanting to Die: Suicide and American Literature." American Suicide Foundation. New York, 11 November 1994.

————. "Psychodynamics of Suicide, with Particular Reference to the Young." *American Journal of Psychiatry* 148 (1991): 1150–58.

————. "Psychotherapy and Suicide." In *Essential Papers on Suicide,* ed John Maltsberger and Mark Goldblatt, 427–41. New York: New York University Press, 1996.

Herman, Judith Lewis. *Trauma and Recovery.* New York: Basic Books, 1992.

Holbrook, David. *Sylvia Plath: Poetry and Existence.* London: Athlone Press, 1976.

Holinger, Paul. "Our Lost Future: Suicide and Homicide among Youth." *Lifesavers* 7 (1995): 4–5.

Holland, Norman N. "Literary Suicide: A Question of Style." *Psychocultural Review* 1 (1977): 285–303.

Hotchner, A. E. *Papa Hemingway.* New York: Random House, 1966.

Hughes, Ted. *Birthday Letters.* New York: Farrar Straus Giroux, 1998.

————. "Sylvia Plath and Her Journals." In *Ariel Ascending: Writings about Sylvia Plath,* ed. Paul Alexander, 152–64. New York: Harper and Row, 1985.

Hussey, Mark. *Virginia Woolf A to Z.* New York: Oxford University Press, 1995.

Jamison, Kay Redfield. *Touched with Fire: Manic-Depressive Illness and the Artistic Temperament.* New York: Free Press, 1993.

————. *An Unquiet Mind.* New York: Knopf, 1995.

Jobes, David A., Alan L. Berman, Patrick W. O'Carroll, Susan Eastgard, and Steve Knickmeyer. "The Kurt Cobain Suicide Crisis: Perspectives from Research, Public Health, and the News Media." *Suicide and Life-Threatening Behavior* 26 (1996): 260–71.

Kafka, Franz. *Letters to Friends, Family, and Editors.* Trans. Richard Winston and Clara Winston. New York: Schocken, 1977.

Keats, John. *You Might As Well Live: The Life and Times of Dorothy Parker.* New York: Simon and Schuster, 1970.

Kelley, Alice van Buren. *The Novels of Virginia Woolf: Fact and Vision.* Chicago: University of Chicago Press, 1973.

Kenney, Susan. "Two Endings: Virginia Woolf's Suicide and *Between the Acts.*" *University of Toronto Quarterly* 44 (1975): 265–89.

King, James. *Virginia Woolf.* New York and London: Norton, 1994.

Koloski, Bernard, ed. *Approaches to Teaching Chopin's* The Awakening. New York: MLA, 1988.

Kroll, Judith. *Chapters in a Mythology.* New York: Harper and Row, 1976; Harper Colophon, 1978.

Kumin, Maxine. "How It Was: Maxine Kumin on Anne Sexton." In *Anne Sexton, Complete Poems*, xix–xxxiv. Boston: Houghton Mifflin, 1981.

Lattin, Patricia Hopkins. "Childbirth and Motherhood in *The Awakening* and in 'Athenaise.'" In *Approaches to Teaching Chopin's* The Awakening, ed. Bernard Koloski, 40–46. New York: MLA, 1988.

Laub, Dori. "Bearing Witness or the Vicissitudes of Listening." In *Testimony: Crises of Witnessing in Literature, Psychoanalysis, and History*, by Shoshana Felman and Dori Laub. New York: Routledge, 1992.

Leder, Priscilla. "Land's End: *The Awakening* and Nineteenth-Century Literary Tradition." In *Critical Essays on Kate Chopin*, ed. Alice Hall Petry, 237–50. New York: G. K. Hall, 1996.

Lee, Hermione. *Virginia Woolf.* New York: Knopf, 1997.

Leenaars, Anton, and David Lester. "Suicide and Homicide Rates in Canada and the United States." *Suicide and Life-Threatening Behavior* 24 (1994): 184–91.

Lesser, Simon. *Fiction and the Unconscious.* New York: Vintage, 1957.

Levertov, Denise. "Anne Sexton." In *Light Up the Cave.* New York: New Directions, 1981. Rpt. in *Anne Sexton: Telling the Tale*, ed. Steven E. Colburn, 54–60. Ann Arbor: University of Michigan Press, 1988.

Lynn, Kenneth. *Hemingway.* New York: Fawcett, 1987.

Malcolm, Janet. *The Quiet Woman: Sylvia Plath and Ted Hughes.* New York: Knopf, 1994.

Maltsberger, John, and Dan Buie. "Countertransference Hate in the Treatment of Suicidal Patients." *Archives of General Psychiatry* 30 (1974): 625–33. Rpt. in *Essential Papers on Suicide*, ed. John Maltsberger and Mark Goldblatt. 270–89. New York: New York University Press, 1996.

———. "The Devices of Suicide." *International Review of Psycho-Analysis* 7 (1980): 61–72. Rpt. in *Essential Papers on Suicide*, ed. John Maltsberger and Mark Goldblatt, 397–416. New York: New York University Press, 1996.

———, eds. *Essential Papers on Suicide.* New York: New York University Press, 1996.

May, John. "Local Color in *The Awakening*." In *The Awakening*, by Kate Chopin, 211–17. Ed. Margo Culley. 2d ed. New York: Norton Critical Edition, 1994.

McCabe, Jane. "'A Woman Who Writes': A Feminist Approach to the Early Poetry of Anne Sexton." In *Anne Sexton: The Artist and Her Critics*, ed. J. D. McClatchy, 216–43. Bloomington: Indiana University Press, 1978.

McClatchy, J. D., ed. *Anne Sexton: The Artist and Her Critics.* Bloomington: Indiana University Press, 1978.

McCorkle, Jill. *New York Times Book Review*, 6 December 1987. In *Kate Chopin*, by Emily Toth, 405. New York: William Morrow, 1990.

McGrath, Lynette. "Anne Sexton's Poetic Connections: Death, God, and Form." In *Original Essays on the Poetry of Anne Sexton*, ed. Francis Bixler, 138–68. N.p.: University of Central Arkansas Press, 1988.

McMahan, Susan Day, and Robert Funk, eds. *Nine Short Novels by American Women.* New York: St. Martin's Press, 1993.

Mellow, James. *Hemingway: A Life without Consequences.* Boston: Houghton Mifflin, 1992.

Meyers, Jeffrey. *Hemingway: A Biography.* New York: Harper and Row, 1985.

Middlebrook, Diane Wood. *Anne Sexton*. Boston: Houghton Mifflin, 1991.

––––––. "On Anne Sexton." Paper presented at "Wanting to Die: Suicide and American Literature." American Suicide Foundation. New York, 11 November 1994.

Milford, Nancy. "From Gladness to Madness." In *Critical Essays on Sylvia Plath*, ed. Linda W. Wagner, 77–83. Boston: G. K. Hall, 1984.

Miller, J. Hillis. *Fiction and Repetition*. Cambridge: Harvard University Press, 1982.

Nietzsche, Friedrich. *The Philosophy of Nietzsche*. New York: Modern Library, 1954.

––––––. *The Will to Power*. Trans. Walter Kaufmann and R. J. Hollingdale. New York: Vintage, 1968.

Oates, Joyce Carol. "The Death Throes of Romanticism: The Poetry of Sylvia Plath." In *Sylvia Plath: The Woman and the Work*, ed. Edward Butscher, 206–24. New York: Dodd, Mead, 1977.

Ohly, Friedrich. *The Damned and the Elect*. Trans. Linda Archibald. Cambridge: Cambridge University Press, 1992.

Orne, Martin. Foreword to *Anne Sexton*, by Diane Wood Middlebrook. Boston: Houghton Mifflin, 1991.

Page, Alex. "A Dangerous Day: Mrs. Dalloway Discovers Her Double." *Modern Fiction Studies* 7 (1961): 115–24.

Parker, Dorothy. *The Portable Dorothy Parker*. New York: Viking, 1973.

Pearce, Richard. *William Styron*. Minneapolis: University of Minnesota Press, 1971.

Pfeffer, Cynthia. "Families of Suicidal Children." In *Suicide in Adolescence*, ed. Rene F. W. Diekstra and Keith Hawton, 127–38. Dordrecht: Martinus Nijhoff, 1987.

Phillips, David. "The Influence of Suggestion on Suicide: Substantive and Theoretical Implications of the Werther Effect." *American Sociological Review* 39 (1974): 340–54. Rpt. in *Essential Papers on Suicide*, ed. John Maltsberger and Mark Goldblatt, 290–313. New York: New York University Press, 1996.

Phillips, David, and Lundie Carstensen. "The Effect of Suicide Stories on Various Demographic Groups, 1968–1985." *Suicide and Life-Threatening Behavior* 18 (1988): 100–114.

Plath, Sylvia. *The Bell Jar*. New York: Harper and Row, 1971.

––––––. *Collected Poems*. Ed. Ted Hughes. New York: Harper and Row, 1981; HarperPerennial, 1992.

––––––. *The Journals of Sylvia Plath*. Ed. Frances McCullough and Ted Hughes. New York: Dial, 1982; Ballantine, 1991.

––––––. *Letters Home*. Ed. Aurelia Schober Plath. New York: Harper and Row, 1975.

Poland, Scott. *Suicide Intervention in the Schools*. New York: Guilford Press, 1989.

Poole, Roger. *The Unknown Virginia Woolf*. Cambridge: Cambridge University Press, 1978.

Raeburn, John. *Fame Became Him: Hemingway as Public Writer*. Bloomington: Indiana University Press, 1984.

Ratner, Marc. *William Styron*. New York: Twayne, 1972.

Reynolds, Michael. *Hemingway: The American Homecoming*. Oxford: Blackwell, 1992.

––––––. "Hemingway's Home: Depression and Suicide." In *Ernest Hemingway: Six Decades of Criticism*, ed. Linda Wagner, 9–17. East Lansing: Michigan State University Press, 1987.

————. *The Young Hemingway.* Oxford: Blackwell, 1986.

Rich, Adrienne. *On Lies, Secrets, and Silence: Selected Prose, 1966–1978.* New York: Norton, 1979.

Rose, Jacqueline. *The Haunting of Sylvia Plath.* Cambridge: Harvard University Press, 1991.

Rosenthal, M. L. "Sylvia Plath and Confessional Poetry." In *The Art of Sylvia Plath,* ed. Charles Newman, 69–76. Bloomington: Indiana University Press, 1970.

Rosenthal, Michael. *Virginia Woolf.* New York: Columbia University Press, 1979.

Rosowski, Susan. "*The Awakening* as a Prototype of the Novel of Awakening." In *Approaches to Teaching Chopin's* The Awakening, ed. Bernard Koloski, 26–33. New York: MLA, 1988.

Ross, Daniel W. "A Family Romance: Dreams and the Unified Narrative of *Sophie's Choice.*" *Mississippi Quarterly* 42 (1989): 129–45.

Rothenberg, Albert. *Creativity and Madness.* Baltimore: Johns Hopkins University Press, 1990.

Ruderman, Judith. *William Styron.* New York: Ungar, 1987.

Ryerson, Diane. "'ASAP'—An Adolescent Suicide Awareness Programme." In *Suicide in Adolescence,* ed. Rene F. W. Diekstra and Keith Hawton, 173–90. Dordrecht: Martinus Nijhoff, 1987.

Schlack, Beverly Ann. *Continuing Presences: Virginia Woolf's Use of Literary Allusion.* University Park: Pennsylvania State University Press, 1979.

Schwartz, Murray, and Christopher Bollas. "The Absence at the Center: Sylvia Plath and Suicide." In *Sylvia Plath: New Views on the Poetry,* ed. Gary Lane, 179–202. Baltimore: Johns Hopkins University Press, 1979.

Sexton, Anne. *Complete Poems.* Boston: Houghton Mifflin, 1981.

————. *No Evil Star: Selected Essays, Interviews, and Prose.* Ed. Steven E. Colburn. Ann Arbor: University of Michigan Press, 1985.

————. *A Self-Portrait in Letters.* Ed. Linda Gray Sexton and Lois Ames. Boston: Houghton Mifflin, 1977.

Sexton, Linda Gray. *Searching for Mercy Street.* Boston: Little, Brown, 1994.

Shattuck, Roger. *Forbidden Knowledge.* New York: St. Martin's Press, 1996.

Shields, E. F. "Death and Individual Values in *Mrs. Dalloway.*" *Queen's Quarterly* 80 (1973): 79–89.

Shneidman, Edwin. *Definition of Suicide.* New York: Wiley, 1985.

————. *On the Nature of Suicide.* San Francisco: Jossey-Bass, 1969.

————. "Risk Writing: A Special Note about Cesare Pavese and Joseph Conrad." *Journal of the American Academy of Psychoanalysis* 7 (1979): 575–92.

————. *The Suicidal Mind.* New York: Oxford University Press, 1996.

————. *Suicide as Psychache.* Northvale, N.J.: Jason Aronson, 1993.

Showalter, Elaine. *The Female Malady.* New York: Pantheon, 1985.

————. Introduction to *Mrs. Dalloway.* In *Virginia Woolf: Introduction to the Major Works,* ed. Julia Briggs. London: Virago Press, 1994.

————. "Tradition and the Female Talent: *The Awakening* as a Solitary Book." In *The Awakening,* by Kate Chopin. Ed. Nancy Walker, 169–89. New York: St. Martin's Press, 1993.

Shurr, William H. "Mysticism and Suicide: Anne Sexton's Last Poetry." In *Critical Essays on Anne Sexton,* ed. Linda Wagner-Martin, 193–210. Boston: G. K. Hall, 1989.

Solomon, Barbara. "Characters as Foils to Edna." In *Approaches to Teaching Chopin's The Awakening*, ed. Bernard Koloski, 114–19. New York: MLA, 1988.

Spangler, George. "Kate Chopin's *The Awakening*: A Partial Dissent." In *The Awakening*, by Kate Chopin, 208–11. Ed. Margo Culley. 2d ed. New York: Norton Critical Edition, 1994.

Spivack, Kathleen. "Poets and Friends." In *Anne Sexton: Telling the Tale*, ed. Steven E. Colburn, 25–38. Ann Arbor: University of Michigan Press, 1988.

Stape, J. H., ed. *Virginia Woolf: Interviews and Recollections*. Iowa City: University of Iowa Press, 1995.

Steiner, Nancy Hunter. *A Closer Look at Ariel*. New York: Popular Library, 1973.

Steinhauer, Harry. Introduction to *The Sufferings of Young Werther*, by Johann Wolfgang von Goethe. Ed. and trans. Harry Steinhauer. New York: Bantam Dual-Language Book, 1962.

Stevenson, Anne. *Bitter Fame: A Life of Sylvia Plath*. Boston: Houghton Mifflin, 1989.

Styron, William. *The Confessions of Nat Turner*. New York: Random House, 1967.

———. *Darkness Visible*. New York: Random House, 1990.

———. *Inheritance of Night: Early Drafts of "Lie Down in Darkness."* Ed. James L. W. West III. Durham: Duke University Press, 1993.

———. "Interview with William Styron." *New York Times Book Review*, 12 December 1982.

———. *Lie Down in Darkness*. New York: 1951; New American Library, 1978.

———. "Marriott, the Marine." *Esquire*, September 1971.

———. *Set This House on Fire*. New York: Random House, 1960.

———. *Sophie's Choice*. New York: Random House, 1979.

———. *This Quiet Dust*. New York: Random House, 1982.

———. *A Tidewater Morning*. New York: Random House, 1993.

Todd, Olivier. *Albert Camus: A Life*. Trans. Benjamin Ivry. New York: Knopf, 1997.

Toth, Emily. *Kate Chopin*. New York: William Morrow, 1990.

Treichler, Paula. "The Construction of Ambiguities in *The Awakening*: A Linguistic Analysis." In *The Awakening*, by Kate Chopin, 308–28. Ed. Nancy Walker. New York: St. Martin's Press, 1993.

Trombley, Stephen. *"All That Summer She Was Mad": Virginia Woolf and Her Doctors*. London: Junction Books, 1981.

U.S. Center for Disease Control. "Attempted Suicide among High School Students— United States, 1990." *Morbidity and Mortality Report*. 40.37 (1991): 633–35.

U.S. Department of Health and Human Services. *Report of the Secretary's Task Force on Youth Suicide Vol. 1: Overview and Recommendations*. Washington, D.C.: U.S. Government Printing Office, 1989.

Uroff, Margaret Dickie. *Sylvia Plath and Ted Hughes*. Urbana: University of Illinois Press, 1979.

Van Dyne, Susan. *Revising Life: Sylvia Plath's Ariel Poems*. Chapel Hill: University of North Carolina Press, 1993.

Wagner-Martin, Linda. *Sylvia Plath: A Biography*. New York: Simon and Schuster, 1987.

———, ed. *Critical Essays on Anne Sexton*. Boston: G. K. Hall, 1989.

Walker, Nancy, ed. *The Awakening,* by Kate Chopin. New York: St. Martin's Press, 1993.

West, James L. W., III. *William Styron: A Life.* New York: Random House, 1998.

————, ed. Introduction to *Inheritance of Night: Early Drafts of "Lie Down in Darkness,"* by William Styron. Durham: Duke University Press, 1993.

Westbrook, Max. "Grace under Pressure: Hemingway and the Summer of 1920." In *Ernest Hemingway: The Writer in Context,* ed. James Nagel, 77–106. Madison: University of Wisconsin Press, 1984.

Wolff, Cynthia. "Thanatos and Eros: Kate Chopin's *The Awakening.*" In *The Awakening,* by Kate Chopin, 233–58. Ed. Nancy Walker. New York: St. Martin's Press, 1993.

Wolkenfeld, Suzanne. "Edna's Suicide: The Problem of the One and the Many." In *The Awakening,* by Kate Chopin, 241–47. Ed. Margo Culley. 2d ed. New York: Norton Critical Edition, 1994.

Woolf, Leonard. *An Autobiography.* Vol. 1, *Sowing, 1880–1904;* vol. 2, *Growing, 1904–11;* vol. 3, *Beginning Again, 1911–18;* vol. 4, *Downhill All the Way, 1919–39;* vol. 5, *The Journey Not the Arrival Matters, 1939–69.* New York: Harcourt, Brace and World, 1960–69.

Woolf, Virginia. *The Common Reader.* 1st series. New York: Harcourt, Brace and World, 1925.

————. *The Common Reader.* 2d series. New York: Harcourt, Brace and World, 1932.

————. *The Complete Shorter Fiction of Virginia Woolf.* Ed. Susan Dick. London: Hogarth Press, 1985.

————. *The Diary of Virginia Woolf.* Ed. Anne Olivier Bell. 5 vols. San Diego, New York, and London: Harcourt Brace, 1977–84.

————. Introduction to *Mrs. Dalloway.* New York: Modern Library, 1928.

————. *The Letters of Virginia Woolf.* Ed. Nigel Nicolson and Joanne Trautmann. 6 vols. New York and London: Harcourt Brace Jovanovich, 1975–80.

————. *The Moment and Other Essays.* San Diego, New York, and London: Harcourt Brace Jovanovich, 1948.

————. *Moments of Being: Unpublished Autobiographical Writings.* Ed. Jeanne Schulkind. New York and London: Harcourt Brace Jovanovich, 1976.

————. *Mrs. Dalloway.* Ed. G. Patton Wright. The Definitive Collected Edition. London: Hogarth Press, 1990.

————. *A Passionate Apprentice: The Early Journals of Virginia Woolf, 1897–1909.* Ed. Mitchell A. Leaska. London: Hogarth Press, 1990.

————. *Roger Fry, A Biography.* London: Hogarth Press, 1940.

————. *The Voyage Out.* Ed. Elizabeth Heine. London: Hogarth Press, 1990.

————. *The Waves.* London: Hogarth Press, 1963.

Wurtzel, Elizabeth. *Prozac Nation.* Boston: Houghton Mifflin, 1994.

Young, Philip. *Ernest Hemingway: A Reconsideration.* University Park: Pennsylvania State University Press, 1966.

Index